CRITICAL QUESTIONS FOR AGEING SOCIETIES

Gemma M. Carney and Paul Nash

P

First published in Great Britain in 2020 by

Policy Press, an imprint of
Bristol University Press
University of Bristol
1-9 Old Park Hill
Bristol
BS2 8BB
UK
t: +44 (0)117 954 5940
e: bup-info@bristol.ac.uk

Details of international sales and distribution partners are available at
policy.bristoluniversitypress.co.uk

British Library Cataloguing in Publication Data
A catalogue record for this book is available from the British Library

ISBN 978-1-4473-5157-3 hardcover
ISBN 978-1-4473-5158-0 paperback
ISBN 978-1-4473-5159-7 ePub
ISBN 978-1-4473-5831-2 ePdf

Cover design: Qube
Front cover image: Gemma Hodge

FSC
www.fsc.org
MIX
Paper from
responsible sources
FSC® C013604

Gemma Carney would like to dedicate this book to the memory of her father, Michael Carney, who faced his illness with grace and courage but who sadly died during the course of writing this book.

Contents

Lists of tables, figures and boxes

Glossary of terms

Active ageing – A globally popular policy which works on the basis that older people should maximise and optimise their opportunities for health, civic participation and security to enrich individual quality of life and to decrease the burden of an ageing population on society and government.

Age/birth cohort – Those people born and living at the same time and so regarded as a collective group. A birth cohort generally refers to people born within a few years of one another.

Ageism – The prejudice or act of discrimination against a person or group based on age.

Alzheimer's disease – A progressive and non-reversible generalised degeneration of the brain, affecting memory and thinking skills, eventually affecting activities of daily living. The most common form of dementia in older adults.

Attitude – A positive or negative set of thoughts and feelings held by an individual that influences and explains their actions.

Austerity – A political and economic term referring to policies enacted to reduce government budget deficits through spending cuts, welfare reduction and tax increases. It was a policy much used by Western governments following the global economic crisis of 2008.

Baby boomer – Refers to a person born between 1946 and 1964, immediately following World War II when there was a marked increase in birth rates.

Bed blockers – A derogatory term used to describe older people who remain in hospital, occupying a hospital bed, because there is not adequate community or family support available for them to finish their recovery at home.

Biological determinism – The theory suggesting that human behaviour is all innate, determined by biological attributes such as genetics and not to do with the social environment (for example, the idea that all women are 'hysterical' because of their hormones).

Brexit – The political process whereby the United Kingdom is rescinding its membership of, and leaving, the European Union.

Care Quality Commission – An independent regulator in England, monitoring the quality of all health and social care services.

Caregiver – A person who regularly provides help and assistance for health and/or social and personal care needs, in either a paid (formal) or unpaid (informal) capacity.

Chrononormativity – The social norm or expectation that people will experience certain life events or partake in similar experiences at the same stages in life.

Civic participation – Where an individual or individuals act to address an issue of social concern. For example, making a positive change in your local neighbourhood.

Comorbidities – The simultaneous presentation of two or more chronic conditions in the same patient.

Consent – Permission, verbal or written, given by a person or their legal representative, for an action to be taken on their behalf.

Coronavirus/COVID-19 – A viral respiratory infection that passed from an animal to humans in late 2019. The virus emerged in Wuhan, China in December 2019 and by March 2020 was named as a global pandemic by the World Health Organization. The outbreak causes widespread death, illness and serious economic and social disruption to the world economy. The virus is more likely to be fatal in older people, those with underlying illnesses, men, and people from Black and minority ethnic backgrounds. At the time of writing (April 2020), there is no known cure or vaccine against the virus.

Cultural gerontology – The term used to describe the growing interest in using arts and humanities approaches, methods and theories to understand ageing societies in gerontology. See also, Gerontology and Social gerontology.

Cultural turn – The shift in focus to include the arts and humanities theories and methods to understand ageing societies.

Cumulative advantage/cumulative disadvantage – The systematic explanation of the development of advantage or disadvantage over a person's lifecourse. How individual divergence and differentiation through social categories (wealth, health and so on) result in advantage or disadvantage over time.

Custodial grandparents – Grandparents who take over the full-time raising of their grandchildren, assuming the legal rights and responsibilities that entails.

Dementia – An umbrella term incorporating a range of diseases including but not limited to Alzheimer's disease, Lewy body dementia, vascular dementia and Parkinson's disease. They are typified by a progressive and irreversible deterioration of the brain resulting in cognitive decline, memory loss, personality change, physical impairment and impairment in activities of daily living.

Demographic transition – This is the change in patterns of mortality, fertility, migration and growth rates within given populations resulting in changes to the demographic stage (see also, Demographic Transition Model).

Demographic Transition Model (DTM) – Maps the total population of a country, incorporating birth rate, death rate, immigration and emigration, all of which are key drivers of demographic ageing.

Dependency ratio – The number of dependants below working age and over retirement age versus the number of people of working age.

Diagnostic Statistical Manual (DSM) – A globally referenced and accepted handbook of mental disorders developed in the US and used by healthcare professionals. This includes symptoms and descriptors allowing professionals to diagnose any mental disorder.

Elder abuse – 'A single, or repeated act, or lack of appropriate action, occurring within any relationship where there is an expectation of trust, which causes harm or distress to an older person' (WHO, 2012).

Embodiment – The relationship between the ageing body and social and cultural aspects of ageing. It has become an important contribution of cultural gerontology to our knowledge of human ageing.

Emigration – The process of leaving one's home country and moving to permanently settle in another (compare, Immigration and Migration).

Encore careers/encore discrimination – Phrases which signify that the longer lifecourse provides more opportunities for multiple experiences (good and bad) at different stages of the lifecourse. For example, women who experience sex discrimination may experience 'encore' discrimination in the form of ageism in later life.

Engaged citizenship – When individuals choose to educate themselves in politics and actively and lawfully participate in forms of political engagement other than standard voting.

European Social Survey – A social science survey spanning Europe that seeks to map attitudes, beliefs and behaviour patterns through different populations over time.

Explicit attitude – An attitude under the conscious awareness and control of an individual, informing the way a person interacts within the social world.

Externalised ageism – Ageism directed towards another person.

Feminist theory – Ideas and concepts about women's rights as used by activists and academics and which take an analytical approach to understanding the roots and impacts of gender inequality.

Filial piety/filial care – This phrase is most often associated with a practice that is common in Confucian countries, such as China and South Korea: the practice of providing care and support within your own family, usually to older parents. Piety, in this case, does not refer to religious observance, rather it means here showing love, compassion and respect for elders by supporting parents who supported you earlier in the lifecourse.

Fourth age – Not directly linked to chronological age, this period of life is defined as the final decline towards death, characterised by dependency and illness/disease.

Gender identity – This is an individual perception about self-gender. It may be the same as the sex assigned at birth or it can be different (for example, a person born with male genitalia may identify as female).

Gender regime – The state of gender relations (power balance) within any given institution or environment. This can include government regulations and workplace rules.

Gender roles – Culturally accepted set of ascribed roles or behaviours characterised as appropriate for men or women (for example, the idea that only men can be Catholic priests).

Generation – The term used to refer to a birth cohort or group of birth cohorts which are recognised as having some common attributes and experiences by virtue of the time into which they are born.

Gerontocracy – The notion that a state or society is governed by older people.

Gerontology – The bio–psycho–social and cultural study of ageing and older persons by medical and social scientists or by humanities scholars (see also, Social gerontology and Cultural gerontology).

Global North – Includes the advanced economies of Europe and North America, characterised by democracy, country-level and individual wealth, technological development, political stability, an ageing population and proliferation of world trade.

Global South – Initially coined to replace the term 'third world', this refers to those countries in Asia, Africa, Latin America and the Caribbean, characterised by low to middle incomes, unstable democracy, less technological development, political instability, and a younger population.

Hegemonic masculinity – A gender regime where the practices of men are designed to maintain their dominance over women, as well as the establishment and maintenance of a hierarchy to privilege those men in power.

HIV – Human Immunodeficiency Virus. A sexually transmitted infection that damages the immune system, compromising the body's ability to fight organisms, potentially resulting in Acquired Immunodeficiency Syndrome (AIDS).

Homogeneity – Sharing the same characteristics and attributes as a broader group or portion of the population. The same as those in a particular grouping. For example, the population of Ireland is homogenous, in that it is 82.2 per cent White Irish (Central Statistics Office, 2016).

Humanistic approach – Focused on the individual, emphasising empathy and the inherent good nature in human behaviour.

Immigration – The inward flow of people (migrants) from one country into another (compare, Emigration and Migration).

Implicit attitude – An attitude not under an individual's conscious control or awareness, which predicts behaviour in unplanned encounters.

In-group – A category of persons or an identity which is seen as core, valid and an important part of the community (so young people are the in-group in a culture where youth is valorised).

Intergenerational – Refers to social exchange or relations between different generations, for instance, relations between grandparents and their children and grandchildren.

Intergenerational solidarity – Also referred to as 'solidarity between generations' it refers to the support that one birth cohort or group of birth cohorts provides to another. This support can include anything and everything from financial aid to care for the very young or very old. At societal level, it refers to support for transfers between generations, such as pensions or child benefit.

Internalised ageism – Ageism directed inward at oneself where the negative stereotypes held about older people and ageing are applied to the self.

Intersectionality – Describes the way in which social categories such as race, age, gender and class are interconnected and impact on individuals to differing extents at different points of the lifecourse.

Intragenerational – Occurring within one defined generational cohort (for instance, intra-generational inequality refers to the idea that some young people live in poverty and others enjoy considerable family wealth).

LGBTQI★ – Lesbian, Gay, Bisexual, Trans(gender/sexual), Queer, Intersex. The ★ denotes other sexual identities falling under the 'queer' banner, including pansexual, asexual and omnisexual.

Lifecourse – A theory developed by sociologists which views ageing as one stage of a series of phases that begin with birth, and which develop through childhood to adulthood and old age.

Loneliness – A level of social interaction or engagement that falls below what an individual desires. A subjective measure/experience.

Long-term care – A full range of services covering medical and social needs for those who are unable to care for themselves.

Macro-level – On a social/societal rather than individual level. For example, ageism can operate at societal level through legislation which bars people from working after a certain age.

Medicaid – A US-based healthcare programme that provides assistance to those on low income to access healthcare services.

Medicare – A US-based federal healthcare programme providing health insurance to those over 65 years and those under 65 who are in receipt of Social Security Disability Insurance.

Menopause – This is the time when a woman's menstrual cycle ceases and she is no longer able to become pregnant. This is caused by a decline in oestrogen levels.

Micro-level – The smallest level of measurement. Information at a local or individual level.

Migration – The process of moving from one country, place or locality to another (compare, Emigration and Immigration).

Narrative of decline – The widely held, dominant view that old age is synonymous with loss and decay, rather than valuable wisdom and experience.

National Health Service (NHS) – A publicly funded national healthcare system in the UK, funded by taxation providing free or low-cost healthcare at the point of access for UK and other qualifying citizens.

National insurance – A UK based, government-operated social security scheme that provides an income 'safety blanket' for everyone, including income support, maternity pay, sickness pay and a national pension scheme.

Neoliberalism – An ideological political project, dating back to the 1980s regimes of Thatcherism in the UK and Reaganomics in the US. It involves making strong ideological arguments which lead to withdrawal of state support for individual welfare such as pensions and healthcare.

Non-governmental organisation (NGO) – A not-for-profit organisation that operates outside and independently of any government to address social and/or political issues.

Osteoporosis – A condition usually experienced in later life as a result of hormonal changes, calcium and vitamin D deficiency, characterised by brittle and fragile bones.

Out-group – A group or category of persons whose identity or beliefs are peripheral or devalued in comparison with the norm (for example, women in a patriarchal culture).

Pension – A regular payment or source of income made to a person following retirement from either the state or a private investment fund.

Person-centred care – A model of caregiving whereby the care recipient is seen as an equal partner and stakeholder in the decisions about, delivery and monitoring of their care to ensure their needs are met.

Political demography – The study of a given population as it relates to government and politics.

Political economy of ageing – The study of how political structures and economic systems conspire to produce inequalities between younger and older people, and among older people as a group.

Population ageing – The general trend seen where the average age of a given population is increasing.

Positive ageism – Where being an older adult leads to positive assumptions about character or ability. For example, an expectation of reliability or trustworthiness.

Post-war consensus – An agreement across political parties to establish a series of national public institutions such as the NHS in the UK from 1945 to 1979.

Prejudice – A set of preconceived ideas or opinions resulting in harm or injury (not necessarily physical) to a person based on their ascribed attributes.

Presbyopia – Farsightedness caused by a reduction in the elasticity/hardening of the lens of the eye.

Population pyramid – A graphical representation of a population, illustrating the gender and age profile at a given moment of time.

Retirement – The point at which a person leaves paid employment.

Risk assessment – A systematic evaluation of potential risk for a particular situation or activity.

Sandwich carers – Those people, usually in middle age, who are providing care and support for their own ageing parents while also supporting their own children.

Self-presentational bias – The process by where an individual portrays themselves in the most positive way for social acceptance within any given environment or grouping.

Sexism – The prejudice or act of discrimination against a person based on their sex.

Sexual orientation – Sexual identity in reference to which gender a person feel attracted to (for example, homo-, hetero- or bisexual).

Social care – Care provided for older people in their own homes. Social care can include personal hygienic care, cooking, cleaning or nursing care. It is an important means of allowing many older people to avoid being placed in a long-term care facility or hospital.

Social contract – A non-written, implicit agreement or understanding between members of a society to cooperate for overall social benefit, defining the limits, rights and duties of each party.

Social gerontology – Social gerontology is a subset of gerontology that studies social processes, issues, practices, and policies associated with older people. See also Gerontology.

Social isolation – An objective state where an individual is separate from others/ lacks social contact.

Social location – The position or status that a person occupies in their society because of their race, gender, religion, income or job.

Social welfare – A set of publicly funded assistance programmes, designed to support and provide care to those citizens within a given society deemed most needful, particularly children, vulnerable adults and older people.

Socio-economic status (SES) – Combines sociological and economic measures to provide an indication of an individual's social position in relation to others. The measure includes: work experience, income level, educational attainment, and occupation, and is used to evidence economic difference.

Stereotype – A set of generalised beliefs concerning the homogenous attributes of a particular group or category and every individual in that grouping.

Stewardship – The idea that each generation is responsible for taking care of the Earth until the next generation takes over.

Structured dependency – Where older adults are forced into dependency on others or the state based on the inability to maintain income or activity level due to structural reasons such as policy or fiscal poverty.

Successful ageing – 'Successful ageing is multidimensional, encompassing the avoidance of disease and disability, the maintenance of high physical and cognitive function, and sustained engagement in social and productive activities' (Rowe and Kahn, 1987).

Universal assessment – The universal assessment or Comprehensive Geriatric Assessment (CGA) is the gold standard of assessment for older adults, providing a holistic screening of medical, psychological, functional and social domains.

Universal design – The design of an environment to enable access and use to the greatest possible extent by everyone regardless of age, gender or disability.

Un-retirement – The process of returning to paid employment following retirement.

Welfare state – The social contract that exists between citizens and government through which provision of public services such as health and education are funded and organised. It is a common system in northern and western European countries, such as the United Kingdom (UK) and countries of the European Union (EU).

About the authors

Dr Gemma M. Carney is a social gerontologist based at the School of Social Sciences, Education and Social Work, Queen's University Belfast. She is a member of the British Society of Gerontology executive committee and of the editorial board of *Ageing & Society*.

Dr Paul Nash is an Associate Professor in the Leonard Davis School of Gerontology at the University of Southern California. His research focuses on both ageism and HIV in ageing populations. This has informed work with the World Health Organization and the production of several White Paper reports.

Both authors won student-nominated teaching awards for their classes in gerontology and social policy in 2019.

Acknowledgements

Like all creative work, this book is a product of much more than the efforts of its two authors. We would like to thank our families, friends and colleagues who encouraged and supported us throughout the project from inception to completion. We first met through membership of the British Society of Gerontology (BSG) and would like to acknowledge the importance of BSG in providing a supportive community for gerontology nerds like us to hatch plans and work together. We urge anyone interested in pursuing research on ageing, independently or in a formal university setting, to join the BSG.

Gemma M. Carney would like to thank her all of her colleagues at Queen's University Belfast, but particularly Paula Devine, Leonie Hannan and Dirk Schubotz, for providing support and encouragement throughout. Special thanks are due to Professor Tony Gallagher who, as Head of School, encouraged the writing of a textbook despite the pressures of the REF (Research Excellence Framework) and who allowed the School of Social Sciences, Education and Social Work to provide financial support for a trip to the Leonard Davis School of Gerontology to work with Paul on the book. Research assistant Callum Briscoe deserves a special mention for compiling Table 1.1 as well as providing expert referencing, scouting out international examples and testing out our review exercises. Thanks to Sarah McKenna, ace gerontology student, for sharing a student perspective on early drafts of key chapters. The image on the cover of the book is kindly provided by visual artist and one in a million friend, Gemma Hodge. Lastly, Gemma Carney would like to thank her husband Neil and sons Ray and Cal without whom all of her life and work would have infinitely less colour and worth.

Paul Nash would like to thank colleagues in both Swansea University, UK, and the University of Southern California, US, as the writing process spanned employment at both. Prof Vanessa Burholt was, and continues to be, an invaluable friend and mentor to Paul, offering much encouragement through the writing process and more widely within academia. Paul would also like to highlight the filial support from mother Kate, sister Sarah and nephew Alex. Despite the geographic distance, all have provided emotional and instrumental support on their many visits to Los Angeles. Their encouragement and unwavering support has made this book possible while juggling many other commitments. The writing process and sacrifices made have illuminated the strength in true friendships and cemented the bonds both personally and professionally around a shared goal.

Preface

From our first discussions of undertaking a book project, we were determined to produce a book which was informative, easy to read and provided students with answers to the questions that most interest them. Textbooks have tended to follow a well-worn path, focusing on health and social care, the family life of older people and services aimed at them. By choosing to base our book on questions put to us by our students we have chosen a different, perhaps more risky, path. In taking this approach, we have made some progress in shedding new light on areas of research and study which are often ignored in textbooks about ageing and older people. We are particularly pleased that this book includes in-depth discussions of diversity, masculinity and cultural gerontology. However, we are confident that this decision gives what follows greater relevance and timeliness. Most importantly, you can rest assured that answering our students' questions has produced an interesting read. However, by choosing to follow the interests of our students, based in Leonard Davis School of Gerontology, University of Southern California, US, and Queen's University Belfast, Northern Ireland, UK, we have, inevitably, had to make some difficult choices, which have resulted in a few compromises.

We acknowledge that our coverage of health and social care is less comprehensive than students taking vocational degrees in health and allied services might expect. Likewise, where we live (UK and US) and the teaching experience we have, which is in social gerontology, means that we have probably offered too many examples from the UK and the US and too few from Canada, Australia or Asia. This is a conscious choice. We have tried, where possible to include as many international examples as are relevant to the learning outcomes we are striving to reach in each chapter. However, we are cognisant that all research and teaching takes place in a particular cultural and geographical context.

On reflection, we decided that it is best for authors to draw on their own research and experience rather than try to be an expert on areas and cultures which they have neither directly studied nor experienced. Likewise, as we explain in the opening chapter, our book is unashamedly post-structuralist in its approach. We wish it to be an important introductory text from the critical gerontology tradition for all scholars of ageing. So, rather than trying to match other texts on issues such as health and illness, we chose to offer a fuller, more student-centred account of recent developments in critical gerontology, which aim to take our understanding of human ageing above and beyond the physiological. That said, we have tried to be as inclusive, broad-minded and comprehensive as possible, bearing in mind that we are two authors working together, playing to our strengths, rather than a long list of international names submitting individual chapters to a handbook.

Lastly, the bulk of the research and writing for this book took place in 2018 and 2019, in the time before coronavirus/COVID-19. We are aware that, unfortunately, the prospects for human longevity may be compromised by the pandemic and some of the projections in the book, made on the basis of publicly available data, may be affected by the impact of the pandemic. At the time of writing, the catastrophic impact of the virus in terms of fatalities among care home residents in most countries is only beginning to be estimated (see Phillipson, 2020). In terms of social policy, the blanket ageism in many of the policies emerging as the crisis unfolds (see British Society of Gerontology, 2020) serves only to support the book's central premise, that we all must take a critical perspective on the impacts and opportunities that arise from population ageing. While we cannot yet provide solid data on the coronavirus crisis, we can urge our readers to use the pandemic as a means of understanding how the ageing of our population has fundamentally changed the social, political and health systems of every country in the world.

We hope that in the final analysis, you will find our introductory textbook both a comfort and a challenge; a sort of bookish friend to which you will return again and again as you improve your knowledge of ageing and older people. Likewise, if you are teaching gerontology, then we hope that you find our book, its exercises, quizzes and questions the most obliging and insightful of teaching assistance in your work.

What is population ageing?
(Demography)

> Many people are afraid of aging … much of the negative attitude is
> generated by a set of myths about individual and population aging
> that are not backed and often squarely contradicted by evidence.
> (Axel Börsch-Supan, 2013: 3)

Introduction

If you are reading this book, chances are that you have signed up for a course
in ageing studies or social gerontology, which is a sub-set of gerontology – the
study of human ageing. Or, perhaps, you are working with older people and
would like to know more about social policy issues related to ageing. You may
even be one of those people who picked up this book because you are curious.
Regardless, you are sure to have some questions about ageing and older people.
In our experience of teaching people about ageing, we have identified a number
of questions to which students want to know the answers, but are too afraid to
ask. These questions range from 'What counts as old age anyway?' to 'Will I have
enough money to retire, and when?'. You probably have more questions of your
own that relate to your personal experience, members of your family or what
you have observed from news or public debate.

Whatever your question, we can assure you of two things: you are probably
not alone in asking it, and the answer will be much more interesting than you
expect. We have been so inspired by the questions that students have put to us
over the years that we decided to use their curiosity to shape our whole book.
Each chapter is written as a response to a question posed by a student to one of
us at some stage in our teaching careers. In every chapter you will find interesting
questions lead to fascinating answers.

It is this constant capacity of the study of human ageing to shock, excite, inspire
and even provoke fear that makes it one of the most interesting areas of scholarship
in social science today. Box 1.1 sets out six shockers to whet your appetite:

Box 1.1: Some ageing factoids
- If you are female and were born in 2000 in Kensington and Chelsea (a wealthy area of
  London, England), your life expectancy at birth is eight years longer than a baby girl born
  just 200 miles north in Manchester, England, in the same year (ONS [Office for National
  Statistics], 2013).

- In the UK, as of April 2019, the full state pension is £167.25 per week. That's about £8,700 per year (Department for Work and Pensions, 2019).
- Population ageing is as much to do with children as it is older people. One of the main drivers for population ageing is actually falling total fertility rates (that is, the number of children born per woman) (Harper, 2016).
- In 2016, more than 30 per cent of the homeless population of the United States (US) were over 50 years old and this is still growing (Department of Housing and Urban Development, 2016).
- According to a 2016 Government Accountability Office (GAO) report, in the US, around 50 per cent of households headed by someone 55 or older have neither a pension nor any retirement savings (Government Accountability Office, 2019).
- Extended life expectancy varies across the globe. A girl born in Swaziland today will be lucky to see her 50th birthday. This compares with a life expectancy of 87 years for a girl born in Japan (United Nations Department of Economic and Social Affairs, 2015).

To check out your own life expectancy, use the tool on the UK's ONS website (www.ons. gov.uk).

Our approach

Throughout this book, we aim to keep you interested. So, we will include lots of boxes with interesting facts, references to relevant online resources, and, crucially, difficult questions for you to think about as you learn more about ageing. In this chapter we are going to lay the groundwork by describing some of the infrastructure that you need to understand population ageing. However, we have left detailed descriptions of some key concepts, such as the 'dependency ratio' and 'birth cohorts', to later chapters. We have provided a glossary of key terms for you to check the meaning of concepts too. As social scientists we are also keen to explain how different approaches in social policy and allied health services such as social work and social care might affect older people, or indeed, whole populations who are ageing. Deciding the legal age at which someone qualifies for a state pension may seem like a simple and straightforward policy decision, for example, but it has very significant implications for the experience of ageing in that particular country. For instance, if you are required to work until you are 67 (the current age at which someone is eligible to receive the state pension in the UK) that may lead you to take a very different perspective on your work–life balance than someone who knows that they can retire at 62, such as pensioners in Greece (OECD, 2017). Retiring earlier also means that you will need to have saved a much bigger pension pot throughout a shorter working life. Likewise, if, like many middle-class people in northern and western Europe, you spend longer in education and so don't start earning a salary until you are in your thirties, the time available to you to make adequate pension contributions is shortened. Our working lives are changing and so our pension policies must too. As you work through the book you will get down to the nuts and bolts of policy questions such as this, but first we need to talk about theories of ageing and how they help us to understand and explain population change.

Theories are vital because they help us to sort and interpret information, evidence and data. Evidence without theory is like jelly without a mould – shapeless and difficult to work with. Arguably, theories are the most important part of the infrastructure of your learning about any topic. That is why in this book, rather than separating theories of ageing into a chapter by themselves, we have grounded each chapter in the relevant theory. So, in Chapter 2 you will be introduced to basic concepts of ageism, Chapter 3 covers the dependency ratio, Chapter 6 includes feminist theories of gender and ageing, and so on. As we are interested in both the theory and policy implications of population ageing we have used practical tools to help you to understand how knowledge of ageing societies is constructed. For instance, towards the end of this chapter we will examine and deconstruct the most popular and useful method of representing an ageing population in graphical form, the population pyramid. You will see in Table 1.1 later in this chapter that we have outlined life expectancy and a human development index for populations all around the globe. These are useful measures of working out which stage of the demographic transition a society has reached. First, let us lay out a few ground rules about the theoretical approach that the book takes: critical gerontology.

An important note on the language of gerontology and ageing

For the most part, in your daily life you will notice that the language around ageing and older people tends to swing between two extremes. On the one hand there are the sensationalist newspaper headlines which suggest that our ageing population represents a 'demographic time-bomb'. The time-bomb analogy is based on the idea of the dependency ratio, which we explore in Chapter 3. The short version is that actuaries suggest that, based on current costs of pensions and healthcare, if more people live longer and fewer children are born, then we will be left with fewer workers per retired person. They envisage pension funds then having a big gap between the expectations of members and the funds available. When this is applied to a whole population, it seems legitimate to claim that there is, indeed, a time-bomb of under-funded pensions.

Critical gerontologists have always critiqued this kind of actuarial reasoning for three important reasons. First, we argue that the predictions do not allow for any change of policy. In fact, if pension policies were adjusted to allow for greater life expectancy, through policies such as making larger employer contributions or workers retiring later, then the gap between savings and expectations should never arise. Second, critical gerontologists recognise that by applying actuarial assumptions to a whole swathe of the population, it is easy for the public to come to the mistaken assumption that older people, as a group, are dependent, a burden in some sense. It would not be acceptable to apply this reasoning to other groups. For instance, can you imagine actuaries saying that all pregnant women and their babies represent a 'maternity benefit time-bomb'? This seems ridiculously sexist and short-sighted. If so, then why should it be perfectly acceptable to apply such a reductionist moniker to pensioners as a group? Third, critical gerontologists are very conscious of the role of language in perpetuating myths and stereotypes about old age. We are aware not just of the structures which confine older people to homogenous categories, but also the processes that maintain and support those structures. So, critical gerontologists take great trouble to analyse policies for older people in a way that reveals potential benefits but also the potential of the policy to be oppressive. A good example of this kind of reasoning can be viewed in the work of Bülow and Söderqvist (2014) in critiquing 'successful ageing'. In their historical overview of 'successful ageing' (a concept introduced through Rowe and Kahn's 1984 paper, 'Human ageing: usual and successful') the authors identify how the language of success, central to the discourse of 'Reaganomics' in the US in the 1980s, managed to shift responsibility for well-being in old age away from society or the state, instead placing it on the individual. The door was then left open for neoliberalism, that ideology of the individual, to claim that those who avoided poverty and ill health in old age were ageing 'successfully'. Critical gerontologists are more concerned with where this leaves the many millions of older people who become frail, ill or poor through no fault of their own, a theme that we develop in some detail in Chapter 4.

Bülow and Söderqvist (2014) make a convincing case for recognising that language is not neutral, particularly when it is being used to evaluate the performance of a particular segment of the population. Their critique applies to other related concepts which built on the successful ageing ideology, such as active ageing, healthy ageing or ageing well. At its heart, the critique of these neoliberal approaches to analysing old age has its roots in the broader claim by critical gerontologists such as Meredith Minkler that to understand human ageing we must see beyond the physiological and particularly the biomedical which tends to reduce old age to 'a series of downward sloping lines' (Minkler, cited in Bülow and Söderqvist, 2014: 146). So, language is important because it links back to ideology as well as to conceptual schema and theoretical approaches. The overall impact is that language serves to empower or imprison depending on the kind of ideology or approach it is describing. As you read through this book, take note of when we use terminology such as 'pension time-bomb' or 'economic burden' to describe a policy response to a particular question facing our ageing societies. We will use quotation marks to indicate that the term being used needs critical interpretation by you as a reader, and by your whole class in discussions and debates.

Ageist language, whether hostile or paternalistic, is the tool used to empower or imprison people in stereotypes of old age. It is an important goal of our book that students learn about the impact of their own words, and how to devise fair and clear language to describe ageing and older people through their study and work. There are some clear examples of the impact of language and particularly how a lack of nuanced understanding of the diversity of older people's lives and experiences has resulted in the use of age as a means of controlling the spread of COVID-19 in 2020 (Carney, 2020). The use and misuse of language in the formation of stereotypes is developed in Chapter 2. The issue of language as a means of empowerment or oppression has come to the fore in recent years with the rise of populist and divisive politics in the Western world. There are many reasons for this, most of which are beyond the scope of this book. However, there is one aspect of this shift which is an important conceptual theme running through this book – the prevalence of neoliberal ideology in government, politics, and society for the past three decades.

A note on neoliberalism and Right versus Left politics

Neoliberalism is an ideology, best understood as the marketisation and commodification of every aspect of our lives, from our social media data to our education and healthcare. It began with a backlash against the economic instability of the 1970s, which saw the UK economy dominated by industrial unrest and the US by repeated economic crises. The antidote to this instability was presented as the free market. This neoliberal ideology was institutionalised in US and UK politics through the leadership of Ronald Reagan in the US and Margaret Thatcher in the UK. Thatcher and Reagan worked hard to liberalise and deregulate markets so that the state had less control over the national economy. The purpose of this liberalisation was to free up the market to provide goods and services in a manner which was more efficient and effective than the state could provide. In the UK, Thatcher claimed that the state had no responsibility for individual welfare, setting out to remove state control from as many aspects of life as possible. State-run utilities and transport networks were privatised and those living in free, local government-owned 'council housing' were encouraged to buy their homes under the 'Right to Buy' scheme. While Thatcher's premiership ended in 1990, her legacy is still visible in every general election held in the UK since, including the New Labour government of Tony Blair which held office from 1997 to 2008. Even Labour, the traditional party of the Left with strong socialist and social justice ideals at its core, opted to embrace neoliberal ideology in order to be elected. Thatcher and Reagan's regimes left a legacy, shifting politics in the UK and the US firmly to the more conservative and free-market Right-wing of the spectrum. This shift has been solidified in elections of Donald Trump in the US and Boris Johnson in the UK. However, the importance of collectivist solutions to major problems has been thrown into sharp relief since the COVID-19 pandemic emerged. Suddenly politicians who won votes on the basis of promises to retract state-run public services are utterly dependent on the state institutions they have spent years depleting, such as the National Health Service (NHS) in the UK. These conditions beg the question whether a post-COVID consensus, like the post-war consensus of 1945, could emerge once the pandemic has passed, or whether the experience of the pandemic will make politics even more divisive and individualistic.

   Throughout this book, we make reference to Right wing and Left wing governments. In general, Left means a government which is more socialist or social democratic, such as those parties associated with workers' rights, women's rights and protecting minorities. This would be the Democrats in the US, the social democratic governments of Sweden and Denmark or the Labour Party in the UK. It is worth noting that there is still a lot of diversity within this, with Swedish socialists being decidedly more collectivist than the US Democrats, who are more liberal than socialist. On the other end of the political spectrum we see parties of the Right, or Right-wing governments. These governments tend to subscribe to ideologies such as free-market liberalism, or more commonly, neoliberalism. Examples of Right-wing governments include the US under Donald Trump and the UK under Boris Johnson. Further to the Right on the political spectrum are governments such as those of Jair Bolsonaro in Brazil or Viktor Orban in Hungary. In these cases governments may set out to erode equality or human rights, such as the policy of Orban to ban gender studies from universities in Hungary (Redden, 2019). While you will need to read on to Chapter 3 to engage with a worked example of neoliberalism, it is worth taking some time to read its full definition in Box 1.2.

Box 1.2: Defining neoliberalism

Neoliberalism is one of those awkward phrases that is widely used but, perhaps through such over-use, has lost some of its analytical weight. In his article, 'What is Neoliberalism?', Kean Birch (2017) outlines many of these issues, but also provides a handy definition of the concept and its uses: 'Neoliberalism is regularly used in popular debate around the world to define the last 40 years. It is used to refer to an economic system in which the "free" market is extended to every part of our public and personal worlds ... Neoliberalism is generally associated with policies like cutting trade tariffs and barriers. Its influence has liberalised the international movement of capital, and limited the power of trade unions. It has broken up state enterprises, sold off public assets and generally opened up our lives to the dominance of market thinking' (Birch, 2017: 1). In short, neoliberalism refers to the monetisation and marketisation of many aspects of human life.

Outline of chapters

Deciding what to include in a textbook is always difficult. It is important to be as comprehensive as possible, but restrictions in space and time mean that no book is truly so. Given these limitations, we chose broad themes. The result is nine chapters, each of which addresses a core area of social gerontology. In each chapter, we lean on seminal work to scope out the field, then update this with current publications and try wherever possible to include worked examples to illustrate how the policy plays out for older people and their families in real life. As stated in the Preface, much of the writing for this book took place in 2018–19. The COVID-19 pandemic is unfolding as we make our final changes to the proofs of the book and so only minor comments can be made on the implications of the pandemic for ageing societies. One thing we can say with some surety is that the pandemic throws a harsh light on the need for society and government to take greater account of the age and health profile of their population when planning where to spend public money.

In this first chapter we demonstrate how making the transition to an older population means that we will need to rethink many of the basic tenets of the welfare state. We outline how thinking and research on ageing populations are constantly developing, and how issues which seemed insurmountable in the past (for instance, gender inequality in life expectancy), have now been replaced with alternative challenges, such as the prevalence of dementia, or the need to improve standards of care in residential settings. We use a number of tools such as population pyramids to demonstrate this complexity and provide readers with an overview of population ageing around the globe. We conclude that the problem is not ageing itself, it is that we use age to structure social, economic, and political life in a way that is neither efficient nor effective (Carney and Gray, 2015).

Chapter 2, 'The ageist zeitgeist', takes up the baton of this problematic approach to thinking about chronological age by addressing the challenge of combating ageism – one of the most pervasive and harmful forms of discrimination. We explain how attitudes and behaviours are interlinked and how socio-cultural norms reinforce what is and is not acceptable behaviour.

One of the ways in which ageism perpetuates is through the use of age as a structural barrier to accessing employment and education. We explore some of these issues in Chapter 3, 'Retirement, active ageing and working longer'. By asking whether retirement is becoming a thing of the past, we examine alternatives such as extended working lives and opportunities for new careers in business or trade. We conclude that active ageing, the core policy in this area for ageing societies since the 1990s, is problematic when it is operationalised within the context of high levels of inequality. As levels of inequality continue to increase, active ageing has become maligned in some circles, and is now often regarded as merely an aspiration for well-off older people rather than a workable policy for ageing societies.

As Chapter 3 reports, most people have little say about when they retire. Quite often retirement is the result of redundancy or ill health. For these reasons, in Chapter 4 we take up the theme of care for older people. We note that most carers of older people are spouses or older adult offspring, who are aged 60 or over themselves. While we note the physiological changes that accompany normal ageing, we frame this as just one of many stages of possible dependency experienced across the lifecourse, from birth to death (Fineman, 2005).

Rights are taken up again in Chapter 5 when we discuss 'Diversity among the ageing population'. Chronological age is a pretty spurious basis on which to place people into one group or 'minority' and so it is hardly surprising that diversity among older people is significant. In this chapter, rather than offering a superficial overview of everything from gender to racial discrimination, we choose to focus on LGBTQI* rights as a means of exploring the process of ageing through a period when gay men's lives transformed from being criminalised to gaining equal rights.

As gender discrimination shapes every aspect of ageing across the lifecourse, we have dedicated Chapter 6 to examining how age and gender intersect to produce different experiences of ageing for men and women. We address important questions such as gender differences in old age and how policies affect older women. We finish with a section on masculinity and ageing, concluding that there are particular challenges for men in old age.

In Chapter 7, we move from the discussion of age discrimination to solidarity between generations, one of the most valuable forms of social solidarity in ageing societies. The chapter elaborates on some core concepts, such as 'generation' and 'birth cohort', explaining how each is related but distinct. The chapter goes on to discuss how some governments, who wish to remove socio-economic rights supported through the welfare state, have attempted to erode solidarity between generations by promoting regressive politics of generational equity which have little foundation in researched evidence.

The fact that public discourse about ageing has been 'ceded to political activists, pundits and journalists, leading often to exaggerated or garbled interpretation' (Teitelbaum, 2015: S87) is explored in Chapter 8, 'Politics of ageing'. By asking why older people vote and younger people protest, we investigate how political participation changes across the lifecourse. We conclude that narrowing the gap between public perception of what it means to live in an ageing society and research evidence about population ageing is going to be key in making a peaceful transition to a new, older, electorate.

In Chapter 9, we take up the challenge of ageism, naïve media interpretation and low levels of public understanding of ageing through the lens of cultural gerontology. We explore how the cultural turn has expanded and enhanced our understanding of what it means to live a long life. Through themes of embodiment and identity, and by exploring cultural critiques of the biomedical model, we show how a deeper and more culturally connected understanding of ageing can enrich this stage of the human lifecourse for everyone.

Chapter 10, the final substantive chapter of the book, pulls together all of the core concepts and information from each chapter under broad headings and themes such as political economy of ageing, and post-structuralism. In this chapter, we also lay out a range of possible research questions and areas for further research, which students may decide to pursue at postgraduate level. We conclude with some critical questions for graduates around how they can have a positive influence on ageing societies.

Chapter 11 is dedicated to helping you consolidate what you have learned. We do this through a series of multiple-choice questions. You can dip into this chapter as soon as you have finished working on a particular topic, or you can wait until you have finished the whole book and use these exercises to test your level of knowledge with an end of term quiz. Either way, you will be surprised by how much you now know about human ageing and the policy challenges it poses for ageing societies.

An online resource of questions and exercises is also available at https://policy.bristoluniversitypress.co.uk/critical-questions-for-ageing-societies/online-resources

As this is a textbook, we worked hard to make it a useful and easy-to-read introduction for anyone interested in the social implications of ageing. To this end, we have added an extensive glossary of key terms which we hope will accelerate your education on ageing.

Let's begin by addressing the first question that students ask in class; why are there more older people around now than in the past? Or, to put it more directly, what is population ageing?

What is population ageing?

Population ageing refers to the general trend across the globe whereby the average age of the human population is increasing. This means that a higher proportion of the population is aged 50 years or more. We tend to take 50 as the marker of the very beginning of old age because it is the point at which life scientists recognise that human beings are beyond reproductive age. This capacity of human beings to live beyond reproductive age has been recognised as significant by all the major international organisations. In fact, the implications of population ageing have been recognised as being so pervasive, enduring and significant that, in 2002, the United Nations launched the Madrid International Plan on Ageing. The World Health Organization (WHO) has led a major international 'age-friendly' initiative in more than 46 countries around the world (WHO, nd). The European Union (EU) has recognised it as a 'grand societal challenge' for researchers under the Horizon 2020 programme of research (European Union, 2019). Most countries in Europe have some form of active ageing strategy (see United Nations Economic Commission for Europe, 2018). For policy makers, population ageing is a major challenge, as it requires changes in how resources are allocated between groups.

The process of population ageing is not a static or linear process; in fact, it has been constantly changing since it gained international recognition at the turn of the century. For instance, the human race passed a major milestone in 2015 when, for the first time in human history, the number of people aged over 60 was larger than the number of babies born. So, population ageing refers to the fact that people are living longer, women are giving birth to fewer children (hence the higher average age), and people are moving around the globe so much that it is affecting the population balance. Let's look at these three conditions that contribute to population ageing in more detail.

- Fertility: The number of children being born per woman (referred to as the 'total fertility rate') has been decreasing around the globe and specifically in western and northern Europe, North America and East Asia.
- Delayed mortality: Populations of these same regions have experienced significant increases in life expectancy over the past century. One hundred years ago a woman born in northern or western Europe could have expected to live to be about 50. Today, she will most likely be over 80 at time of death. Her children can expect to live to be over 100 years old. This is an increase of over 30 years in one century. It is helpful to think of this in simple, global terms, provided by leading critical gerontologist, Chris Phillipson. So, in 1900 1 per cent of the world's population was aged 65 or over. By 2000 it was 7 per cent (Phillipson, 2013). This does not allow for regional variation. In some countries, such as Japan and Italy, more than 20 per cent of the population is aged 65 or over. Table 1.1 illustrates these regional differences.
- Migration: The third driver of population change is migration. This does not seem as obvious a cause of population change as extended life expectancy and falling fertility. However, people's decisions to stay in or leave a certain country can have a major impact on the population balance. For instance, one of the main ways that older populations in western Europe can maintain their demographic balance is to 'import' younger people from eastern European countries such as Poland which have traditionally have high levels of emigration. The result is that the population in Poland is now ageing quickly as older people are left behind following the exodus of young people to pursue higher wages and better prospects in richer countries of the European Union (World Bank, 2012).

There are so many interesting points to note about this representation of life expectancy around the globe in Table 1.1. You will see that we use the Human Development Index (HDI) to show not just how long people live, but also the quality of life they are likely to enjoy. The HDI was put forward by leading social scientists such as Amartya Sen, who claim that there must be a strong connection between the means and the ends of human development (Anand and Sen, 1994). Therefore, the HDI is a measure of whether a country's economic progress, measured by Gross Domestic Product (GDP), is accompanied by a society which allows each individual human being to develop their achievements, freedoms and capabilities. The HDI measure is a score between zero and one, offering a useful shorthand for understanding whether human beings are thriving in a specific country. Countries with a score nearer to zero are more likely to have high levels of infant mortality, low levels of access to basic education, and higher maternal mortality rates (for example, Ethiopia and Sierra Leone). On the other hand, countries with low infant mortality, higher levels of tertiary education and literacy

Table 1.1: Life expectancy in selected countries

Region	Country	Life expectancy at birth	Human Development Index	% Population aged 65 or over
Europe	Switzerland	83.6	0.944	18.6
	Italy	82.2	0.880	23.3
	France	82.0	0.901	20.1
	United Kingdom	81.2	0.922	18.7
	Germany	80.5	0.936	21.7
	Poland	76.7	0.865	17.3
	Russia	70.1	0.816	14.6
North America	Canada	82.5	0.926	17.4
	Cuba	79.9	0.777	15.2
	United States	78.5	0.924	15.8
	Mexico	77.3	0.774	7.1
	Jamaica	76.1	0.732	9.9
	Haiti	63.0	0.498	4.9
South America	Chile	79.7	0.843	11.5
	Argentina	76.7	0.825	11.3
	Brazil	75.7	0.759	8.8
	Colombia	74.6	0.747	8.0
	Bolivia	69.5	0.693	6.8
	Guyana	66.8	0.654	5.4
Oceania	Australia	82.5	0.939	15.7
	New Zealand	81.7	0.917	15.6
	Vanuatu	72.3	0.603	4.5
	Fiji	70.4	0.741	6.4
	Micronesia	69.3	0.627	5.1
	Papua New Guinea	65.7	0.544	3.9
Asia	Japan	84.1	0.909	27.5
	Singapore	82.9	0.932	13.6
	China	76.4	0.752	11.2
	India	68.8	0.640	6.2
	Afghanistan	64.0	0.498	2.6
Middle East	Israel	82.6	0.903	12
	United Arab Emirates	77.4	0.863	1.2
	Iran	76.2	0.798	5.7
	Turkey	76.0	0.791	8.4
	Syria	71.0	0.536	4.5
	Yemen	65.2	0.452	2.9
Africa	Algeria	76.3	0.754	6.4
	Egypt	71.7	0.696	5.2
	Ethiopia	65.9	0.463	3.5
	South Africa	63.4	0.699	5.5
	Democratic Republic of the Congo	60.0	0.457	3.0
	Sierra Leone	52.2	0.419	2.5

Sources: http://hdr.undp.orgorenorcountries (HDI); https://data.worldbank.orgorindicat//sp.dyn.le00.in
(Life expectancy); https://data.worldbank.orgorindicat//SP.POP.65UP.TO.ZS?view=map (% of over 65s)

in the population will score closer to 1 (for example, Japan and Switzerland). By including HDI in our table of life expectancies, we hope to open your eyes to the possibility that countries with the oldest populations, both in terms of life expectancy and percentage of the population aged 65 or over, often offer the best opportunities for human development.

As you read through the book, no doubt you will refer back to this table to check life expectancies, and to wonder why certain issues such as gender inequality, diversity, or lack of adequate care might produce a lower life expectancy or a smaller population of over 65s.

Box 1.3: When does old age begin?

Alert readers will, by now, have noticed that we are referring to older people inconsistently. Sometimes we refer those who are 50 years or over as older people, at other times it is over 60 or over 65. People aged 80 or over are often referred to as if they belong to a separate category. The question of when old age begins depends on which population you are referring to. In Sub-Saharan Africa, old age begins in your thirties, or not at all, as a relatively high proportion of the population never makes it to adulthood, never mind old age. The answer to the question of when old age begins also depends on who you ask. Life scientists who study senescence (the biological decline associated with old age) will say that old age begins once a human being has moved beyond their reproductive years. So, for much of the wealthy industrialised world, this is aged 50 or over. For policy makers, age tends to be used as a means by which it is decided whether someone qualifies for a benefit. The most important benefit for older people is the state pension. It is so important in the UK context that retired or older people are generally referred to as 'pensioners'. As the pension age has (up until very recently) been set at 65, for policy scholars in UK and European countries more generally, 65 is the age at which old age begins.

Myths and facts about population ageing

One of the great things about studying population ageing is that, while it is a relatively new phenomenon, the scale and size of the 'longevity revolution' (Butler, 2004) means that there have been major investments in research in the area. From the perspective of social scientists, the most important studies are longitudinal. Longitudinal studies are long-term programmes in which researchers find a group of people who are willing to be poked, prodded, questioned and analysed, not just once in a lifetime, but once every two to five years. Longitudinal studies are viewed as the gold standard in research on ageing populations because they allow you to see if there are major changes in a population over time. There are numerous such studies around the globe, and some are specifically designed to investigate population ageing. These studies recruit participants aged 50 or over and follow their progress for as long as they live. In the US, there is the Health and Retirement Study (HRS). The comparable study in Europe is called the Survey of Health, Ageing and Retirement in Europe or SHARE (www.share-project.org/). There are many country-level studies in Europe too, including The Irish Longitudinal Study of Ageing (TILDA) (https://tilda.tcd.ie/), the Northern Ireland Cohort for the Longitudinal Study of Ageing (NICOLA) (https://www. qub.ac.uk/sites/NICOLA/) and the English Longitudinal Study of Ageing (ELSA) (https://www.elsa-project.ac.uk/).

The architects of these studies had the foresight to design them to be comparable. This means that researchers can compare the physiological, financial and socio-economic status of older people in a number of different regional and national contexts around the world. Comparative longitudinal data is invaluable if we are to start adapting and changing our policies to adjust for an older population. So far, findings from these studies are revealing that older people are a more diverse and complex section of the population than envisaged. The stage of life known as 'old age' is proving to be more productive, and have a more varied experience, than previous generations could have imagined.

At the time these studies were launched (SHARE began in 2004, the HRS in 1992) researchers rather naively believed that adapting to an older population merely meant that we needed to find out more about that older population. Once we had the facts, it was thought that we could then use good quality social scientific evidence of the needs of the over 50s and adjust social spending accordingly. As with most things in social policy (and life) it turned out to be a tad more complicated than that. We will begin to discuss these issues by answering a common question asked by students: 'Why is population ageing a big deal?'

Why is population ageing a big deal?

There are a number of reasons why policy makers and politicians are anxious about population ageing. Basically, any change in the demographic balance of a state's population impacts on family structure, the labour market, the organisation of social welfare, the supply and demand of goods and services, and pretty much every aspect of resource allocation in society. In democracies which operate on the basis of 'one person, one vote', a changing demographic profile could also cause big shifts in voting patterns. We will deal with these issues in Chapter 8, which focuses on the politics of ageing. For now, let's concentrate on what having an older population might mean for the political economy, or the financing and resource allocation decisions that produce the 'welfare state' – the social contract between state and citizens which provides publicly funded supports and services to citizens, including pensions, healthcare and education. In truth, ageing is only the latest in a series of incremental but seismic changes to the global population since death rates started to decrease, followed by a logical decrease in fertility rates. The overall process is referred to as the 'demographic transition' and is said to occur in four stages (Harper, 2016; 1); see Box 1.4.

Box 1.4: The four stages of the demographic transition

- Stage 1: 'Life is nasty, brutish and short' (Hobbes, 1651). High death rates from famine, disease, lack of hygiene and malnutrition, accompanied by high fertility rates. This was the situation in England up until about 1780.
- Stage 2: A rapidly expanding population because of improvements in public health, and a reduction in deaths from communicable disease, but fertility rates are still high. However, child mortality rates are also still relatively high. Examples include 21st-century Sudan and 19th-century UK.
- Stage 3: Mortality rates stay low, but fertility rates now also begin to drop. This is where we begin to see the ageing of the population. This was the situation in Europe or the US in the 20th century, or present-day Uruguay.
- Stage 4: By stage four, the fortunes of the European population have completely turned around from the time of Hobbes: life is now healthy, peaceful and long. Death rates and fertility rates are both low but the population is relatively stable, albeit at a high level. This is the stage we have reached in Canada, the US, and western Europe in the 21st century.

Source: Harper, 2016

The main point to note from Box 1.4 is that reaching stage 4 of the demographic transition is where we begin to see important implications for the welfare state. That said, the recent COVID-19 pandemic has given some of countries with the oldest populations in the world, such as Italy and Japan, a bitter taste of the past, when infectious diseases were widespread killers of vulnerable groups. However, if, as expected, a vaccine for COVID-19 is found and we return to low death rates from communicable and infectious disease, then we are likely to continue to have larger numbers of older people. Making the transition to an older population means that we will have to rethink some basic elements of the social contract that underpins the welfare state. One of the major points of contention is the 'dependency ratio' (the ratio of people of working age to those not of working age). Traditionally, working age in the UK is taken to mean those aged between 16 and 64 years. In Chapter 3, we will discuss why calculating a dependency ratio can be problematic.

At the beginning of the third stage of the demographic transition, it was thought that having more people aged 50 or over would have a major, negative impact on the public purse. Some people even thought that the onset of population ageing might lead to a 'demographic time-bomb' (itself a troubling phrase) whereby a disproportionate number of older people would demand healthcare and pensions, at the expense of younger populations. In some quarters, this deficit hypothesis still prevails. It is now recognised that the assumptions underpinning such a phrase are essentially ageist, as they work on the basis that being older automatically implies dependence and need rather than independence and productivity. However, more recently it has been noted that the 'baby boomers' of the early 21st century (those born between around 1946–64) have not been replaced. So, the increase in the proportion of over 60s in societies that experienced a strong baby boom will begin to reduce after 2030 or 2040 (Reher, 2015). Even so, demographers such as Reher (2015) argue that countries which experienced a strong post-war baby boom, such as the UK, the US and many western European countries, should prepare for a 'tidal wave' of growth in the number of cases of certain chronic or degenerative illnesses typical of persons of advanced age. Note that 'tidal wave' holds similarly negative connotations as 'time-bomb' and reflect the negative associations with older cohorts.

Perhaps the solution is for policies to be tweaked to serve an older demographic profile? Such an approach is preferable to blaming a growing minority of the population for simply living too long. This thesis is gaining traction in gerontology. For instance, Carney and Gray (2015) argue that the problem is not the age of the population itself, but rather how age is used to structure social, political and economic life. We will discuss these issues in more detail in Chapter 2 on ageism and again in Chapters 6, 7 and 8 on gender, solidarity between generations, and the politics of ageing, respectively.

Population ageing in the context of population change

For now, the main point to note is that population ageing is the result of the interaction of a number of drivers including declining mortality rates, decreased fertility rates and migration. The impact of migration should not be underestimated. It has been argued (Carney, 2017) that the issue of falling numbers of 'working age population' (aged 20–64) could be solved by opening up to inward migration. However, this approach may lead to new imbalances. For instance, countries such as Poland have a population that is ageing rapidly due to the exodus of young, educated people to more economically healthy member states of the EU, such as Ireland and the UK, since 2004. Conversely, in countries where immigration is a politically contentious issue, the link could be made between relaxing immigration laws and increasing the number of younger people in the population. Of course, gerontologists would also argue that there are many other means of increasing productivity, such as providing opportunities for older people to gain further education, to remain independent and to enjoy encore careers into their eighties and nineties. This philosophy of 'active ageing' has been the official policy of major international organisations and supranational institutions such as the WHO and the EU since the late 1990s. While this approach is not without its critics (Bülow and Söderqvist, 2014;), active ageing is useful for helping us to challenge notions of old age as a period of dependency (Foster and Walker, 2015). In fact, many older people are independent and active throughout their lives. Related to this is the issue of access to education, which tends to be focused on the early decades of the lifecourse. However, looked at from the perspective of long-term demographic change there are two compelling reasons which suggest that education should be lifelong. First, there is a 'positive correlation between education and the likelihood of a long and healthy life' (Reher, 2015: S66). Second, access to education allows ageing societies to improve their capacity to adapt to challenging circumstances (Coleman et al, 2015: S4). Taken together, changes to any or all of these policy areas – particularly education and migration – could have a major impact on the rate at which a population is ageing.

It is generally recognised within social gerontology that ageing is a gendered experience, and that women suffer particular discrimination and disadvantage in old age. This is, perhaps, why there is a whole journal (the *Journal of Women & Aging*) dedicated to the analysis of women's ageing. In more recent years, scholars such as Laura Hurd Clarke have identified gender issues arising for older men, though this work is less abundant (Hurd Clarke and Lefkowich, 2018). The absence of a gender analysis is problematic for lots of reasons, not least that it tends to cause scholars to be blindsided in their analysis of the causes and consequences of demographic ageing. For instance, in his otherwise robust account of the role of baby booms and baby busts in the ageing of the developed world, Reher (2015: S57) cannot account for the abrupt decline in fertility rates from the 1970s onwards. Other scholars have identified an important role for women's fertility choices in precipitating this change. The 1970s saw the advent of the second wave women's movement in the very countries that experienced a sudden dip in their fertility rates, leading Carney (2017: 2) to conclude that 'gender relations can and do shape demographic trends'.

State, citizen and age relations

The welfare state was designed on the basis that people would live for a relatively short period after retiring. Prussian Chancellor, Bismarck, who is largely credited with introducing the first pension in 1889, was working on the basis that most people would be dead long before qualifying for a state pension (von Herbay, 2014). At that time, life expectancy was 68 and the state pension age was 70. Even up until the time welfare states were established following World War II, life expectancy was much lower than it is today. Moreover, people tended to die suddenly of critical illnesses, such as heart attack or stroke. Fast forward to the 21st century and our population is not just older, it is entirely different in terms of physical health, socio-economic status and the older person's expectations of retirement. For example, the male breadwinner model which was a cornerstone of the welfare state allowed the state to delegate large amounts of unremunerated work to women. Thanks to the work of campaigning second wave feminists from the 1960s onwards, this set of norms is no longer acceptable and more women are in employment. This change in the employment status of women has a positive impact on the dependency ratio (Spijker and MacInnes, 2013) but raises major questions about who will provide care to current and future generations of older people.

Extended life expectancy means that we are now living for up to 30 years after retirement. In countries with established health and welfare systems, people are less likely to die suddenly of heart attacks and other cardiovascular diseases. Nowadays, people have much higher survival rates across a range of illnesses, from cancer to pulmonary disease and stroke. Nevertheless, we are more likely to live with a chronic condition such as type 2 diabetes or dementia. Of course, our trusty longitudinal studies have captured all these changes. However, it is proving very difficult to translate this complexity into public understanding of what it actually means to be older. Health is just one area of change, and there are also major challenges in terms of our expectations of wealth, how we have organised housing, and experiences of loneliness and social isolation, as well as more recent problems such as the digital divide. The big question for ageing societies is that a changing demographic balance will require a reallocation of resources. There is no point in building lots of schools if there are not enough children to take up places. At the same time, we need to start investing in lifelong learning and training programmes if delayed retirement is to become a workable policy solution to increased longevity. Crucially, we need to convince voters and taxpayers that this demographic change justifies a change in resource allocation away from early years and towards older people's services. Unfortunately, this task has been further complicated by the fact that some pundits have decided to use older people as a means to justify the retraction of the welfare state, with disastrous consequences. For instance, the systematic underfunding of social care for older people in the UK has long been a campaigning subject of critical gerontologists, an issue that has been thrown into sharp relief by the thousands of unnecessary deaths in care homes during the COVID-19 pandemic (Phillipson, 2020).

The lack of public understanding of the complex range of issues that arise from an ageing population goes well beyond politics; indeed, it affects every aspect of life, business and community. A major challenge for gerontologists (and a good reason for writing this book) is to help people to understand the implications of ageing for themselves, their families, communities and societies. We are not alone in seeing this gap. In fact, this book contributes to a growing literature which seeks to directly address the gap between public understanding of ageing and its actual, observable implications. Such is the lack of public understanding of what it means to have an older population that Axel Börsch-Supan (the architect of SHARE) felt compelled to write an article aiming to 'demystify popular fallacies' about our ageing population. In that article, Börsch-Supan (2013) outlines a number of myths that have endured, despite ample evidence to the contrary provided by SHARE and other longitudinal studies. *None of the statements in Box 1.5 is supported by research evidence.*

Box 1.5: Common myths about ageing populations
- To make a peaceable and successful transition to an older population policy makers need to plan for changes to the lives and behaviours of older people only.
- Older workers are less productive than younger people.
- Retirement is bliss.
- Keeping older people in the workforce leads to higher youth unemployment.
- Older societies have more intergenerational conflict.

Source: Börsch-Supan, 2013

Börsch-Supan (2013) is not alone in expressing frustration with the misinformation and half-truths that are peddled as 'facts' in relation to population ageing. As social scientists, you will be interested to hear that some of those most sceptical of the 'demographic time-bomb' hypothesis are hard data enthusiasts. For instance, Spijker and MacInnes (2013) have described population ageing as the 'time-bomb that isn't'. Scepticism also comes from demographers such as Teitelbaum (2015) who argue that public debate on population ageing, one of the most significant and impressive developments in human history, has been reduced to a series of crises for the public purse framed in ideological terms (see Willetts, 2010, or Howker and Malik, 2010, as examples of this kind of ideological writing). Teitelbaum (2015: S87) traces the difficulty in producing reliable public information about demographic ageing to its complexity, which had led many pundits to fall for the 'seductive temptation of long range demographic projections, demographic dystopias and garbled demography'.

One of the most important ways of countering this trend is to communicate (and interpret) factual evidence about population ageing in formats that can be understood by a general audience. Population pyramids are a great way to do this as they allow demographers and gerontologists to sketch a graph of how populations in different countries, regions or time periods are ageing.

Population pyramids

Every academic discipline has its signature device that draws in new scholars and keeps those already engaged interested for years, decades, and even lifetimes. Geographers have maps, economists have supply and demand curves, historians have archives and demographers have population pyramids. As demography is the study of the changing structure of human populations, the use of population pyramids has filtered into general use by gerontologists (scholars of ageing). Indeed, population pyramids are so integral to understanding and explaining population change that we have provided the tools for you to create your own population pyramid at the end of this chapter.

What are population pyramids?

Population pyramids are a simple graphical device for demonstrating how many people are alive at a particular period of time in a certain location. A basic population pyramid like the one shown in Figure 1.1 has the number of people on the horizontal x-axis and age cohorts on the vertical y-axis.

Pyramids are generally colour-coded into male and female divisions. There are some websites which allow you to surf different population pyramids by country and region (see https://populationpyramid.net). If you play around with these you will find some fascinating (and sometimes alarming) differences between the gender and age balance of different populations around the globe. For instance, a population pyramid from the US in 1950 will show a high birth

Figure 1.1: An illustrative population pyramid

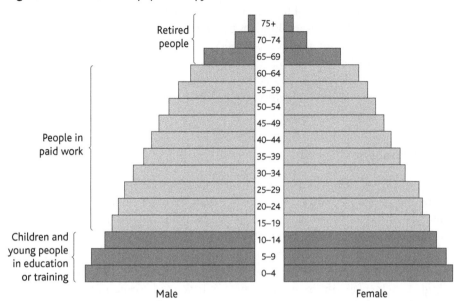

rate, as indicated by the wide base on the x-axis. If you change the year to 2010 you will see major changes at the top and the base of the pyramid. Now there are some 60,000 people living in the US reaching the age of 100 or more. In 1950, the highest age bracket recorded on the pyramid was 80+. This means that while some of those living in the US might have survived up to 100 and beyond at that time, they were so few in number that they could not be recorded meaningfully on the pyramid.

Population pyramids are also really useful for helping us to understand why some countries can be viewed as 'old' countries while other countries still report themselves as having 'relatively young populations'. Once you have mastered the art of deciphering population pyramids you will be able to check out these facts for yourself. Population pyramids also help us to understand the relationships between different birth cohorts, the overall balance of the population and the ratio of young people to old people. These figures are important as they are used by policy analysts and economists to calculate something called 'the dependency ratio', which we will explain in more detail in Chapter 3. For now, take some time to learn how to read a population pyramid, create your own population pyramid, and compare and contrast population pyramids across the globe.

Of course, population pyramids are only one way of demonstrating what a population structure looks like. There are many other methodologies available to researchers of ageing societies. For instance, evolutionary biologists (scientists who study the development of the human race) have a hypothesis that humans have evolved to live beyond the age of sexual reproduction because our ancestors worked out a way to make themselves useful. The detail of the theory is that grandmothers found ways of helping their adult daughters to take care of their offspring (Hawkes, 2003). This adaptation meant that there was a purpose for older members of the tribe and humans began to live longer. Of course, as scholars of ageing we are interested in human ageing in the present day. In particular, we are fascinated in the implications that having an older population may have for social policy. We are also interested in how the experience of ageing may differ from country to country and from region to region. All of these issues will be explored in subsequent chapters.

A final thought

In this chapter we have tried to whet your appetite for investigating what it means to live in an ageing world. We have introduced some of the most important elements of research infrastructure, tools and methodologies that researchers use to explore and understand population ageing. To do this, we have given detailed examples and instructions on how to construct and interpret a population pyramid. We have explained the main drivers of population ageing and how they produce a higher average age in the population. We have made some important detours into critical thinking by asking you to consider when old age begins and to begin to tackle the perennial problem of differentiating myths from facts about our ageing world.

So, we hope by now you are convinced by the United Nations (2002) claim that population ageing is worth studying because it is 'pervasive, enduring' and has 'profound implications'.

REVIEW EXERCISE 1

Creating a population pyramid. See Appendix 1 for detailed instructions.

When am I officially past it?
The ageist zeitgeist

(Ageism and ageist stereotyping)

… older individuals with more positive self-perceptions of aging, measured up to 23 years earlier, lived 7.5 years longer than those with less positive self-perceptions of aging. This advantage remained after age, gender, socioeconomic status, loneliness, and functional health were included as covariates. (Levy et al, 2002)

Introduction

It is a well-known fact that all older people will develop dementia. It is equally well known that when you pass the age of 60 you no longer have sex and lose the ability to function behind the wheel of a car (the two are not linked). These statements are untrue, but they represent commonly held misconceptions about what ageing is and what waits for us on the other side of turning 60. If these statements are false, how do they become so widely accepted? There are many reasons why these myths become 'realities'; together we will explore the key components. In this chapter we will examine attitudes, stereotyping and prejudice, issues that unfortunately affect the lives of older adults and, indeed, of our own future selves.

Ageism is a prejudice unlike any other. A white person will never know what it is to live as a black person. A straight person cannot walk a day in the shoes of a gay person. A man will not experience the same glass ceiling of lower pay and slower progression faced daily by women in the workplace. However, given good fortune, we will all experience the ageing process and therefore ageism will affect us directly at some point. So why is it something that we as a society both perpetuate and fail to challenge? It certainly isn't a minor issue. Ageism is widely acknowledged as globally pervasive by civil society organisations and could be called the last socially acceptable 'ism'. Recent policy changes indicate that international organisations such as the WHO are waking up to the issues being created by failing to challenge ageism. In 2016, the WHO called for cooperation in a global campaign to combat ageism.

Consider the myths in Box 2.1. These are widely held stereotypes and misconceptions of ageing which are addressed throughout this chapter. For now, just read these myths. You can check your thinking with a cheat sheet (Box 2.2) at the end of the chapter.

Box 2.1: Myths about ageing

1. Most older adults will suffer with dementia.
2. The average older adult is either uninterested in or physically unable to have sex.
3. Older adults disengage from the community as they age, preferring to spend more time alone.
4. Generally older adults are all alike (homogenous).
5. Memory loss is to be expected as you age.

(See Box 2.2 for reflections on these myths.)

What is an attitude?

Broadly speaking, an attitude is an internal affective orientation explaining an individual's action (Reber, 1995). Essentially this means that an attitude is a feeling we have towards an 'attitude object' (the target of the attitude, for example, an older person) that directs our behaviour towards this object. An attitude is constructed of four component parts that combine, dictating the strength and direction of that attitude. Using ageism as the logical example, this means the attitude held will dictate whether the feeling is positive or negative, how strong that feeling is and whether or not, in any given situation, we are likely to act upon it. First is the cognitive component. This is the thought process one goes through when looking at prior knowledge, information, education and experience. Essentially, this is the thinking process behind the attitude. Second is the affective component. This includes the emotions, values, desires and preferences associated with the attitude, which are grouped as feelings. The third is the evaluative component. Simply put, the evaluative component is whether the attitude is positive or negative. Arguably, the most important is the fourth, 'conative', component, which is the drive and predisposition towards action. In other words, the conative component is what decides whether or not you are likely to act on your attitude.

Linking attitudes to prejudice

We cannot look at attitudes, especially when addressing the conative component, without analysing how those attitudes link to prejudice. Prejudging a person based on previously held group stereotypes and associated attributions is the cornerstone of ageism. Using the same four component parts discussed in the previous section, the predisposition towards action (conative) is largely driven by the salience of the attitude object, that is whether it is important enough to the individual to act upon. This in turn can be mediated by the group you are with as well as the context you are in; these can dictate the social acceptability of expression. For prejudice to take place, however, it requires more than just holding an attitude. There are two conditions that must be fulfilled. First, grouping or othering must occur. This is the application of rules to form an 'in-group' (those who are us) and an 'out-group' (those who are not us). Without the formation of different groups, there cannot be a target for prejudicial action, and indeed we cannot differentiate between ourselves and those in the out-group. Second, there has to be artificial exaggeration of inter-group differences. Here we create the notion of 'in-group homogeneity', whereby everyone in our own group shares the same positive attributes, and 'out-group differentiation', where those not in our group have the negative characteristics, often in opposition to those attributed to in-group membership. When these criteria are met, the personal affect is high, acceptability of attitude is felt and there is motivation for action, meaning prejudicial behaviour can ensue. We discuss this in the following sections, splitting attitudes into their two subsets of implicit and explicit expression.

Explicit and implicit attitudes

There are two subsets of attitude to consider: explicit and implicit. Explicit attitudes are those that spring to mind when talking about attitudes. This subset consists of attitudes which are under the individual's conscious control and which, when expressed, are done so with total intent and thought. Implicit attitudes are those which are conversely not under the individual's conscious control. Concisely put by Greenwald and Banaji (1995: p 8), implicit attitudes are 'introspectively unidentified (or inaccurately identified) traces of past experience that mediate favourable or unfavourable feeling, thought or action toward social objects'. So, a person can have implicit and explicit attitudes about the same things. They may be the same (both positive) or they could be different (one positive, one negative). In terms of ageing, what we see generally is a positive *explicit* attitude (where the respondent knows what is being asked and responds in a socially acceptable way) and then negative *implicit* biases against older people. This dissonance exemplifies that the implicit bias is one that the person is unaware of but which can be an underlying driver for behaviour (Banse et al, 2001). The main difference between the two subsets is whether the person with the attitude is consciously aware of the gap between their implicit dislike of old age versus their outwardly expressed view that older people are great. There are further differences in the way that these attitude subsets are expressed. Explicit attitudes are less enduring across both time and situation. This means that they are susceptible to contextual cues, such as whether it is acceptable to express a certain perspective in a certain place. For example, you may express different attitudes when you are with co-workers in the office as opposed to friends at a social gathering. Explicit attitudes are potentially expressed differently when a societal shift of acceptability changes, so the individual is able to maintain social standing. In addition, explicit attitudes are more malleable. This means that they can be shaped by the performer to meet their needs.

Self-presentational bias is the process by which an individual wishes to be seen in the best possible light and fit in with those around them to be accepted. In

Figure 2.1: Attitudinal pathways

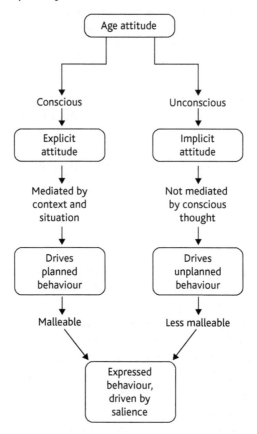

this situation, a negative attitude may be modified or not expressed at all in order to fit the situation and benefit the attitude holder. People who are particularly adept at this are referred to as 'high self-monitors'. Finally, explicit attitudes are also very useful at predicting planned behaviour. For example, if you were going to a conference of gerontologists and older adults you would know the type of people you are likely to encounter and as such you would have a positive explicit attitude towards older people and act based on that. In essence, in a known situation, what you say will inform how you act.

When looking at the implicit subset, these attitudes are far more stable and enduring. As they are not under the performer's control, they are not subject to self-presentational bias or social acceptability. Instead, this subset is built through exposure, something addressed later in the chapter when looking at models of acquisition. Implicit attitudes also differ in their predictive ability in that they are better indicators of spontaneous behaviour. Given the same example of age, picture an emergency admission into hospital. The medical staff will never know which demographic of the population they will see on any given day. They often have to make split second decisions based on experience, knowledge and gut feelings. It is action in this situation that is driven by the implicit subset.

Measuring explicit attitudes

From this it is clear that implicit and explicit attitudes are separate constructs within the larger attitude concept. Because of this, psychologists measure them in two distinct ways. When addressing an explicit attitude, 'Likert scales', such as the Fraboni Scale of Ageism (Fraboni et al, 1990), are often used. These are scales whereby a respondent is presented with a statement and they indicate on a numerical scale the extent to which they agree or disagree with the statement. As with expressions of attitude, explicit scales are subject to self-presentational bias (Paulhus and Reid, 1991). There is also evidence that people may provide socially desirable responses when it is clear what the questions are asking and what kind of response would be deemed appropriate (Paulhus and Reid, 1991). For example, a person might answer positively when questioned about their attitudes towards older people when it is clear that you are trying to work out whether they are ageist or not. Also when faced with completing a questionnaire, respondents face the 'authority principle' as demonstrated iconically by Stanley Milgram (1963). The authority principle means that people respond, not necessarily in the socially desirable way, but in the way they perceive the authority figure (in this case the survey administrator or experimenter) wishes them to. This does not mean to say that such scales are without use or merit, just that they have their limitations. As previously mentioned, explicit attitudes are a good predictor of planned behaviour and are a strong component of an overall attitude and as such should be measured. In terms of ageing research, much is conducted using the Fraboni Scale of Ageism (Fraboni et al, 1990). This consists of 20 items, some of which are purposely worded in a way to minimise socially desirable answers, to assess the perceptions an individual holds about older adults as well as some reflective behavioural items. Items such as 'I sometimes avoid eye contact with older people when I see them' attempt to measure behaviour, whereas items such as 'Many old people just live in the past' seek to ascertain both understanding and opinions of ageing and older adults.

Measuring implicit attitudes

A Likert scale, however, is not appropriate or sensitive enough to assess an implicit attitude. To do this, measures have been developed to tap into an individual's social implicit cognition. The Go/No-go Association Task (GNAT) (Nosek and Banaji, 2001), Affect Misattribution Procedure (AMP; Payne et al, 2005) and Sorting Paired Features (SPF) task (Bar-Anan et al, 2009) tests have all been developed and used with differing degrees of uptake. However, the Implicit Association Test (IAT) (Greenwald et al, 1998; Nosek et al, 2007) is widely accepted to be the most accurate, reliable and consistent, and is broadly used throughout the implicit cognition literature. The IAT relies on measuring 'response latencies' between congruent and incongruent pairings of words and images to ascertain the direction of preference between two categories. This measure, unlike the explicit measure, is not susceptible to self-presentational bias. Indeed answers can only be controlled when a respondent is specifically instructed on how to do so and even then the time taken renders those responses void.

It is important to remember that these are subsets of the same attitude and not distinctly separate. An individual may hold different implicit and explicit attitudes towards the same attitude object. However, in this situation we are able to measure both parts of the whole and we should be able to better predict behaviour and more accurately map the whole attitude.

Where a negative attitude is held towards older adults, it is called ageism. At the other end of the spectrum there are heroic representations of ageing, where older people are presented as benevolent, wise or vulnerable. In a seminal work, Palmore (1990) identified this as positive ageism. Negative ageism is the more straightforward identification of old age as a bad thing and older people as inferior in some way. Positive ageism is a way of using a person's chronological age as if it gives them specific but generalised traits, for instance, by describing them in patronising or heroic terms based on their wisdom, longevity, survivorship or some other exceptional trait that is linked to their age. Both forms of ageism are harmful as they rely on stereotypes rather than encouraging accurate representations of ageing and indeed the recognition of the heterogeneity of ageing.

At this point, it is also worth recognising the fact that ageism is a two-way street. Both younger and older people are subject to ageism related to societal expectation around their behaviour. This book, however, is centred on ageism against older adults.

What is ageism against older people?

Coined by Robert Butler in 1969, ageism was defined as stereotyping of and discrimination against individuals or groups on the basis of their age (Butler, 1969). Although there are various permutations of this, the crux remains the same: using chronological age as a basis for discrimination. In terms of ageism against older adults, this means that those who are classed by themselves or by society as 'older' are discriminated against purely on the basis of stereotypes or expectations based on that old-age categorisation. As mentioned earlier, ageism is unique in that those younger people who engage in ageist action and rhetoric are actually discriminating against their future selves and building on the social acceptance of this practice.

It is helpful to see ageism as having two main pathways: externalised and internalised ageism. The former is the way in which an individual expresses negative age stereotypes or behaviours towards another and the latter is when an individual internalises those negative attributes and assumes them within themselves as they age. There are massive consequences to the older person when subjected to both externalised ageism from others and the internalising of stereotypes that they themselves associate with ageing.

The reason we opened the chapter with a quotation from Levy and colleagues (2002) is because it is one of the most cited statistics about old age. Levy et al (2002) identified that older adults who demonstrated negative attitudes towards ageing lived less long than those who exhibited a positive age attitude. Their study tracked 660 people over the age of 50 in a longitudinal design establishing that those holding more positive self-perceptions about ageing and the ageing process lived seven and a half years longer on average than those in the sample who expressed negative self-perceptions on ageing. This is a shocking statistic but when it is unpacked, it is not all that surprising. Internalised ageism has been shown to increase levels of cardiovascular stress and reduce levels of self-efficacy (Levy et al, 2002) in line with stereotyped expectations as well as significantly decreasing activity, productivity and ability; this is known as the stereotype embodiment theory (Levy, 2009). Some physiological declines such as dementia are widely reported in the media in a way which suggests that every older person either will, or is sure to, live with dementia. This influence is one of the reasons why the stereotype exists that all older adults will have dementia. Dementia is not normal ageing, but the idea of living with dementia has begun to reflect assumptions of normal ageing. This becomes ingrained in the social mindset and creates self-fulfilling prophecies whereby older people are expected to become socially isolated, lonely, lack physical ability, live with cognitive decline and ultimately become a fiscal burden on family and state alike (Levy, 2009). The physiological and psychological impacts of ageism are not minor, nor are they confined to lesser developed countries or lower socio-economic groups.

Arguably, ageism becomes an issue for society, limiting the research done and questions asked in order to formulate policy to support older adults. Ageist assumptions and attitudes prevent societies from embracing the opportunities of an ageing demographic around the world. Instead, an ageing population is presented as a problem. This negative view is supported by out of date heuristics (stereotypes and mental images). As gerontologists who study the activities and lives of older people, we know that older adults have the capacity to make huge contributions to society. Embracing the wealth of knowledge, experience and ability that is within the marginalised older community will only further advance those ageing societies willing to embrace the opportunity afforded to them.

How do we acquire attitudes?

As with measurement, acquisition of attitudes is slightly different for both implicit and explicit subsets. Two schools of thought around attitude development exist, the averaged account and the summation account. The averaged approach suggests that attitudes are formed from the average evaluations of the attributes (or characteristics) associated with an attitude object (for example, an older person) whereas the summation approach suggests that an attitude is the sum of evaluations (positive and negative) associated with salient outcomes of observed behaviours (including both media and personal experience). Explicit attitudes are formed through the averaged approach, whereby conscious cognition is used to shape the direction and strength of the attitude held. Implicit attitudes are formed through the summation approach, whereby no conscious thought process is required and it is, moreover, the sum of the experiences observed which influence the attitude held.

When looking at the items leading to both forms of attitude acquisition, these are wide and varied. Observing salient actors or models, such as family members, friends and even celebrities, can shape the attitudes held and developed as we age. Media, and increasingly social media, bombard us with images, text, opinions and information that all inform attitudes. With regard to ageing, these can be explicit, like stereotypes that shape our perceptions of age and ageing. Classic examples are grey hair, using a walking aid or exhibiting cognitive decline. In addition, they can be implicit, whereby only younger models are used in commercials for beauty products, cars or other desirable items. This implicitly reinforces the notion that young is attractive and therefore to look old, and by proxy to be old, is bad. Each time age is presented in this way (old = bad versus young = good) it reinforces the stereotypes of older people as undesirable or having traits which are negative. The opposite is the image of a younger person who is presented as the pinnacle of social desirability. As mentioned earlier, ageism does work both ways. Where older people can be seen both as wise or doddery, young people can be seen not only as physically attractive and strong but also as 'snowflakes' and 'moaning millennials'. When ageism is targeted at older people, however, where it has both the most effect and the most traction, it is a harmful social practice, corrosive to both the older person and society more widely. Arguably, it is middle-aged adults, those stepping away from being prejudiced against for being young but not yet old enough for 'standard ageism', who are the catalyst for both youth and older age discrimination. Stereotyping will be discussed later in the chapter, but it is worth remembering that stereotypes must be taken with more than just a pinch of salt, applying context and subsets of attitude to both their adoption and expression.

Though the averaged and summation approaches are eloquent in their explanations, in this book, the authors propose a holistic model of attitude acquisition and reinforcement across the lifecourse. While acknowledging the same sensory inputs from media and salient influencers, this new model proposes an overarching approach to how reinforcement continues through the lifecourse leading to the internalisation of negative associations (see Figure 2.2).

The Acquisition, Internalisation and Reinforcement (AIR) model of ageism in Figure 2.2 illustrates the lifecourse approach to attitude development. From childhood, we make observations and assimilate information which feeds into the creation of stereotypes and attitudes about older people. These are expressed once acquired (even through social anecdotes or humorous quips) resulting, as we age, in internalisation of our own worth according to our chronological age stereotypes. The acceptance of these traits as belonging to older people becomes

Figure 2.2: AIR (Acquisition, Internalisation, Reinforcement) model of ageism

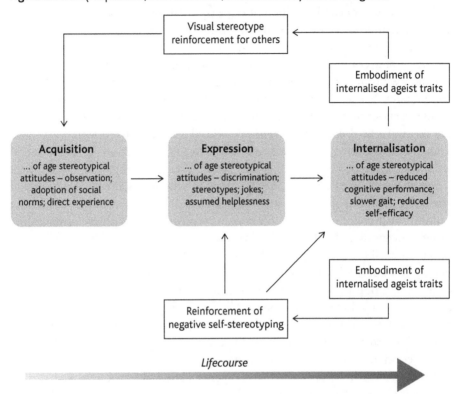

internalised as we accept our own transition into older age, resulting in an array of negative physiological and psychological consequences. The embodiment of these traits then has a dual effect. First, exhibiting age stereotyped traits feeds into the observations of others' acquisitions of negative ageist attitudes. Second, exhibiting the traits also reinforces one's own beliefs about the ageing process and the effects it has, deepening the internalisation and expression of age negative opinions towards others of the same age group. As an exemplar, an older person internalises the stereotype that as you age, you become less stable on your feet and less mobile. This becomes a self-fulfilling prophecy whereby they walk less often, as they lower expectations of themselves. The result is a gradual loss of mobility and independence. All the time this is being observed by other older people and those in the social out-group. The model identifies the feedback loops, which lead to deepening and perpetuating stereotypes and further lead to societal observations of stereotyped behaviour.

What are stereotypes and why do we use them?

Stereotypes are the labour-saving devices we all use in our daily lives to help us comprehend the huge amount of stimuli we receive. We create cognitive schema and heuristics to 'chunk' information units together, creating rules about values and attributes associated to different objects, situations and people. Stereotypes are created and, as we progress through life, we use these as a platform to seek additional information, strengthening stereotypes and associated attitudes. If we encounter contradictory information then, unless undeniable or massively salient, we dismiss it as an exception that proves the rule. We do this for the same reason that we create stereotypes in the first place. Humans are inherently indolent, choosing the path of least resistance, and stereotypes assist us in reducing the cognitive load. Basically, stereotypes are like a kind of short-circuit way of categorising ourselves and other people so that we can make sense of the world around us. Stereotypes regarding older people are also subject to the ultimate 'attribution error' (Pettigrew, 1979). This is where negative behaviour and attributes of an out-group (in this case, older people) are attributed to intrinsic causes. The thought process is, 'that's typical of an older person', and positive out-group behaviour and attributes are exceptional cases or due to the environment or situation. This is to say that the in-group ('youth') to which the observer belongs is associated with positive traits and values with the opposite being true of the out-group ('not youth'). For instance, stereotypes of older people being behind the curve in terms of understanding and using technology allow younger people to feel more in control of what is important in life. In making these associations, stereotypes are maintained, attitudes are strengthened and the AIR model continues the cyclical trajectory.

There are further issues with stereotyping about older people that can be far more serious than assuming all older people use walking aids or become forgetful. Negative implicit attitudes and negative age stereotypes have been shown to be prevalent in the health care setting, with diagnosis and treatment not being based solely on presented symptoms but also on perceptions about the patient's age (FitzGerald and Hurst, 2017). Sex is one obvious example. Few people want to think of their parents having intercourse and as an extension of that, they don't think of or acknowledge that older generations engage in intimate sexual relationships. However, this is simply not the case. Physical intimacy and indeed sex have been shown to be important in the maintenance of successful relationships as well as for cognitive and physical well-being (Gott and Hinchliff, 2003). Where it is impossible for someone in their 90s to get pregnant, they are capable of having sex and so run the same risks as younger people when it comes to contracting sexually transmitted infections (STIs). In fact, there is an alarming rise in the rates of STIs on the older adult population (Bodley-Tickell et al, 2008). Dependent on the STI, symptoms can range from sore joints to cognitive impairments similar to those caused by dementia; as such, STI symptoms may be mistaken as signs of 'typical' ageing. If doctors are not taking a sexual history and are discounting STIs as a potential cause then not only are we doing an injustice to older people but we are potentially jeopardising their health and the health of others for the want of an open mind, some safe sex advice and some antibiotics.

The take-home message from this section is that stereotypes can be useful and they have to have some basis in truth. A stereotype that is not reflective of at least part of the target group wouldn't be a stereotype; there would be too much incongruence with observed reality. So, stereotypes are processing shortcuts that can be useful in a complex world. However, if stereotypes are overwhelmingly negative and used in an uncritical way they can serve to diminish the credibility of a person, or indeed, an entire group. We have all seen an older person who has grey hair or is walking with a stick or living with dementia. To use these observations to generalise isn't too much of a stretch. We fall into the trap of ageist stereotyping when we judge the whole person by their grey hair or walking stick. This is how stereotyping can be incorrect and damaging to this and future generations of older people, ourselves included.

Is it all doom and gloom?

As alluded to earlier in this chapter, attitudes can be changed. It may take a little bit of work (even more work is needed if you want to shift those internalised attitudes) but it can be done. This is why high-profile campaigns like that from the WHO are invaluable in turning the social tide. In 2016, the campaign to combat ageism was launched by the World Health Assembly (part of the WHO) in an attempt to turn the tide on ageism. They proposed an information gathering exercise to collate all of the known expertise in the area to synthesise effective action to challenge ageism. They aimed to develop a global coalition, harnessing a free communication and discourse to improve data working and make structural changes in policy delivery. This was the first time such an ambitious undertaking had been attempted, but the WHO understood that it was going to take a concerted effort from all sides at the same time to make any impact, as a piecemeal change would be undermined by the pervasive ageist narrative. Challenging the overwhelming negative associations with age needs an intergenerational approach and a desire from all parties to engage. Education needs to change in terms not only of formal information about ageing but also in the way media portray ageing to more accurately reflect what it is to be an older person. Policy makers, employers and the public need to engage with counter-stereotyped images of older people. This is not to say extreme counter stereotypes. Just as when forming stereotypes, counter-stereotypical imagery needs to be plausible and possible, otherwise it will not be salient enough to challenge the existing heuristic and will be dismissed.

A final thought

So what does ageism mean in the face of increasing longevity? Are we destined to feel worse and spend more scarce health resource combating a form of prejudice that is known to reduce quality of life in old age but which is totally preventable? It would seem so. With the growing tide of ageism (especially implicit) and the seemingly tacit understanding and acceptance of ageism socially, this pernicious condition is set to make more of an impact as the number of older people grow. Does this have to be the case? Totally not! There is a band of researchers aiming to develop interventions to break this cycle and produce programmes to challenge this last bastion of socially acceptable prejudice. However, it will take more than this. A step change in public opinion is required. A realistic view of ageing and 'prospective self-ageing' is required to shake the acceptance and challenge the stagnant norms. The 'cultural capital' (Bourdieu, 1986) that older people have to offer is dependent on society's ability and willingness to cash in on it. The population is ageing, the quality of this ageing is largely dependent on accepting this and on how different countries challenge these myths and embrace ageing as a positive and contributory part of the lifecourse.

Box 2.2: Debunking the myths of ageing

These are the facts behind the myths presented in Box 2.1.

1. Dementia is NOT a natural part of ageing. It affects only approximately 6 per cent of those over 65, and 40 per cent of those aged over 80 have a diagnosis of dementia at any one time. Life can cause us to forget things. This is the same no matter what age we are and is not synonymous with ageing. Similarly, no older person should be described as 'suffering' with dementia. It is like any other disease, and an older person can live well with dementia provided they have support and the understanding of those around them.

2. Sexual attitudes and patterns do not change significantly with age. Sex is rated as important by older adults and is part of subjective and measurable well-being. Among older people, the main change in sexual behaviour tends to happen following the death of a partner. Older people are less likely to engage in new relationships of a physical nature than people in their thirties and forties. The problems that arise with not acknowledging older adults as sexual people are evident: older adults are experiencing the largest percentage growth in number of STI diagnosis, and one in four adults living with diagnosed HIV in the UK is aged 50+.

3. Desire for social contact remains stable throughout the lifecourse. Some people will seek it, others will not. If social limits occur, this is usually due to mobility issues or loss of friends or partner and not through lack of interest.

4. As we progress through life, we make decisions that shape the direction of our lives. As an older person, we have made a life full of the decisions that differentiate us from one another. With this in mind, those aged over 50, 60 or 70 are no more alike as a cohort than any other age group.

5. Memory loss is not a predictable part of the ageing process and instead is linked to medical issues. However, the process of retrieval does slow with age. This is where the little acorn of truth exists to grow the oak of misinformation that old age equals memory loss in all cases.

REVIEW EXERCISE 2

Media outlets are a vast source of information for all ages. In terms of ageism, all forms of media (social and otherwise) hold a mix of positive and negative imagery about ageing. For a seven-day period, note down every time an older person is seen, mentioned or referenced on radio, TV or online. Make a note of whether this is positive, negative or neutral. Include anything you think is an example of stereotyping. This can be blanket media like the TV or it can be tailored media searched for on Facebook, Twitter, YouTube and so on. You should locate at least 10 references to allow you to make a comparison. Are these presentations largely positive or largely negative? What are the predominant character representations?

Group: Divide into groups of four. Pool your findings and discuss. What provided the 'best' examples of ageism, fashion sites, healthcare settings, TV, Facebook, and so on? Which examples do you think are more serious? Can you create a hierarchy of the incidents of ageism, from those which you think are most serious to those which, in your view are less damaging? Have you found any incidents of ageism against younger people?

Solo: Make a table of references to ageing and older people, allocating them to negative, neutral or positive categories. Post on social media to challenge the very media you have analysed.

Will I ever have enough money to retire?

(Retirement, active ageing and working longer)

We are entering the age of no retirement. The journey into that chilling reality is not a long one: the first generation who will experience it are now in their 40s and 50s. They grew up assuming they could expect the kind of retirement their parents enjoyed – stopping work in their mid-60s on a generous income, with time and good health enough to fulfil long-held dreams. For them, it may already be too late to make the changes necessary to retire at all. (Hill, *The Guardian*, 29 March 2017)

Introduction

This chapter will describe the wide breadth of experiences of retirement around the world. For some people, particularly those who live in a country with a long-established welfare state and who enjoy good health, retirement can be a relaxing time where work-life balance is improved. For others, who live in a place where the statutory pension is miserly or non-existent, retirement is a continuation and sometimes worsening of grinding poverty. Disadvantageous circumstances are, in such cases, compounded by failing health and increased frailty that sometimes accompanies old age (Betti et al, 2015). So, the quality of retirement is intrinsically linked to the availability of an adequate income, commonly paid in the form of a pension. From the perspective of policy makers, pensions are important because they represent large proportions of governmental costs, as much as 46 per cent of social expenditure in some European countries (Ebbinghaus, 2015: 58).

In this chapter we will show how pensions can be interesting and easy to understand. We will do this by providing you with some of the key concepts underpinning pension policy. We start by offering you a brief history of pensions in the UK and elsewhere. Next, we will introduce the concept of the 'dependency ratio', which is at the heart of most arguments about the affordability of pensions. Related to this, we will provide you with an overview of some sociological tools to help you to work out whether and when people should retire. The concept of the 'institutionalised lifecourse' will be used to explain how we unconsciously live our lives according to 'chrononormativity' – the tendency for society to expect people to engage in certain activities at certain stages of their lives (Leonard et al, 2017). Our historical perspective on pensions will also demonstrate how social statistics have played an important role in the introduction of pensions, the very first form of social welfare payment. Please note that, though gender is a major issue in terms of the experience of retirement and access to pensions (see Foster, 2010), we have decided not to deal with gender and retirement here, but to cover it in Chapter 6, gender and ageing.

This chapter is a good place to further explore some of the core concepts introduced in other chapters. We will return to ideas such as the demographic transition established in Chapter 1. We will also draw on some of the issues raised in Chapter 8 about the political will needed to change policies in ageing societies. We will apply some of the concepts from Chapter 2 on ageism, in order to understand decreasing demand for workers as they grow older. Towards the end of this chapter, we will outline some key concepts for understanding the ageing workforce, such as the lifecourse perspective and the over-bearing influence of neoliberalism in defining what constitutes work (Polivka, 2012). The importance of solidarity between generations will also emerge in our discussions of extending working life. As the chapter progresses, you will learn that pensions occupy a crucial position at the very apex of social policy in ageing societies, somewhere between political decision taking and economic policy making but with deep implications for social welfare.

Pensions

While pensions are reported as one of the first social benefits to be paid by the state, they are still a relatively recent invention. Early pensions served a dual purpose. Primarily, they were designed to avoid destitution of people who were too old or too sick to work, but they also facilitated labour market turnover, allowing employers to replace older workers (Macnicol, 2015). In policy terms, pensions had an important effect in producing a new category of citizen – a 'pensioner' – which became recognisable as a distinct social group (Townsend, 1981). Arza and Johnson (2006) argue that the reason old age poverty trumped other social ills of the period was because pensions became politicised. It is only because politicians could see the electoral value of pensions that the payment became codified in social policy. In the UK, there was support from across Labour and Conservative political parties that pensioners should not be subject to the Poor Law (Arza and Johnson, 2006: 7). Similar situations existed in countries which were among the earliest adopters of pensions, such as Germany, where pensions were introduced in 1889. It has been said that conservative Chancellor Bismarck introduced pensions in order to steal votes from socialist parties (Arza and Johnson, 2006). The dates of pension introduction around the world can be seen in Box 3.1.

Box 3.1: Pensions around the world

German Chancellor, Otto von Bismarck, is generally credited with having introduced the first pension for lower income workers in 1889 (Arza and Johnson, 2006: 2). But the idea of a state pension was slow to take hold around the world. The first wave of pensions were introduced in the early 20th century – New Zealand, 1898; Australia and the UK, 1908; France, 1910; Italy, 1919; Poland, 1927. However, pensions were not distributed equally, often only applying to men. In European countries, women did not qualify until much later than men. Race also plays a role in determining access to pensions. For instance, white South Africans received a pension from 1928, but Black South Africans had to wait until the 1950s.

A brief history of pensions in the UK

When the UK old age pension was introduced in 1908, citizens qualified when they reached the age of 70. At that time, average life expectancy in the UK was about 79 years of age, so policy makers expected to have to pay out for only a few years. Given these parameters, to guarantee a pension to a small section of the population seemed like a prudent piece of policy making. Campaigners such as Charles Booth played an important role in convincing policy makers that pensions were necessary (Lain, 2016). Charles Booth's 1887 survey provided empirical evidence that old age was the single greatest cause of poverty, as 38 per cent of paupers were aged 65 or over (see Lain, 2016). His findings were supported by 1899 research undertaken by Seebohm Rowntree (in Lain, 2016); Rowntree demonstrated that many of those in poverty were trapped by circumstances (such as old age or widowhood). At that time, the general view was that people were responsible for their own poverty, which was a result of laziness or lack of self-control. The idea of a publicly funded pension challenged this view. In terms of providing a basis for supporting pension policy, this was a very significant shift.

If older people are not responsible for their own poverty, then their welfare becomes the responsibility of the state. This is certainly the case if the social norms of that society will not accept hordes of destitute older people as a fact of life. Booth's and Rowntree's research (which Lain (2016) identifies as early social science), therefore, provided evidence of this reality and so played an important role in radically improving the lives of older people in the UK (Arza and Johnson, 2006). The work demonstrates that social science research evidence does matter. It can have an influence on policy and people's lives, particularly if it informs policy development.

By the time the State Pension Act was passed in 1908, Booth's original idea of a flat-rate pension that was not related to previous earnings had been significantly watered down. The final pension was set below a subsistence level and means-tested. No one was going to enjoy a 'comfortable' retirement on this pension. This was in tune with Victorian ideals, which maintained that people were best helped by experiencing enough discomfort to motivate self-reliance. Likewise, anyone deemed not to be of 'moral character' was excluded from qualification. Historian Karen Chase's readable history of old age in Victorian times charts the 'halting movement towards public provision for old age through a system of universal pensions' (Chase, 2009: 6).

The story of UK pensions continues in this miserly vein through the 19th century, though major gains for retired workers were made in 1925 when contributory pensions were introduced for workers and widows. Pemberton et al (2006: 5) recognised gender inequality as a root cause of 'extensive relative poverty of older women' as it meant anyone exclusively involved in unpaid work was unable to make social insurance contributions and so was effectively excluded from the system. In any case, it was not until the Beveridge Report of 1942 and the subsequent Social Insurance Act of 1946 that pensions became the norm for UK citizens (Pemberton et al, 2006).

Politics played an important role in establishing public support for pensions. The principle of a pension for all citizens was most likely politically possible because of cross-class solidarity that was established through the sacrifices made by all citizens during both world wars (Lain, 2016: 24). However, the usual tussles between Right- and Left-wing governments continued. Labour introduced the 'basic state pension' in 1946. This went through several iterations, eventually becoming linked to prices rather than earnings by a Conservative government in 2010. Arza and Johnson (2006) offer a succinct and useful overview of the series of events that have led to the UK pensions systems becoming one of the most complex in the world. Politicians who introduced pensions never foresaw the extension in life expectancy to the extent where most people would live for 80+ years. As public expectations of having a pension grew, so did the number of people surviving to pension age. For most of the 20th century this was not a problem, as the extension of coverage meant that the proportion of those paying into the system also increased. However, these workers eventually reached retirement age, the birth cohorts coming through behind them were smaller, and so contributions were lower (Arza and Johnson, 2006: 8). Policy makers engaged in a number of policies to fill the gap between demand for pensions and supply of pension payments; 'public pensions in most high income countries were seen by the 1990s to be facing multiple problems – population ageing, system maturity and rising costs' (Arza and Johnson, 2006). Pensions became complicated and costly, gaining a reputation as a major drain on national funds. The stage was set for reports such as the World Bank's (1994) *Averting the Old Age Crisis*, which laid the blame for rising pension expenditure firmly at the door of older people themselves. Of course, with the benefit of hindsight, this is not a supportable position, nor was it intentional. If societies develop health and welfare systems that increase longevity, we can hardly blame beneficiaries of good healthcare and social welfare for living beyond an age costed for in our national budgets.

The debate about pensions continues to this day because publicly funded pensions were never established as a right of all citizens. Instead, UK pension provision became a combination of below subsistence means-tested state pensions which the better off supplement with generous occupational pensions (Lain, 2016). Governments of both Left and Right appear to have expected the private sector to fill the gap left by an inadequate state pension (Pemberton et al, 2006).

The result is a high degree of inequality within birth cohorts in the UK. The most obvious inequality is between those with private occupational pensions and those without. The result is that some pensioners are quite well-off, while the majority, particularly older women and especially widows, still live precariously on the edges of poverty (Arza and Johnson, 2006; Pemberton et al, 2006; Macnicol, 2015). In the next section, we explore the concept of the dependency ratio, which is used to understand, explain and plan pensions around the world.

The concept of the dependency ratio

The dependency ratio is the concept used to describe the balance of the number of people of working age versus those in retirement and those still in school or training. The United Nations definition of the dependency ratio states that 'the dependency ratio relates to the number of children (0–14 years old) and older persons (65 years or over) to the working-age population (15–64)' (United Nations, 2013).

Policy makers find the dependency ratio a useful concept because it allows them to estimate who is likely to need access to social support (that is, those not in jobs) and how many taxpayers will be available to fund that support. A high dependency ratio means that there are fewer workers to support those outside the labour market. A low dependency ratio is most desirable in the eyes of policy makers because it means that there will be more workers to support dependents. Ultimately, this means that because there are more people of 'working age' (that is aged between 15 and 64 years), the assumption is made that there will be more taxpayers' money available to support everyone.

The relationship between population change and the dependency ratio is complex and ongoing. For instance, at the early stage of the demographic transition, the dependency ratio declines. This is referred to as a 'demographic dividend' because there are fewer children to support, and there are plenty of adults still at work. As fertility continues to decline, mortality also decreases and we see the effects of population ageing taking effect as workers begin to reach retirement age. It is at this point that economists start to get anxious about population ageing because they see dependency ratios rising. The economist's perspective is summed up by Hurley (2012): 'After plateauing around 2010, the share of those of working age is predicted to decline steadily from 67 per cent to 59 per cent by 2040. A growing number of dependents, most notably retirees, will be accompanied by a declining number of persons of working age' (Hurley, 2012: 3).

Of course, there are some researchers who take a lateral view on this issue and argue that much of what is lost in terms of 'older workers' over the past 60 years has been regained in terms of women now being economically active. Indeed, Spijker and MacInnes (2013; 2) have shown that 'the proportion of the entire population who are at work is similar now (48%) to what it was 60 years ago (46%)'.

A note of caution: critical limitations of the dependency ratio

There are some limitations to the dependency ratio as a proxy for indicating the 'economic burden' of an older population, not least the point made in the opening chapter of this book, that using language like deficit, burden or time-bomb creates a negative expectation around ageing and older people. Moreover, the model assumes that all under 15s and all over 65s are economically dependent. This is, most likely, not the case. In some countries people will start working at 13 or 14, while in others many young people spend longer in education, only beginning to pay social insurance (and tax) in their twenties or thirties. Another problem with the dependency ratio is that it tends to classify only paid work as economically useful. There are many other activities that make a contribution to the economy, which are not counted as paid work. Some examples include caring for an ailing relative, caring for children or grandchildren, doing housework, managing household accounts, growing food in the garden, volunteering in your local library or charity shop. If we were to include all of this unpaid work as economic activity, the dependency ratio in an older society would look quite different. The dogmatic belief that paid work is the only activity of any value is closely linked to the dominant ideology of the late 20th and early 21st century, neoliberalism. In the next section we look at how the values of neoliberalism have been applied to the institution of retirement.

Neoliberalising retirement

Macnicol (2015) argues that the concept of the dependency ratio has been used disingenuously by neoliberal ideologues who wish to dismantle the whole institution of retirement. Macnicol (2015) builds a strong case for taking a sceptical look at some of the 'demographic facts' presented by policy makers and politicians who wish to use population ageing as an excuse to remove social welfare from the hands of the state.

   Macnicol (2015) expertly and relentlessly lays out how the concept and practice of neoliberalism, as both an ideology and a stage of capitalism, impacts on the status of old age as a life stage and older people as economic entities:

> In general, pure neo-liberalism tends to view categories like 'old age', 'disability', 'unemployment' and even 'poverty' as mischievous welfarist constructs that encourage a false notion of rights. When applied to older people, this prescription implies that old age should be defined down to a residual category, and that older people should work as late in life as possible. (Macnicol, 2015: 20)

The reality of this policy is starting to seep into public understanding of the changing nature of retirement. Newspaper articles leading with headlines such as 'A World Without Retirement', like that cited at the beginning of this chapter, are increasingly common, particularly in regions such as North America and western Europe where the over 60s have already reached sizeable minority status of between 15 and 22 per cent of the population. Ebbinghaus (2015) sums up the challenge as particularly difficult for countries with 'pay as you go' pension systems where the working population finances current pensioners. The pressure on pension systems has increased since the financial crash of 2007–08, when many private pension schemes lost much of their value at very short notice (Ebbinghaus, 2015).

Does everybody get a pension?

Of course, as scholars of ageing and social policy, you will, by now, have realised that there is almost always a solution to social problems. In the case of financing retirement, the solution is to increase pension contributions, particularly those made by the state and employers, and to remove barriers to labour market participation such as lack of skills and expensive childcare. As illustrated in Box 3.1, in countries like Sweden, every retiree receives a pension. This contrasts with Kenya whose government, having ignored older people for generations, introduced a universal old age pension in 2018. Anything is possible. It is not that financing retirement is impossible, but it is difficult. Reforming or creating a viable and fair pension system requires brave political decision making. It requires governments to take a long-term perspective on the welfare of future generations. Failure to take a long-term view is a perennial problem, given that politicians tend to work on the basis of five-year electoral cycles (Rajan, 2010). In short, the end of retirement is not a natural outcome of population ageing; it can at least partially be attributed to the decline of the collectivist political will needed to provide public support for the financing of pensions or, indeed, any other social welfare payments on the basis of need (Taylor-Gooby, 2016).

When successive neoliberal governments' dismissal of retirement as too costly is combined with wage stagnation and rising inequality, we reach a situation where even people in employment cannot afford to make adequate pension savings. Ebbinghaus (2015) offers a useful analysis of how neoliberal policies have engaged in both privatisation and marketisation of pensions. As governments realised that the 'free lunch' – where citizens paid more in social insurance than they drew down in the form of pensions in the earlier stages of the demographic transition – had ended, they sought to encourage private providers to fill the gap of inadequate state pension payments (Arza and Johnson, 2006). This left the door open for pensions to become a market-based commodity, which only those with surplus income can afford to finance. Given the reliance on short-term or zero hours' contracts and the rising costs of housing, it seems unlikely that current generations of workers will have adequate retirement savings and so pensions, or rather the lack of adequate pensions, look likely to be a major challenge for future generations of older people.

For all of these reasons, it is important that you are aware of neoliberalism as both a stage of capitalism and as a political ideology (Macnicol, 2015). As you delve more deeply into policy options in ageing societies you will go on to read about many of the 'problems' presented by an older population, such as retirement, extending working life and the issue of age discrimination in the labour market. Being mindful of the role of neoliberal ideology in counting the cost of ageing, rather than the value of older people, will help to give you a balanced perspective on whether these problems arise from changes in our population balance or from political problems such as rising income inequality and retraction of the welfare state. Take a look back at the HDI scores and percentage of the population aged 65 or more in Table 1.1 to convince yourself that many older societies are also stable and prosperous societies.

Pension reform

By the 1980s, the legitimacy of retirement as a social institution was being slowly eroded. This has manifested in a number of ways, most clearly through arguments about the rising costs of pensions as people live longer after retirement. Again, the problem rests with an absence of long-term planning. For instance, in the 1990s, in an effort to deal with the large 'baby boomer' birth cohort's need for employment, employers expanded early retirement programmes where older and 'out of date' employees, who were not well versed in information technology, were phased out. This practice had the effect of bringing forward retirement so that it now began as early as the age of 50. This societal norm is observable in a range of contexts. From the perspective of policy makers, from the 1990s onwards anyone aged 50 or over is deemed to qualify as an 'older worker'.

At the same time, early retirement schemes also sent out the message that older people were disposable workers who were unlikely to be able to cope with the demands of information technology. Once they were retired, older people were designated as inactive in the labour market, thereby entering the debit column on the actuaries' dependency ratio calculator. With the benefit of hindsight, we can now see that the 1990s was an inopportune time to implement these changes. Early retirement schemes were introduced just as life expectancy was reaching 85 years of age or more. The combination of growing numbers of older people and their inactive status made for convenient circumstances for those trying to argue that welfare states were economically unsustainable. If you find this confusing, you are not the only one. Ebbinghaus (2015) remarks: 'Although they have advanced in tandem in response to the public finance problem, demographic ageing and the diffusion of neo-liberal economic doctrine, the two should remain analytically separated.' He has a point, but for the purposes of understanding the lived experience of reaching retirement age in ageing societies, it is worth noting that neoliberal ideology is likely to use any change in population balance (whether that is a rising number of migrants or older people) to justify the further retrenchment of the welfare state in favour of free market alternatives. In terms of pensions, the doctrine is clear – the welfare state will no longer provide an adequate pension. Therefore, it is down to the individual to finance their own retirement through a private pension, sale of assets or simply delaying retirement until they are too old or too sick to work. Some scholars, recognising the need for some way of demonstrating the value of retired people to a market economy, governments and policy makers, have devised 'active ageing' as an alternative to work in old age (Foster and Walker, 2013).

Box 3.2: Fact checking neoliberalism

Take a few minutes to see if neoliberal ideology influences public thinking about the ageing workforce. A quick Google search for 'grey tsunami' will yield many results such as the headline in the October 2012 edition of *Discover Magazine*: 'The gray tsunami: the world faces a wave of aging, and with it wrenching social and economic changes'. In this article, the author chooses to ignore the subtleties of demographic projections, instead choosing to treat estimates of future need as forecasts. We will discuss this in more detail in Chapter 8, but suffice to say, there are numerous examples of how population projections have been way off the mark in the past. Instead, we argue that you should look to other evidence of what older people can contribute to society and economy, not just count the cost of their needs. For instance, in the UK, the Royal Voluntary Service (2011) commissioned a report which found that older adults were a net contributor to the economy. Where total welfare costs were found to be £136.3bn, the net contributions were circa £175.9bn, including informal social care totalling £34bn and volunteering estimated at about £10bn. When looking at the projections to 2030, they suggest that this net benefit will increase to £75bn, with the costs of welfare increasing to £216bn but the benefit reaching in excess of £291bn. This highlights the importance of a balanced narrative and the recognition of a wide range of contributions made by older people outside of the traditional workplace. Further, it also advances the discussion about the value of informal caregivers, something discussed in more detail in Chapter 4.

Active and successful ageing (and their many detractors)

The idea of older people as active agents in their own lives and the lives of their communities underpins the globally popular concept of active ageing: 'Active ageing is the process of optimizing opportunities for health, participation and security in order to enhance quality of life as people age' (WHO, 2012: 12). One of the main markers of living under a neoliberal regime is what Beck and Beck-Gernsheim (2003) have referred to as the 'risk society', where people are individually responsible for their own welfare. This implies that the state and collectivist solutions to social problems are replaced with more efficient and cost-effective solutions that rely on individual responsibility for individual welfare. From this perspective, older people, rather than being viewed in a paternalistic way, should be encouraged to enjoy their freedom, independence and agency through working longer or contributing to society as volunteers, unpaid carers of grandchildren or through any other productive activity.

At the time at which the idea of active ageing really took hold as the core policy response for ageing societies, there was growing scepticism that older people were in need of any social protection at all. Through the postmodern lens of sociologists such as Gilleard and Higgs (2000), who sought to deconstruct existing assumptions around ageing, an image of older people as a cultural grouping concerned with individual desires and frivolous activities such as holidays and shopping was projected. This scholarship adhered to the mantra that whatever came before must be deconstructed by postmodernists. In this way, these authors unwittingly opened the door for neoliberal ideologues to present retirement as an expensive luxury rather than a well-earned rest. For example, Gilleard and Higgs (2000) proclaim: 'People who are retiring at the end of the twentieth century are able to access a material culture that is more extensive – richer – than ever before' (Gilleard and Higgs, 2000: 32). While it is difficult to argue with this, it is also fair to remark that anyone living in the UK at the end of the 20th century had a similar experience. By foregrounding age and making it synonymous with leisure (through retirement) Gilleard and Higgs seem to suggest that, by virtue of their elevated age, older people are somehow less deserving of material wealth. The response to Gilleard and Higgs (2000) by theorists of the political economy of ageing (such as Alan Walker) (Foster and Walker, 2015) was to support the idea of active ageing – whereby the loss of social and economic status through retirement could be compensated for by 'working' as a volunteer, through self-care and making a contribution to community and family in old age. Neither side of this debate in social gerontology which ran throughout the 2000s managed to deal with the fact that active ageing is superimposed on a very unequal world, although Walker, in particular, did make a valiant effort (see Walker, 2012). While retiring at that time may have been a boon for those with occupational pensions, for most people, retirement was a continuation of poverty, bad health and social exclusion.

Human ageing: usual and successful

The roots of the active ageing versus old-age dependency debate can be traced back to a seminal paper by Rowe and Kahn (1987). The authors argued that there was too much focus on the losses associated with old age when in fact, 'human aging' is 'usual and successful'. This approach is widely identified as the precursor to what became active ageing in the 1990s and 2000s. Some problems identified with the successful ageing model include the fact that high levels of inequality mean that it can never be a universal experience. For older people who are well resourced and have access to high quality health and social care it is possible to remain active and independent. On the other hand, those in ill health, with debilitating conditions, no occupational pension and poor or inappropriate housing can be utterly beaten by the onset of any one of a number of likely events of old age, such as loss of a spouse or age-related disability. These observations led to some robust critiques of active and successful ageing, such as that by Bülow and Söderqvist (2014) who clearly outline how the reliance on 'successful ageing' as a barometer for ageing well inevitably leaves some older people doomed to failure. Bülow and Söderqvist are particularly mindful of how the moral message that those who are ageing well are doing so because of their own hard work is attached to active ageing. They go so far as to argue that it has seeped into research and policy making in ageing societies. In their view, a critical perspective is needed so that active and successful ageing can be '… understood as a practice that was also political, normative, and with concrete consequences for the lives and social policy of ageing individuals' (Bülow and Söderqvist, 2014: 146). Despite these shortcomings, active ageing is still the go-to policy for policy makers in ageing societies and is now integral to most national policies on ageing. There is now an Active Ageing Index which measures how societies are helping their older populations to remain independent for as long as possible (https://www.unece.org/population/aai.html). Foster and Walker (2013, 2015) and Foster (2018) have completed extensive work on active ageing in national, supranational and international organisations.

Work, retirement and the institutionalised lifecourse

One of the major issues to consider when looking at the impact of population ageing on retirement is to critically evaluate the place of work in our lives. It seems sensible to remember that – as well as your age – your gender and citizenship status, and other factors such as the historical juncture when you were born might affect your life and career trajectory. Fortunately, there is a rich literature in this area. Following on from the seminal work of Matilda White Riley on age stratification (1971), the concept of the institutionalised lifecourse was developed by German sociologist Martin Kohli (1988). In making the case for a sociological (as opposed to merely economistic) understanding of ageing, Kohli argued that work structures the lifecourse. Kohli (1988) demonstrated that our lifecourse is institutionalised into three distinct stages over which we have little control. Other authors argued that the welfare state plays an important role in enforcing structure on the roles and activities expected of us at different points in the lifecourse (Mayer and Müller, 1986, cited in Mayer, 2009: 415).

So, life trajectories are shaped by when you are born, your gender, issues such as age segregation, the structure of welfare state institutions and other factors. To be a child means to meet social expectations to go to school, to become educated and be prepared to work on reaching adulthood. In industrial societies, this education is clearly linked to the next stage of life, productive adulthood. This is a long period of life where one is expected to produce goods and services and earn money as well as pay taxes which support the welfare state. Finally, the third stage is retirement, where one is deemed to be too old to work, but to have made enough contributions to earn a basic income in the form of a pension. Figure 3.1 shows the three stages of the institutionalised lifecourse in industrial societies.

Figure 3.1: Kohli's institutionalised life course

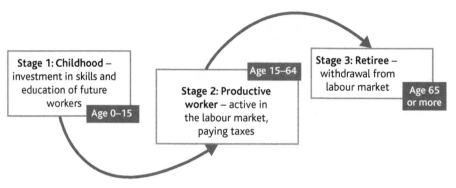

Source: Visual representation of Kohli's institutionalised life course (Kohli, 1985, 1999)

The institutionalised lifecourse

The three stages of the institutionalised lifecourse are integral to the structure and operation of the welfare state as each stage facilitates the next. So, it is only through the tax and social insurance contributions of people of working age that we can finance the healthcare and education of children and the retirement of older people. In this sense, solidarity between generations (see Chapter 7) is at the very heart of welfare states. The welfare state is central to allowing people to make transitions between significant life stages unscathed. Through child benefit, maternity benefit, unemployment assistance, health, education and other public services as well as pensions and healthcare in old age we are supported by the welfare state. In establishing this theory, Kohli (1999) drew on Elder's (1999) classic study *Children of the Great Depression*, first published in 1974, which established the lifecourse approach, an increasingly important branch of ageing studies. This approach has since been developed by Dannefer (see Baars et al, 2006) and Hagestad (2018).

Lifecourse sociology is now an important aspect of understanding not just population ageing, but also how social institutions work with the welfare state to produce social policy outcomes (Mayer, 2009). Thanks to the work of lifecourse sociologists we now know that age is not the only factor to take into account when considering someone's welfare. The time at which that person was born will also have a big impact on their expected income, their access to social security, and their ability to earn their own living (Laslett, 1991). So, a woman born in the US today is much more likely to be free to work and save for a pension than women who married in the 1950s. However, her wages may be too low and her childcare costs too high for her to afford to save for retirement. Likewise, people who came of age around 2010 have hit a very difficult job market following the Great Recession of 2008. The 'baby boomers' – born 1946–64 – are a particularly large birth cohort, which explains why there is so much hyperbole in the media about everything they do. More recently, psychologists have attempted to identify iGen – the birth cohort born between 1995 and mid-2000s, whose whole life experience has been shaped by how we interact with information technology. We will look at a number of further examples of these issues later in the chapter when we examine case studies of older apprentices who retrain in middle age, physicians who seem reluctant to retire, and women who say they never get to retire from housework (Leopold and Skopek, 2016). The institutionalised lifecourse has also proven to be very useful to scholars struggling to work out the implications of population ageing for social inequality. For instance, women's experience of work in industrialised societies does not leave them as well prepared for a comfortable retirement as men's. We will delve into this in more detail when we deal with gender issues in Chapter 6.

Box 3.3: What is a birth cohort?

A birth cohort refers to a group of people who are born in the same year, years or decade. They are defined as a 'cohort' because the historical juncture at which they are born when combined with their year of birth means that they share social and cultural experiences and events. Researchers prefer to use the term 'birth cohort' rather than 'generation', to discuss social policy. 'Generation' is more correctly applied within the context of family generations such as parents, grandparents and great-grandparents (Bengtson et al, 2005, in Katz et al, 2012).

Extending working lives: supply of and demand for older workers

There has been much discussion among policy makers about how to convince people to retire later. Moreover, there is overwhelming evidence that people tend to be inconsistent in terms of their approach to planning for retirement. Jansen (2018) drew on the European Social Survey to try to distinguish the role of national culture in attitudes towards retirement. His results suggested that people state that they wish to retire before statutory pension age, with many people mentioning 60 or younger as the ideal age at which to retire. In some countries, such as Russia, as many as 59 per cent of people reported that 60 was a good age at which to retire. This contrasts with Ireland where the statutory pension age was 66 in 2019 and is set to increase to 68 by 2028, which is broadly in line with the rest of western Europe. The results of Jansen's survey are completely out of line with stated government policies that are designed to *increase* the age at which citizens can retire. The gap between public and government expectations of retirement is best understood by looking at supply of and demand for older workers. The supply side refers to the willingness of older people to work longer, though issues such as physical fitness may hamper this (McLaughlin and Neumark, 2018). The demand side refers to the willingness of employers to retain or recruit older workers.

When it comes to demand for older workers, a major issue is the prevalence of age discrimination in the workplace. There is research evidence that employers tend to favour younger workers (Loretto and White, 2006) and older workers have reported being sidelined in favour of younger colleagues (Loretto et al, 2007). In a scoping review of 43 research articles on ageism in the workplace, Harris and colleagues found that older workers 'are more likely to be precariously employed in part-time, entrepreneurial or contract work' (Harris et al, 2018: e1). When large corporations or institutions are cutting back on their wage bill they tend to offer 'voluntary' schemes aimed at older workers which encourage early retirement or voluntary redundancy. In the case of high value jobs, these packages may be fairly attractive, particularly to workers who have been in the same role for several decades and feel inspired to try something new. This leads to the other side of the equation, which is the supply of older workers.

Are older workers willing to work longer? In some cases, workers may be forced to take redundancy or to retire on the grounds of ill health. There have been some interesting studies in this area in recent years which point towards there being some major challenges to stated government policies to extend working life to the age of 68, 70 and in the longer term even as far as 80 years of age. Some researchers have even begun to study 'un-retirement' – the practice of returning to paid employment after retirement (Platts et al, 2017).

In fact, there have been studies which show that some older workers are unwilling to retire. In a study of academic physicians in Canada, Pannor Silver and Williams (2018) found that many older doctors were unwilling to retire because they could not face the future without the high status that accompanies their job. In some cases, the physicians (who would be on excellent salaries) reported not having enough retirement savings to give up work. The study authors concluded that the doctors' over-commitment to their work and their employer meant their personal lives were almost non-existent. These doctors had, socially and culturally, nowhere to go if they left their jobs. This led the study authors to ask an important question, which is central to the difficulties governments have experienced in extending working lives:

> Do medical institutions have a responsibility to regularly replace physicians who are not at the very top of their game or who might die in order to ensure patient continuity in care and develop cutting edge medical treatments? Or does pushing academic physicians toward retirement to benefit the institutions constitute an ageist or oppressive approach? (Pannor Silver and Williams, 2018: 327)

A social policy scholar might respond by saying that medical institutions have responsibilities to both parties, while a social gerontologist might give more credence to the physicians' claim that arbitrary age limits on our working lives are a form of institutionalised ageism.

Are 'encore careers' the solution?

If extending working lives is to become a viable solution to the pensions crisis, providing new opportunities that are genuinely attractive to older workers seems like a viable policy option. The quality of work available to older people plays an important role. Pannor Silver's study of Canadian CEOs showed that those with well-paid jobs which they found interesting and rewarding did not enjoy the experience of retirement (Pannor Silver, 2019). Leonard et al (2017) undertook a study of older workers who were keen to retrain in order to reenter the labour market in a different role. Their study of older apprentices, undertaken in England, sheds light on a number of factors that affect older workers. As apprentices are usually 16 years old when they begin their training, the experiences of older apprentices, who were all at least 40 years old when they started training, brought to light the predominance of 'chrononormativity' in barring access to lifelong learning for older people. The apprentices reported feeling isolated for being 'out of step' with their peer group. The research demonstrated how social norms prevail around issues such as when is an appropriate time in one's life to take on certain roles: 'Personal histories are made legible through state-sponsored timelines which serve national economic interests by framing lives as chronological sequences of "productive moments"; normalising the "prime" age at which, for example to start a career, attain promotion or think about "winding down" in terms of labour market participation' (Leonard et al, 2017: 1671). It seems that Kohli's institutionalised lifecourse acts to curtail the extension of working lives at a cultural level.

The older apprentices described, in vivid detail, how Kohli's (1985) differentiated lifecourse is institutionalised. Barry, aged 48, reported that, 'You get to a certain age and you get discarded' (Leonard et al, 2017: 1678). Being older meant that the past had a big influence on the apprentice's current skills and experience. In some cases this was advantageous. In many cases, older apprentices were presented as positive to the business case of managers because of their high level of reliability. This is evidence of what Palmore identified as 'positive ageism' (1990), where being older leads to positive assumptions of passivity or reliability. This image of the reliable older worker can become a trope for an 'ideal type' of employee for low status jobs. Partly because the labour market is not fully open to them, older workers can be more loyal and reliable than younger workers who may have more choice and control over their lives.

Weller et al (2018) found higher levels of entrepreneurship among older Americans than younger cohorts, recognised as 'un-retirement'. They attributed a return to work after official retirement to the fact that 'insufficient retirement savings and a desire to remain productive at older ages may simultaneously lead older households to consider working longer'. Through working for themselves, older people can avoid ageist company bosses, have greater flexibility of hours, more independence and greater self-esteem. Older people are also more likely to have access to capital to start a business. So, entrepreneurship seems to be an adaptation to both supply and demand of older workers discussed earlier.

Overall, there are supply- and demand-side issues to consider when thinking about how to increase the number of years that people work. Demand-side factors, particularly access to training and protection from age discrimination, must be tackled. Supply-side factors tend to be overstated by neoliberal policy makers, though people do express a desire to retire early in public attitude surveys. With appropriate reforms to social welfare, extending working lives could be positive for older people and society, but it must be managed appropriately. Older workers must be paid fairly and protected by equality policy and legislation which counters age discrimination in the workplace.

A final thought

This chapter has offered an overview of the main issues surrounding work and retirement. A brief history of pensions in the UK showed that the pension was a significant development in early welfare states. The introduction of pensions also played an important role in establishing the causes of poverty more generally in the UK. For instance, Thane (2005) reports that, as early as 1870, British policy makers had investigated the possibility of compulsory saving for retirement. However, the very low level of wages, particularly of women, revealed that British workers would not have the spare cash to save for retirement (Thane, 2005). It is somewhat alarming to note that this is still a major issue for workers in 21st-century UK, where zero hours contracts make it impossible for people to save for their pension. It also demonstrates that the principle of conditionality, which limits some people's access to pension income, still clouds the payment of pensions in UK economy and society.

REVIEW EXERCISE 3

Go onto a pension calculator website to work out how much you need to save for retirement. What age would you like to be when you retire? How much weekly or monthly income do you think you would need to live on? Can you guess what major challenges exist for you in securing a decent income in old age? Think about where you are now in your life and evaluate which choices you should make in order to improve your chances of having a comfortable retirement? Is it better to remain single, or to get married? Is your gender likely to affect your income in old age? Write a chronological report of what you think the best steps are for you to guarantee a secure income in old age.

Group: Discuss this in a group, making reference to age, gender, ethnicity and the other issues that might affect the capacity to save.

Solo: Based on your research using the pensions calculator, write a short reflective piece on how governments might improve public understanding of pensioner poverty.

4

Will I need care when I am old?

(Care and support in later life)

There are only four kinds of people in the world – those who have been caregivers, those who are caregivers, those who will be caregivers, and those who will need caregivers. (Rosalynn Carter, 2011)

Introduction

In the opening paragraph of his book *The Human Tide: How Population Shaped the Modern World*, Morland (2019) offers a vivid description of population change in the UK since the mid-18th century. He gives the example of a typical young woman, Joan Rumbold, and her struggle to survive. In 1754, Joan was 19 years old and lived in London. There she met John Phillips, who gave her the dual gifts of a pregnancy and gonorrhoea before abandoning her. Like many desperate people at that time, Joan found herself falling on the mercy of the local workhouse. After some time, she was offered a job as a servant but, in order to take up the job, was forced to leave her son, John Junior, in the workhouse. He died there a couple of years later. Morland (2019: 3) draws the not surprising parallel that, 'this unexceptional story of desperation, abandonment and infant death would today scandalise most societies in the developed world, triggering heart-searching and finger-pointing from both social services and the press.'

Morland's (2019) book is an historical perspective on demography. Joan Rumbold's story offers us a vivid, personalised account of what it was like to live without the welfare state and without the combination of scientific discovery and medical advances. It also gives us a flavour of what life was like for women when they had few rights, or none at all. Morland (2019) argues that since the time of Joan Rumbold's life and death, life in England has for most people, transformed from being 'nasty, brutish and short' (Hobbes, 1651) to being relatively peaceful, healthy and long, though recent experience with the COVID-19 pandemic has, in many ways, taken us back to 1918 and the era of uncontrolled infectious disease. The purpose of this chapter is to offer a critical, exploratory introduction to the implications of this change in length and quality of life in terms of care. The opening section will offer a detailed overview of the physiological changes that come with ageing, as opposed to declining health. In many discussions of health and ageing, these two issues are conflated, and old age has become synonymous with ill health. In fact, it is possible to reach a very old age in full health, notwithstanding some changes to the acuity of our senses, our mobility, our living arrangements and our social lives. It is this last aspect of healthy ageing – the social context – which is of most interest to us in this chapter.

Even now, in the 21st century, too often, older people find themselves in hospital beds, in residential care homes or on medication not because of disease or ill health, but because of a lack of social care, community or family supports. It seems that ageing societies find it difficult to understand how a person can be well, but in need of care. The spectre of 'apocalyptic demography' of which we are so critical throughout this book underpins this obsession with maintaining independence in old age. Throughout this chapter, we argue that we all need care at some point in our lives. Lloyd (2012: 4) counters the neoliberal obsession with risk and personal agency by adopting a 'feminist ethics of care approach'; this rejects 'the characterisation of humans as essentially self-sufficient and independent' instead working on the basis that 'in order to achieve independence and autonomy human beings must first be cared for'. The usefulness of such a feminist ethic of care is very clear if we travel back in time to Joan Rumbold's experience in 18th-century England. Women had few rights, poverty was the norm, and infectious diseases were common killers of children under five. All human beings are vulnerable at some point in the lifecourse, most of us at several points, and none of us is truly independent (Fineman, 2005).

The question which shapes this chapter – 'Will I need care when I am old?' – is a serious and empirical one. It gives rise to another question, this one more moral and political: 'If I do need care, *who* will care for me in old age?'. If you take a few moments to think about it, the answer to both questions is related to human rights, women's rights, social justice and more recently recognised questions around justice and fairness surrounding the division of unpaid work within the private sphere of the family. Elder abuse, carers' rights, women's rights to pursue their own economic life through paid labour outside the home, the rights of migrant care workers, the vulnerability of older women who raised families and cared for older relatives earlier in the lifecourse – all provide a veritable stew of problems and unresolved political and moral questions for ageing societies. All of these questions straddle private and public life, forcing us to think critically about whether who provides care to older adults is a personal issue for individuals to resolve or a broad-based political problem requiring a policy response. The final point, also enunciated clearly by Lloyd (2012), is that many of the questions around eldercare which we deal with in this chapter are related to a key problem in ageing societies, covering such things as the provision of care for older adults, the environments in which it is delivered, the systems upon which older people rely, and who indeed provides such care.

There is a long-term problem with how we think about care. In many ways, as with other areas of interest to feminists, care is often seen as a woman's issue, something that occurs within the private sphere. On the other hand, policy making for older people, or indeed anyone needing care, takes place in the public sphere. In fact, the experience of giving and receiving care involves a constant ebb and flow across the threshold, to the workplace or institution, requiring generations to work together or to care for one another. The day that societies and governments can recognise that care is a public good, with huge economic, social and moral value, is the day that we finally see an end to the unnecessary human suffering that is an everyday experience of older people, their carers, families, and friends.

For all of these reasons, in this chapter we have chosen to focus on care, rather than health. There are many excellent books written on the health of older people, but the decision not to include a whole chapter on health was a conscious one. First, as we said in the preface, health and the prevention or cure of disease lies firmly within the biomedical approach to understanding ageing and older people. Medical gerontology is a very important part of research on older people, and without it, many of the older people we study and work with would not be with us today. However, there is a particular narrowness of focus which comes with medical gerontology which can be problematic for critical gerontologists. Estes and Phillipson (2002) do a good job of explaining this – that many of the 'problems' of older people, such as cognitive impairment or depression, are identified as having medical causes, when, in fact, they could well be the result of poverty, inadequate housing, social isolation, or any number of other deficiencies in policy provision. Many of these problems may be more to do with race or gender than illness. Likewise, there is a clear distinction to be drawn between issues that arise for people because of the onset of old age, rather than the onset of illness. In the next section we outline some of the physiological changes which are normal consequences of ageing. Our main aim in sharing these with you is to help you understand that ageing and ill health are two quite distinct trajectories. It is possible to be perfectly healthy in old age but to nevertheless need some social care to help you deal with loss of mobility or sensory capacity due to old age.

Focusing on the contrasts between the US and the UK, we will highlight the differences between public and private provision of health and social care, taking time to outline the differences that exist in a system where healthcare is still seen as a public good (UK) versus a system where healthcare is sold as commodity on the open market (US) (Lloyd, 2012). In doing this, we will aim to break down yet more myths about who cares for whom, and how. Throughout this chapter we refer to research reports from civil society organisations such as the Alzheimer's Association and carers' associations for statistics on who cares for whom. It is worth noting that these data, while timely and useful when accessing a hidden population such as home carers, are not as reliable as data from articles which have been through the double-blind peer review process of most academic journals.

In order to understand why care is such an important aspect of social policy making in ageing societies, we first need to understand why we are more likely to need care as we grow older. One place to start is to examine the physiological changes that lead to changes in our senses.

Physiological changes that may accompany ageing

As we age, our senses change. Our senses (touch, taste, smell, vision and hearing) are the ways in which we interact with everything around us; as such, any impairment in these can interfere with the way in which we experience and enjoy the world. As we grow older we can expect impairment in all our senses (with, for example, the most severe reductions in odour detection being reserved for those who develop Alzheimer's or Parkinson's disease (Iwamoto et al, 2013). Each of these physiological changes impacts the ways in which an older person can support themselves independently.

Visual deterioration occurs in several ways as we age. The lens itself starts to harden, leading to a condition called presbyopia (Robert and Allen, 2016). This hardening can lead to issues with focusing on near items so that object recognition may become more difficult, as indeed could focusing on stairs and so on. The typical ageing process is also associated with a yellowing and thickening of the lens (Ruddock, 1965). This can change the way in which colours are seen (Page and Crognale, 2005), the clarity in which we see the colours and shapes around us (Spear, 1993), and the way we detect any motion (Snowden and Kavanagh, 2006). These changes in the structure of the eye affect the function and the way in which we can interpret and interact with the world around us.

Hearing loss often occurs as part of the ageing process. Around two thirds of adults over 70 have impaired peripheral hearing (Wilson et al, 1999). While this does not necessarily result in becoming deaf, it does impact the way in which we engage with the outside world, including our ability to hear those who are not directly in our sight, and who may be trying to get our attention.

Ageing also produces other changes to our hearing. It has been found that ageing affects what is known as the temporal fine structure (Grose and Mamo, 2010) and the temporal envelope (Füllgrabe and Rosen, 2016), even in those older adults who are not affected by peripheral hearing loss. Simply put, the changes in the temporal envelope and the temporal fine structure trigger changes in the amplitude and frequency of how we hear sound. As this becomes less sensitive over time, it results in changes in perceptions of loudness, pitch and timbre. These are key perceptions when engaging in conversation: this is where we find the nuances in language, as well as being able to disentangle several auditory inputs when in a noisy environment. Similarly, these perceptual changes mean that we are less likely to engage with nuanced music or indeed get the same rich understanding from music being played.

When we look at sight and hearing together, it is known that loss or decline in one can lead to a compensatory action in the other (Dickinson and Taylor, 2011). However, as we age, this compensatory function is limited due to the proliferation in dual sensory decline (Dawes et al, 2015). What is also of note is that dual sensory decline in later life has also been linked to cognitive decline (Moore et al, 2014). This makes sense when you think about how much we need our hearing and vision to engage with the world around us. What we see from this is that, as we age, impaired sensory input through vision and hearing negatively impacts on cognitive tasks (Schneider and Pichora-Fuller, 2000).

Olfactory decline, or loss of sense of smell, is something that is commonplace as we age. Broad (2017) conducted a systematic review of the field, highlighting that this age-related olfactory decline is associated with a decrease in quality of life and a deterioration in the perception of flavour, a point to which we shall return shortly. She also noted that through behavioural modification, changing diets and drug therapy, this can be reversed, at least in part, leading to a regaining of the quality of life associated with smells. The perception of flavour is a really important idea to keep in mind too. This is a combination of smell and taste. Predictably, as we age, our taste sensitivity to all five tastes (sweet, sour, salt, bitter, and umami) also declines (Ogawa et al, 2017). Ogawa et al (2017) identify that this can have a huge impact not only on quality of life but also on the nutritional intake of older adults. Biological factors such as reduced numbers of taste buds (Feng et al, 2014) interact with disease states (Lalla and D'Ambrosio, 2001), prescription medications (Tomita and Yoshikawa, 2002), olfactory acuity (Kaneda et al, 2000), and lifestyle factors such as smoking (Sato et al, 2002) and poor oral hygiene (Akar and Ergul, 2008), resulting in this age-related change.

As Ogawa et al (2017) highlight, the change in the ability to taste foods severely impacts the enjoyment of eating and as such the social aspect of food – sharing food, eating with friends and even the basics of sufficient nutritional intake – thus affecting health as well as well-being.

Finally, tactile discrimination in our touch or grip also changes with age (Decorps et al, 2014). It is suggested that this occurs due to decreases in the speed of nerve signal transmission (Besné et al, 2002) and the overall changes in the amount of grey matter in the brain (Yang et al, 2010). In combination with the other sensory declines, this can simultaneously increase the risk of falls and decrease quality of life and well-being (Correia et al, 2016). These sensory changes are age related and although some interventions can be effective in slowing them down, they will affect the majority of older adults in a way that will challenge their quality of life (Correia et al, 2016). That said, as discussed later in this chapter, the majority of older adults are able to maintain independent living either in their own home or with a spouse or family member. Where many believe that the majority of older people live in supported living environments, this is not true. With that in mind, however, the chance of requiring short-term respite, rehabilitation, or even long-term care does increase as we age.

Physiological decline is one of the core stereotypes associated with ageing and one of the core components of negative associations or attitudes towards older people. We explore this in more detail in Chapter 2, but it is important to consider it here too. Physiological change and decline is an inevitable part of the human ageing process; however, the extent to which this occurs and the accommodations that can be made to preserve 'normal' functioning are often ignored or overlooked. Fear of this decline can be a central pillar of gerontophobia, the fear of age-related self-degeneration. This fear is, again, a central tenet of the ageist stereotypes and prejudices experienced by older people.

Dementia

If you tune into public debates on health and social care for older people, you will notice that care for people living with dementia often dominates this debate. There are myriad reasons for this, not least that dementia (a catch-all term for various diseases and conditions that affect the ageing brain) is still very much in the grip of biomedical approaches to understanding human ageing. Ever since Robert Butler (1975) succeeded in having Alzheimer's disease (AD) recognised as 'the disease of human ageing', millions of dollars have been invested in trying to find a cure for dementia. This contrasts with more critical gerontological perspectives, which tend to argue that this investment has been misdirected: by the time most people present symptoms of cognitive impairment, the disease is too far advanced for anything to be done. Instead, the investment should be in improving quality of life for people living with dementia. Investment in research on AD has raised public awareness to the extent where there is now something of a moral panic among the general population. Lloyd (2012) makes the sensible point that Alzheimer's remains a disease that stigmatises, and increased scientific understanding has done nothing to counter negative cultural norms around AD and other forms of dementia.

Box 4.1: Dementia in focus

(The figures in this box are taken from the 2018 *Alzheimer's Disease Facts and Figures Report* from the Alzheimer's Association, and refer to the US only.)

Dementia is one of the leading causes of institutional or residential long-term care for older people. With the numbers of those living with dementia continuing to rise, this is not something that is likely to change in the near future. Dementia is an umbrella term for a number of neurodegenerative diseases including Alzheimer's, Parkinson's, Lewy body dementia, and Pick's disease. Each has a range of causes but the common strand is that they reduce cognitive functioning, produce changes in perceptual abilities, and are progressive, non-reversible and non-curable.

As dementia is a progressive disease, people living with it require increasing amounts of support and care as it progresses. The Alzheimer's Association reports that, in 2018, the cost of care for those with Alzheimer's alone was $277bn, with $186bn being a direct cost to Medicare and Medicaid. It is important to note that this does not include the cost of informal caregiving, as discussed in this chapter. By 2050, the Alzheimer's Association further predicts that the total cost of caring for persons with dementia (including long-term and hospice care) is likely to be in excess of $1.1tn. Given that, in 2017, the cost of caring for a person with dementia to the end of their life was $341,840 and 70 per cent of that was met by the individual and their family, we are looking at a huge bill with very few options currently presented to match that need. Putting this individual cost into context, nearly half of those caregivers looking after someone with dementia have an annual household income of less than $50,000.

Ageing in place

According to a special report on those over 65 from the 2010 Census in the US, only 3.1 per cent of this group live in nursing or assisted living facilities, with many choosing to remain at home or age in place with the option of in-home care support (West et al, 2014). This is a snapshot or 'rolling' figure (that is, at any one point in time, this is the case as some people will die and others will take their place) meaning that although the people themselves will change, the percentage will remain fairly constant. What this does mean, though, is that those who are in receipt of care in nursing homes are generally the most sick or unwell, requiring much more concentrated care than those who are able to be supported in their own homes with informal care.

There are many reasons why people wish to remain in their own home not least for familiarity and financial reasons. Think about it. Would you prefer to age 'in place' in your own home or to move to a residential care facility? I think most of us would answer, yes, we would prefer to grow old in our own homes. Each of these options will be explored further, later in the chapter. To help people to age in place, to remain in their community and stay engaged, the WHO proposed eight domains within a 'liveability framework' that can be split between the built environment and the social environment. Details of this can be found in Appendix 2.

World Health Organization approach to healthy ageing

The WHO's approaches to healthy ageing have widely been adopted as the factors that need to be considered holistically if an environment is to be truly 'age friendly'. AARP, a leading ageing-related interest group in the US, has adopted these and developed a network of age-friendly communities across the US and beyond. Further, it has a comprehensive tool for the liveability index, which enables people to see and rate their community in terms of its ageing friendliness. While these approaches are extremely useful for conceptualising a world where we can all enjoy a healthy old age, it is worth noting that some scholars have been critical of the WHO. For instance, Navarro (2008) is mindful that, unlike the World Bank or the IMF, the WHO lacks the political clout to actually change policy and resource allocation at national level. Rising socio-economic inequality is a major cause of health inequality and gender inequality where the burden of caring falls disproportionately on women, many of whom are either paid very little, or not at all if the care is within the family. In this sense, there have not been many major changes in who cares for whom since Joan Rumbold was left caring for her son in London in 1754. The critical question remains – do major policy initiatives actually make it easier for older people and their carers to enjoy good health?

Policy aside, what actually is an 'age-friendly community'? Essentially, these are places where older people are actively involved, where opportunities are created for them and where they are valued and supported rather than placed on a periphery (Alley et al, 2007). This means thinking about public transport, pedestrian accessibility, and local services. In a global initiative largely spearheaded by AARP and the WHO, the aim is to maintain the engagement of older adults in the community, keeping them active and facilitating social contact. Recent research has revealed not only the importance of physical and mental activity for ageing well, but also how environments impact the objective and subjective well-being of older people (Golant, 2015). By creating an environment that is supportive of both exercise and social engagement, older adults will be facilitated to remain both socially and physically healthy, potentially reducing incidences of illness in later life.

There are those who will complain that more money is being spent on 'boomers' rather than supporting other age cohorts. However, if there is more public transport, would that not benefit those of all ages and social strata who do not or cannot drive? Would it not potentially decrease the number of cars on the road thus decreasing pollution (now seen as a significant long-term health risk for all ages) and making roads safer? If there are services that are more accessible, local, and less focused in a city centre where there is limited parking, would this not also benefit people other than the older adult population? The main question being, then, does 'age-friendly' not just mean accessible? Where there are benefits to thinking about older adults' usage of space, these benefits then extend to, for example, disabled people as well as the wider population.

Looking back at the WHO's aim, it is essentially to make an environment in which people of all ages can actively participate. With this definition, age becomes less about older people and more about simply reflecting the entire lifecourse. In many ways, labelling places as age-friendly may be a double-edged sword. It gets people thinking about what it takes to engage and support older adults in the community, but it also increases the risk of 'othering' older adults and seeing them as in receipt of special consideration. With the post-World War II 'boomer' generation reaching old age, and many choosing to remain in their own homes as they age, the notion of facilitating them to do this is becoming ever more urgent. Whether the system be state-sponsored or privately funded, one thing is sure: no long-term care system, of any country, can support all older people simply because their community has become less accessible.

Existing long-term care policies in the US and indeed around the world are largely inadequate to meet the changing demographic needs of the population, as discussed in Chapter 1. There are many factors that will affect an individual's ability to age in place, however. These include whether or not there is a long-term care facility available, how much this costs, and what the quality of that care will be. The US, partly due to its size, lacks a cohesive plan for long-term care, offering a fragmented, expensive, and limited range of options with varying levels of quality provision. Instead of a national approach, there is a community-based patchwork quilt of services with wide-ranging eligibility criteria, costs and (again) availability. This fragmentation is also caused by the monetisation of the system, running for profit and not for the health outcomes of an individual – indeed individuals pay more and receive less and less value (Stange, 2009). It is exactly this fragmentation that results in the rising unmet need, with Feldman et al (2004) highlighting that around 50 per cent of older adults with physical limitations are not receiving the assistance that they require.

Long-term care

The UK: a mixed system

In contrast with the US, in the UK long-term care is a mixture of public, private and charitable provision. Long-term care covers a sweeping gamut of care and support services. These can range from high level care such as those received in nursing and EMI ('elderly mentally infirm') facilities through to Extracare, and care in the community. Services provided in each of these delivery settings are complex, and the responsibility of who pays for what is also adding to the reticence of some in seeking care. Equally, it adds to the inability of others to collect what is rightfully theirs. Care in the UK is provided through a mixture of the NHS, local authority or council, and private and voluntary organisations creating a veritable smorgasbord of potential options. Most people in the UK are completely unaware of cut-offs, availability, and options until such a point where they or their loved ones require assistance. This may lead to hasty decisions being made without all of the information being available for what is the best outcome in that situation. These options and cut-offs are explained later in this chapter.

Home care encompasses a huge list of services, including respite care, community nursing, day centres and even home delivered meals. With regard to who picks up the tab, 60 per cent of the publicly funded portion is met by the local authority with the remaining 40 per cent by the NHS. Direct delivery by the local authority is now rare; instead the model of contracting this to local private and voluntary organisations is preferred. This enables cost savings and also for specialised services to take care of each task. Local authorities are increasingly dealing with budget cuts and as such are increasingly passing the costs on to the end consumer. A report in the *Financial Times* indicated that 'between 2010 and 2020, councils will have lost nearly 60p of every £1 that central government previously provided for services' (*Financial Times*, 2019). The same report also highlighted the case of Liverpool where £174m is raised in Council Tax each year but of that, £172m is directly spent on adult social care due to cuts in direct funding from central government. Since 1993, local services have been largely targeted on those who are most frail, providing free services to fewer and fewer people. Instead, as we will discuss later in the chapter, informal carers are stepping in to meet the unsupported need. Early reports suggest that all of these retractions of welfare for the most vulnerable older people have resulted in the social care sector experiencing very high death rates during the COVID-19 pandemic (see Phillipson, 2020).

In terms of nursing, EMI and Extracare provision, these are all a little different but essentially are about meeting needs of the older adult population in a residential setting. Extracare is a facility where an individual lives with their own lockable front door. They have a house or apartment as part of a wider complex and have their own living space, bedroom, bathroom, and kitchen as well as access to a range of communal services. These communal services differ based on facility, as there is still little formal definition as to what constitutes 'Extracare', but these can include restaurants, beauty salons, swimming pools, recreational spaces, clubs and groups. All of this is provided in an environment where there is a scheme manager and staff who are on hand to provide support. If a resident requires additional support and nursing care, this can be provided in the person's own home and on site. Essentially the aim is to have older adults remaining active in their own environment and to enable them to receive additional support in that same environment should they require it. However, the level of facilities and the ceiling of care support provided will differ between each facility with there being no standard minimum. Nursing and EMI are essentially very similar in terms of physical provision. Residents will have their own room, sometimes with a private toilet facility but rarely with ensuite bathroom. Relaxation, dining, personal hygiene, and socialisation are all in communal areas. Activities in these environments are largely led by staff rather than the resident-led approach common within Extracare facilities. The main difference comes in the type of care provided. Nursing is more about physical care needs and supporting physical limitations, although cognitive decline is often supported too. EMI is specifically set up to support those with cognitive impairment so staff are more highly trained in this area.

So, who pays for what when it comes to long-term care in the UK? Well, sit back, as this is where it all gets a little bit complicated. While reading this, imagine what it would be like as an older person who needs assistance to navigate the system. Keep in the back of your mind that they may want to pass some money on to those they care about after they die. Local authorities are the gatekeepers to support funds for health and social care. If the needs an individual presents with require continuing care or are significantly related to health, then these costs (or at least part) may be met by the NHS. The local authority conducts the assessment to see if the needs are within a nationally agreed framework and, if so, they must assist the older adult in claiming the health and social support that is required. Also, the amount a person pays varies based on the country in which they reside in the UK. As of 2019, if savings or income exceeds a set maximum, then the total cost of the care is met by the individual. There is slight variance across the four countries of the UK; cut-off points range from £23,250 (around $28,300) in England and Northern Ireland to £24,000 (around $29,200) in Wales and £27,250 (around $33,100) in Scotland.

Contributions are calculated based on a comprehensive financial assessment. These take into consideration regular income such as pensions but also any welfare state benefits that may be received, such as Personal Independence Payment or Attendance Allowance. Also considered are capital assets such as cash savings, investments, stocks, and even homes, including the principal private residence of the applicant or any holiday or second homes. As a homeowner, if you require care for longer than 12 weeks, which is deemed to be a permanent move into a long-term care facility, then your home will be classed as part of any assets. That said, it won't be counted if a partner, another person over 60 or a person under 16 whom you support lives there too, or if an ex-partner lives there and they are a lone parent. So, again, it's not as simple as it first seems. What if you are assessed as requiring a local authority paid place? Well, at that point, the local authority will pay; however, all income (except a small living stipend determined by the local authority) is taken by the local authority to contribute. So in essence, if you have any form of pension income, you are still going to be paying for your care.

Overall the provision and funding systems are complicated in the UK, not ideal for older people with care needs to navigate. Having an individual means-based assessment is also complicated and reliant on different local authority assessments and funding structures. There are proposals around potential alternatives and these will be addressed later in the chapter when we have looked at what a largely private provision, such as that of the US, entails.

The US: a private system

If you thought the UK was complex, think again. Where the UK has a well-established safety net to try to ensure everyone has access to the care that they need, this is not really the case in the US where there are different systems that may not always work together in the ways intended. Although there are different terms used in the UK and the US, essentially the types of physical accommodations offered in both countries are similar. Respite care facilities, skilled nursing facilities (SNFs), retirement villages and Extracare all exist, albeit on somewhat grander scales. Similar to the UK, there is also great variability under these broad headings. (Quality of provision will be discussed later in this chapter.) In the US, there are two types of public system when it comes to supporting long-term care for older adults: Medicare and Medicaid. These have distinct differences and meet differing needs, but should in theory work together to ensure need is met.

Medicare was established in 1965 and is a social health programme to support those over the age of 65, and younger people with disabilities or those who need end-of-life care. It is funded through payroll taxation to essentially spread the cost of this care across society to protect everyone. It is specific in what it covers, namely only medically imperative skilled nursing care and home health services. Nursing homes are only paid for up to the first 100 days, with a 'co-pay' between days 21–100. Co-pays are co-payments made by a service beneficiary (in this case, older person or their family) in addition to that which is paid for by health insurers (in this case, Medicare). When it comes to home care, this is only supported where skilled care is needed, not social or personal hygiene care. There are also eligibility criteria. To access Medicare, you need to have been working for a minimum of ten years to pay into the system as well as being over the age of 65 (Grabowski, 2007). This is an immediate disadvantage if you are a migrant and have an older relative that you have brought over and are supporting in the US. It also has disadvantages for those who have chosen not to engage in paid work, but to stay home and support their family and raise children. This may also be a consideration for women when they are thinking about divorce in later life and what access to insurances and health support they may or may not get.

Medicaid is not age-based and is essentially a public welfare assistance programme for those without fiscal independence (Grabowski, 2007). It is jointly funded by the state and federal government through taxation. It is accessed by a means-tested welfare assessment system only when any assets are spent even if this results in people having to sell everything that they have built up in their lifetime. It is the largest source of funding for health and allied health services for those of limited means. It is the largest funder for long-term care services but has a skew towards institutional care provision where costs can be more easily predicted and managed. Similarly to the regional differences in caps on care experienced in the UK, Medicaid is managed by the individual states and as such there are differences in coverage decisions, service provision and eligibility, largely based on state budgets. In 2019, this meant that Minnesota and Massachusetts offered the most accessible and comprehensive health care through Medicaid or affiliated schemes, with the least access (and most expensive services) being offered in North Carolina and Alaska. The basic tenet behind Medicaid is that it is a safety net for those who are unable to meet their own needs. The wealthy are able to support their own long-term care needs or have insurances to meet it. Those with mid-range socio-economic status are generally left worst off, having to rely more on informal care. We will discuss later in this chapter.

So far, so simple. But this is where the private providers also come into play and any partnerships make the system less navigable. Private providers and insurance companies are prolific in the US and when it comes to long-term care they all work in a similar way, irrespective of the level of coverage. They provide some level of care for institutional and home-based care and claims on policies for either are triggered on assessment of cognition and ability to manage activities of daily living. Dependent on the provider and the level of cover, they can provide benefits from years to a whole lifetime but may have clauses about not covering anything up to the first 90 days of care. Here, the devil is in the detail.

For those who don't meet Medicaid requirements, but cannot afford full insurance, partnership programmes were established in the 1990s as a way of aiding affordable long-term care provision. These fall into two camps. 'Dollar for dollar' is the basic system and most simple to understand. If a person purchases $250,000 worth of cover they would get $250,000 worth of care. If they required more than this level, they could apply for Medicaid while still retaining $250,000 worth of their assets. This is a good way of ensuring that all assets are not spent down. The second type is 'total asset protection'. This is more comprehensive. Essentially these policies will fund three years of nursing or six years of home care, after which point Medicaid can be applied for and as much as 100 per cent of a person's assets are protected. In 2010 there was a further option provided called Community Living Assistance and Support Systems (CLASS Act). This is less comprehensive but was designed to offer cover to more people. This would be offered as an opt-out to all employees and taken directly from earnings. To claim on this, employees must have been working for three years and have paid premiums for five years, but the benefits were only limited to $50–75 a day as a contribution towards care needed.

Who cares for whom?

We have looked at the formal care structures in two different countries to show the variations between a largely state-funded system (UK) and a largely private system (US). However, with the majority of people remaining in their own homes, who is actually providing the care and support that is so instrumental to the well-being of the older adult cohort? Informal caregivers are the backbone that supports the long-term care system in the UK and the US (as well as many other countries around the world). These can be friends, family, spouses or neighbours who provide support to older adults. This care can range from instrumental activities, including shopping, cooking and cleaning, through to traditional caregiving activities, such as bathing, toileting and feeding. Caregiving does not have to be performed by a live-in carer, nor does it have to be provided 24 hours a day. It is important to recognise who are caregivers, however, due to the burden that can be placed upon them and the issues that this can cause for their own health; both points we will address later in this chapter.

That said, do caregivers see themselves as caregivers? Although we have explored the definition of a caregiver, providing a *portrait* of a caregiver is much more complex. Many caregivers do not actually identify themselves as caregivers as they are simply living with their spouse. This is also true in situations where there is a non-specific care family relationship, such as where a child 'pops in' to look after a parent, rather than there being a live-in husband or wife providing care. Many people see this provision of care and support as part of a family obligation or indeed just as 'something you do', rather than self-identifying as a carer. Where does the line get drawn? Providing emotional support, friendship and companionship? Giving medical support like changing wound dressings? Assisting toileting or bathing (ADLs – activities of daily living)? Picking up groceries or helping with finances (IADLs – Instrumental Activities of Daily Living)? All of these form part of the caregiving spectrum. Whether done daily, at regular intervals or even sporadically when needed, these still amount to caregiving activities and the person giving them being a caregiver. But who is the typical caregiver? Schulz and Eden (2016) found many gender implications of caring, not least that women do more hours caring than men. Generally, caregivers have other roles too, including full-time employment, and the majority of caregivers do not live with the person for whom they care. Depending on the reason for providing care, the average length of a caregiving role or responsibility is about four years, but there is high variation, depending on the care recipient and reasons for which care is needed. Lloyd (2012) reports that in many countries in Europe and North America there is a growing recognition that ageing societies can no longer expect families to provide the majority of care for older people.

Using the US as a case in point, as of 2019, there were around 41 million caregivers providing care to adults. Of those, approximately 15.7 million were caring for someone with Alzheimer's or other forms of dementia (Reinhard et al, 2019). The Family Caregiver Alliance report (2015) highlighted that the value of this unpaid care exceeded the monetary value of both paid home care and total Medicaid spending combined. The National Caregiver Alliance is a US non-profit organisation, serving as a one-stop shop specifically for caregivers in California to access information and services to support them directly, signposting support across the US. With an increasingly ageing population, the number of those providing informal care is set to continue to rise. Currently, when not utilising services, these patients can be invisible in national level statistics, which is why we often have to rely on data gathered by civil society organisations to include them in research. It is also worth putting informal caregiving into the context of payments as outlined above. Where many Americans struggle with insurances, co-pay, and accessing formal care, 66 per cent of people with disabilities requiring support receive it solely from their informal care support network. Twenty-six per cent rely on some combination of formal and informal support systems and less than ten per cent receive all of their care needs from the formal, paid-for sector (Doty, 2010). This can be mapped as an historical change when we look at the number of older adults (65+) who have informal caregivers as their only form of support. Between 1994 and 1999 there was an increase from 57 per cent to 66 per cent, a figure that was inversely mirrored from 36 per cent to 26 per cent in those who used a combination of formal and informal care services (Federal Interagency Forum on Aging-Related Statistics, 2015). This demonstrates the move away from formal support, which is in part due to the cost and complexity of the system. While there are benefits for having informal caregivers who know you and with whom you are comfortable, there has to be consideration given to the caregiver too. With 30 per cent of those caregivers caring for older adults in receipt of long-term care at home themselves being over 65 (The Retirement Project, 2007), the implications are not difficult to imagine. When looking at the crudest of measures, caregivers lose out financially on income and benefits totalling around \$283,716 for men and \$324,044 for women (AARP, 2011). These are not insubstantial figures but they only reflect the direct loss of income, and not the other factors that can impact upon a carer. Much of the literature concurs that those who are caregivers will experience increased levels of depressive symptoms as well as poorer physical and mental health outcomes as they age (Roth et al, 2015).

Indeed, the evidence suggests there is more support for worsening mental health in those who identify as caregivers than there is for their decline in physical health. These psychological concerns include depression and increased anxiety surrounding day-to-day tasks as well as the quality of the care that they are able to provide. They also often report social isolation due to caregiving responsibilities taking them away from other social activities for themselves. This phenomenon is known as 'caregiver burden', the perception of stress by the individual providing care and the negative social, financial, emotional, spiritual, and physical outcomes associated with this. Contrast this with Roth et al's (2015) report that there is extensive evidence of increased longevity for caregivers.

Caregiving, then, is very much a tale of two halves. It is evident that in the majority of cases, having a loved one with a chronic illness or debilitating condition will be stressful, but it is not so clear-cut as to whether this is down to providing care or simply the stress of the condition on their loved one. Amirkhanyan and Wolf (2003) illustrated that having a close family member who was seriously ill with dementia or any other serious disability would lead to an increased incidence of depressive symptoms and increased stress regardless of whether a caring role was undertaken. Roth et al (2009) similarly found that 33 per cent of both spousal and non-spousal carers reported no strain in providing care, with the National Opinion Research Center (2014) reporting that 83 per cent of caregivers rated caregiving as being a positive experience. When asked, caregivers have also said that caregiving has been affirming of their family ties and individual identity, resulting in a feeling of fulfilment rather than filial obligation, the societal expectation that adult offspring will care for their parents. So, caregiving can be both positive and negative.

Given the complexity of caregiving, how do caregivers cope? Most interventions to improve the health of a caregiver are multifaceted (Liew and Lee, 2019). They include time alone as well as time with others outside the care relationship, and continued education and planned activities of self-care. When tailored to the individual, these interventions become effective and have been shown to reduce overall stress and perceived burden, increase self-care behaviours, reduce anxiety, and improve the competence and efficacy of the caregiving too. In a study of interventions which helped alleviate the depression that is experienced by some carers of people with dementia, Liew and Lee (2019) found that providing a range of different supports, including emotional and practical support, was most effective in reducing depressive symptoms of carers. As they are providing such an important form of social support, it seems obvious that informal carers should not be taken for granted, and certainly not ignored nor abused. There should be respite consideration given under each and every one of the private and publicly funded schemes, given the amount of work that caregivers do and the contributions they provide to the wider society and systems they support. There are, however, very few schemes in any country that meet the needs of caregivers or even acknowledge the burden which they are under and indeed the burden they are taking away from formal state or private care infrastructures. Lastly, the resilience of caregivers and receivers, the pure toughness of human beings in stressful situations is often ignored. It is important to consider how taking care of carers will produce better quality care. Next, we will consider the quality of care, surely the most important aspect of any care system.

Quality of care

It is not just the financial aspect of care that is important. We have discussed how sensory decline impacts our quality of life as we age, and how important that is; equally, the quality of the care that is received is just as important in long-term care. In both the UK and the US, the key way in which this quality is achieved is through a series of standards that are enforced by an inspectorate. The premise behind this is that, prior to registration, any long-term care facility will have to demonstrate that they have met the minimum standards criteria before they can accept residents. Following this, there are regular inspections to ensure that minimum standards are maintained to provide safeguards and assurances to residents and family members that the needs of residents are being met. That said, there are differences in the types of standards as well as to the degree in which those standards are met.

In the UK, the Care Quality Commission (CQC) has a set of fundamental standards below which care must never fall. These are the basic levels that all residents can be assured that their services will meet (see Appendix 3 for details). These standards are there to protect the older person but also to provide a contract between the provider and the resident to outline the minimum expectations. The facilities are initially inspected within the first six months of registration and then every six, 12 or 30 months depending on whether they have been rated 'inadequate,' 'requires improvement' or 'good (or outstanding)' respectively on their last inspection. The standards cover functional, structural, procedural and personal aspects of the delivery of care to underpin the holistic nature of that care.

In the US, however, the care standards outlined by the Joint Commission's Long Term Accreditation Program are somewhat more structural. What we don't see in the Long Term Care Accreditation Program are policies such as person-centred care, the rights of the resident, or indeed markers associated with the quality of the care. Many of the quality indicators are left down to the individual facility, almost as a way of marketing how good that they are rather than as a framework through which to conduct inspections. Wagner et al (2012) investigated the role of standards monitoring on the quality of care provision in the US. They found that nursing homes that signed up to the Joint Commission's Long Term Accreditation Program were more likely to keep up the good work after accreditation and well into the future. Providing standards for nursing home providers to meet and exceed is an important way of providing quality care. As you will see from our next discussion, even where standards are clearly outlined, some older people will still be vulnerable to mistreatment or neglect, commonly referred to as 'elder abuse'.

Elder abuse

On the far end of the quality of care spectrum is the neglect and mistreatment of older people in care, referred to as 'elder abuse'. This can broadly be defined as any violation of an older person's human or civil rights by another person. It is such a broad term, encompassing everything from physical and psychological abuse through to financial abuse and discrimination. Due to its all-encompassing nature and the lack of cohesive governance to catch and manage those guilty of it, Cooper et al (2009) suggested that up to 25 per cent of older Americans in receipt of care had been subjected to significant levels of abuse. This figure was revised in 2016, estimating that around ten per cent of Americans aged over 60 have experienced some form of elder abuse (National Council on Aging, 2016). This is a really serious statistic, not least when one considers the implications. Not only are there social well-being implications but, in terms of the health outcomes, even modest abuse increases the risk of death by 300 per cent when compared to a control group of older people who have not been identified as being abused (Dong et al, 2011). It is clear that there are failures in the long-term care settings, not just from these sample statistics, but also from the increased incidences being reported. There are arguments that this is partly due to increased awareness and improved reporting mechanisms, but whatever the reason, the human cost for this is just too high.

However, when looking at it from a delivery point of view, it is not just the human cost that is high. An estimated $5.3bn from the US annual health expenditure was attributed to treating violent injuries to older adults as a result of elder abuse (Office of Inspector General, Department of Health and Human Services, 2014). The same report also mapped a 12 per cent increase between 2008–09 in the annual financial loss by victims of financial exploitation, then totalling $2.9bn, a figure the report reflects has only continued to rise. It is clear that a systemic change is needed to safeguard older adults in receipt of long-term care, be that in residential facilities or ageing in place in their own homes and receiving services there. With increasing numbers of older adults and the current trends, it is evident that the numbers of cases, and the personal and financial costs of these, will only continue to rise unless something is done.

Before his death in 2008, leading UK social policy scholar, Peter Townsend completed an important piece of work outlining the prevalence of elder abuse in the UK. Townsend (2006) found that older people in the UK were at risk of abuse both within the family and in institutions. Drawing on reports from older people's charity Age UK, he found evidence of older people in homes being forced to eat dinner while sitting on a commode. Sometimes neglect is the cause – the report listed cases of older people dying of dehydration after being admitted to a care home. In one case this was because care staff failed to note that a woman needed help eating and drinking (Townsend, 2006: 171). Townsend concluded that a human rights framework was the best way to protect older people, as it afforded them the protection of internationally recognised rights. 'The EU continues to extend access to economic and social rights and integrate these with other, better institutionalised civil and political rights (e.g. the proclamation of the EU Chapter of Fundamental Rights in 2000)' (Townsend, 2006: 170). Unfortunately, we have yet to see his suggestions being implemented. Moreover, the UK's decision in 2016 to leave the EU means that future generations of older people will not have the protection of the European Court of Human Rights, one of the pillars of the system of human rights protection over the past few decades.

New models of care

It is clear that there are pros and cons to each of the market-based and publicly funded systems. The main disadvantage is the same for each – that the levels of complexity in each of the systems make them more than just a little difficult to navigate, for both older people and their families alike. People who are eligible for help are not claiming what they can because they are not sure of what options are available. Shifting from a means-based assessment to a universal model would add more clarity, and this is being adopted in some countries to prevent the confusions highlighted above. Partnership between public and private organisations seems to be a more sustainable way of spreading the cost and allowing there to be incentives for self-care, as the responsibility has to be shared with the individual too. National level rather than regional strategies provide consistency in care and in the equity of distribution, enabling fair access to care and support services for long-term care. Whether direct payment or service delivery, there are systems that can be implemented based on assessed best practice to empower older people and maximise the effectiveness of care. What is certain is that the demand for long-term care in any of the guises outlined is only going to increase, so taking a head-in-the-sand approach really is no longer an option.

A final thought

In this chapter we have laid out the reasons why, as an introductory text for critical gerontology, we have chosen to focus on care, rather than health, in old age. We have offered detailed evidence of how there is an important distinction between ageing, and the physiological changes that accompany the passage of time, as opposed to acquiring disease, which is a distinct and separate human experience. We do this in order to mark out how biomedical and critical approaches to understanding human ageing place a different emphasis on health and care. For biomedical gerontologists, the emphasis is on health and the curing and prevention of disease. For critical gerontologists, the emphasis is on human rights, carers' and women's rights, and the prevention of elder abuse. There was some discussion of the various global policy frameworks that surround ageing and older people, focusing specifically on the WHO's age-friendly cities programme. The chapter concluded with a detailed comparative discussion of long-term care systems in the UK and US, drawing out possibilities for new models of care funding and provision in the future.

REVIEW EXERCISE 4

Go online and review inspection reports of local nursing homes. Would you like to live in a nursing home? What alternatives are there to providing care for older people? How would a model like foster care for older people work? How did the warehousing of older people into large residential homes contribute to the high death rates in care homes during the coronavirus pandemic 2019–20?

Group: Have a class debate on the motion: 'Why I look forward to spending my final years in a nursing home'.

Solo: Compare the nursing home reports with two newspaper articles on nursing homes. Which source are you inclined to believe? Which source would leave you better informed were you searching for a nursing home for yourself?

All old people are pretty much the same, aren't they?

(Diversity among the ageing population)

> Aging populations are becoming more diverse in terms of color, culture, identity, disability, and socio-economic standing. As a result, the need for culturally competent professionals and businesses that serve and provide products for older adults is increasingly important. (American Society on Aging, nd)

Introduction

This chapter addresses an issue that is too often ignored in textbooks about ageing. Even gerontologists – in fact, you might argue, *especially* gerontologists – might decide that it is convenient to group everyone over 60 into the single category of 'older people'. Such categorisation is misleading. There is as much diversity and inequality in the older population as there is in the general population (Erber and Szuchman, 2015). For instance, rising inequality within birth cohorts is one of the biggest challenges facing policy makers in the coming decades. This means that we are seeing bigger income gaps between rich and poor retirees than between younger and older cohorts from the same class background (Walker, 2012). What this means on the ground is that we can see greater wealth disparity between classes. For example, those who were able to buy property or make investments during their working lives are retiring with substantially more resources than those who were unable to make the leap onto the housing ladder. Likewise, those whose income stagnated at subsistence rather than savings level are less likely to enjoy a financially comfortable old age.

We can see this when looking at the US market in terms of the disparity between white and African American homeownership. In 2018, total homeownership in the US was 64.2 per cent, a steady rise from the financial crisis a few years earlier (National Association of Home Builders (NAHB), 2019). When broken down by race, the NAHB report highlights that white (non-Hispanic) homeownership was 73.6 per cent, while African American home-ownership rates were as low as 43.6 per cent and indeed all minority ethnic groupings fall below the American average. Forbes (2019) attributes this to rising house prices which mean that even first-time homes are often out of the reach of minority ethnic groups in many regions of the US. Even when help to buy schemes are in place, the researchers found this often results in financial overstretching among minority homeowners, especially when maintenance or housing taxes are due. Ultimately, higher rates of foreclosure are seen. Even when people in the African American community are able to get onto the housing ladder, they are older when they buy their first home, and are purchasing houses of lesser value (Choi et al, 2019). With the continuing wealth accruing from homeownership through increasing home values, this disparity then increases through the lifecourse, in a pattern of accumulated disadvantage. Further, if stretched, it is less likely that minority ethnic homeowners were able to save as much. This is shown concisely when looking at Table 5.1, illustrating the average house wealth at age 60.

Table 5.1: Average housing wealth at age 60 by ethnicity and age at which home was purchased

Age at buying first home	Black	White
Less than 35	US$72,729	US$125,920
35-44	US$46,632	US$116,888
45+	US$26,668	US$104,866

Source: Choi et al, 2019

When retiring, this means that older adults from higher income backgrounds are able to do so more comfortably. A higher income means greater access to both preventative and treatment-based medicine (something not afforded to those in lower brackets in countries using a payment model, such as the US). Further, when taking a lifecourse approach to diversity, it can be argued that older people are the most diverse of any chronological age group. As we will discuss through this chapter, ethnicity, gender and sexuality are among the factors which differentiate individuals within each birth cohort. However, as we age, we make a series of life decisions which, like the branches of a tree spreading out, further differentiate us from others within our cohort, irrespective of the other cultural or biological characteristics we may share.

Life does not happen in a vacuum. Our geographical location, political landscape, global situations and societal norms impact the ageing trajectory and associated health and social outcomes experienced by every person. The majority of this chapter discusses how those in the minority LGBTQI* community age and the challenges, the barriers and health concerns being faced. Many of the challenges explored within the LGBTQI* community can be applied to other minorities and diverse populations. We have chosen to focus on this group because the sweeping global changes in levels of social and legal acceptance of homosexuality offer a perfect example to explore how the impact of different structures can affect those ageing within a diverse minority group. Box 5.1 provides a brief summary of how this impact may be experienced in the context of the legalisation of homosexuality.

Box 5.1: Experiences of homosexuality between birth cohorts in the UK

From 1533 until 1967, same-sex sexual activity between consenting men was illegal in England and Wales. It is interesting to note that this was only the case for men; women may have shared the social stigma, but not the legal ramifications of same-sex activity. Those men born during this period and identifying as gay have had a very different life trajectory to those born since. For a man born in the 1930s and 1940s, their formative years would have been spent in an environment where homosexuality was not just frowned upon or socially unacceptable, but punishable by law. The gay world was very much underground, with people fearing being discovered by friends, family or the police. The social recriminations could lead to being ostracised within social and workplace circles in addition to receiving a criminal record. Many gay people led double lives and, even where families were aware, there was a distinct practice of 'don't ask, don't tell'. This would make it increasingly difficult to develop and maintain meaningful sexual relationships due to having to be hidden. Even after legalisation, the social narrative still continued to cause issues, especially into later life, when seeking medical treatment, acting as next of kin, buying a house, and simply living everyday life, being gay presented social and legal problems. Many would not think twice about such things, but as a gay man and especially through the ageing process, these things were constant battles. The accumulation of this prejudice across the lifecourse did not evaporate with legalisation and many older people who required institutional residential care were forced back into the closet. Prior to legalisation this was due to the statutory rule of law but after this point it was more of a social concern. Older men felt that they would be ostracised by their peers or would have to come out again, something that they may have found hard enough to do previously with the support of friends, let alone within the confines of a supported living facility where they cannot escape from other residents. Further, concerns about care staff opinions and provision of care often left those without the social support required from partners or 'family of choice'.

Contrast that to a gay man born in the UK in the 1990s or 2000s where same-sex marriage is legal (as of 2013) and social acceptance is fairly universal, for example, with 45 openly gay members of parliament (2017 general election). There is no longer the fear of acquiring a criminal record because of who you love. There is not the social stigma or repression of personality. There is not the fear of reprisals in health or professional settings. Just this alone reflects the impact of social norms and government policy on lifecourse trajectories as well as health and well-being in later life.

For a full discussion of how the passage of time has affected research on gay and lesbian communities see Martin and d'Augelli (2009).

It is not that any one generation 'has it worse' than those pre(pro)ceding them, it is more accurate to say that each generation has different challenges, opportunities and obstacles. These are often linked to political or macro-level systemic changes that occur at particular time points during the lifecourse but which are also shaped by social narratives. Explored through this chapter we shall be addressing intersectional social change in the form of women's rights, global challenges, race relations and LGBTQI* rights. In each of the aforementioned there were or are both times and places where discrimination and even persecution was an acceptable social norm but, in each case, paradigm shifts have been seen which transform social and political perceptions, ultimately changing the lived experience of those within each of those groupings.

Where genetics clearly play a role in equalities or inequalities in ageing, the environmental, political and economic drivers we experience through our lives have a significantly more prominent impact on our experience of ageing (Marmot and Wilkinson, 1999). The impact of formative education can set up a life trajectory, and social mobility is influenced by the social class, standing and employment type of your parents. As previously discussed, the impact of cumulative and intersectional disadvantage through the lifecourse (gender, race, sexuality, age) has increasing impact through mid-life, not least on employment opportunities. Those with fewer disadvantages have a greater earning potential, and consequently more financial resources to save through the working life which increases the potential for a well-funded retirement. This chapter will focus on sexual orientation and gender identity, providing a global context to explain this. With the huge changes that have occurred (both positive and negative) within the lifetimes of the current older adult population, this provides an ideal spotlight on the impact of social, cultural and political change in terms of diverse populations. Furthermore, concurrent medical advancements also allow us to discuss new ageing populations, that is, those who would not previously have lived into later life.

Sexual orientation and gender identity

No longer are the clear-cut dichotomous variables of gender and sexual identity the dominant narrative of most of the world. Gay or straight; male or female. Outdated concepts that have been replaced with the understanding of gender as a fluid domain and a sliding scale of sexuality and orientation. Up until 1987, homosexuality was considered as an illness under the Diagnostic Statistical Manual (DSM) classification of mental illness. Homosexuality was illegal in the UK until 1967 when it was decriminalised in England and Wales only. Scotland and Northern Ireland followed in the 1980s. In the US, homosexuality was criminalised until 2003 across all states. As of 2019, it is still illegal in 71 countries around the globe. Where illegality is still part of the social fabric of being gay, this does not only affect the support available to gay men but also the potential punishments, which can range from imprisonment to violent public executions. Being gay where homosexuality is illegal adds to the stresses endured through the lifecourse.

Sexual orientation has important repercussions for family life, and hence for expectations about care. Those identifying as LGBTQI* are more likely to be estranged from their family, less likely to have a partner in later life, less likely to have children and less likely to have custody or contact with any children they may have had from previous heterosexual relationships (Orel, 2017). The 'traditional' family structure, formally in some cultures or informally in others, results in varying forms of filial care responsibility in later life or as required through the lifecourse. As we age, the likelihood of requiring additional care and support increases. When a family is not apparent, 'family of choice' (see Box 5.2) is called upon to meet social care needs. However, family of choice often comprises people of the same or similar ages and may be unable to provide the same level of support or indeed may require additional support themselves. As such, those LGBTQI* identifying older adults may have higher levels of unmet care needs compared with their heterosexual counterparts, who may have adult children who are available to care for them.

Box 5.2: Family of choice

A family of choice is essentially a non-kin network of friends that is built up by members of a community who may not have the usual family connections. Such a network provides the intimacy, care and support that would be traditionally provided by a family and is usually more robust than a circle of friends. This kind of network is most commonly observed among the gay community due to a shared experience and shared history, something that creates a solid connection even if a genetic family is still part of an individual's life. That said, these family of choice networks are increasingly being seen in dispersed migrant communities, those ageing without children and increasingly fragmented families. It is worth noting that some researchers have shown how these families of choice can mix with given families to establish a rich and varied set of networks which the researchers refer to as 'personal communities' (Pahl and Spencer, 2003).

Moreover, gay people can experience severe discrimination in terms of recognition of marriage and civil partnership for next of kin. Huge strides have been made in terms of civil partnership recognition and legal marriage bills; however, this is a political realisation of a social movement that has only occurred (as of 2019) in relatively few countries around the world. Even in those countries where legal status is possible, where partners have not undertaken official marriage or civil partnership, as is often the case for older people currently, it is difficult to get the same rights of visitation, sharing of medical information and financial sharing as is afforded to either married or 'common law' heterosexual partners in what is still a heteronormative culture. Times when older people most require the support from their family of choice can be the hardest moments for them to receive it, especially where someone's biological family does not accept their personal definitions yet whose relationship is respected more by law than those of unregistered partners.

Within the realm of healthcare, older adults can face issues within residential settings too. Within the universal assessment prior to admittance into long-term supported living environments, sexuality is not broached and a universal heteronormative assumption is not uncommon. Where an LGBTQI★ older person living in the community with a social support network may feel comfortable living openly, this may change when living status changes. Considering that, at the time of writing, the majority of openly 'out' older persons may have lived through a period where their sexual identity or orientation was classified as illegal, they have already been through a significant social and emotion upheaval in coming out. Table 5.2 draws on the work of a collaborative on-line community of LGBTQI★ rights activists, who have established a fascinating website and discussion forum history and experience of the fight for LGBTQI★ rights around the globe. You can see that there is a wide variety of approaches and attitudes towards homosexuality depending on religion and political culture in different countries (Kohut, 2014).

Table 5.2: Decriminalisation of homosexuality around the globe

Country	Year homosexuality was decriminalised
Kingdom of France	1791
Netherlands	1811
Italy	1890
Iceland	1940
Greece	1951
England and Wales	1967
Cuba	1979
Ukraine	1991
South Africa	1998
US (Nationwide)	2003
India	2018

Source: 'LGBT rights by country' at equaldex.com

To further elucidate this, Box 5.3 shows a brief timeline of events in the LGBTQI★ history in the US. Taking this in context, it shows the life trauma that older adults who identify as LGBTQI★ in 2019 may have been through with their identity and legal standing in the US.

Box 5.3: A brief timeline of LGBTQI* history in the US

1924 – The first gay rights organisation formed
1952 – American Psychological Association categorises homosexuality as a 'sociopathic personality disturbance'
1953 – President Eisenhower bans homosexuals from working for federal government

1961 – Illinois is the first state to decriminalise homosexuality

1967 – Black Cat Tavern, LA. Demonstration against police harassment of LGBTQI* community

1969 – Stonewall riots in New York

1973 – American Psychological Association removes homosexuality from list of mental disorders

1975 – Sergeant Matlovich forcibly discharged from US Air Force for revealing his sexuality

1979 – First national march on Washington DC for gay rights

1993 – President Clinton signs the 'Don't ask, don't tell' policy

1996 – President Clinton bans federal recognition of same-sex marriages

1998 – Mathew Shepard tied up and beaten to death in Wyoming because of his sexuality

2003 – US Supreme Court decriminalises homosexuality

2004 – First legal same-sex marriage conducted in Massachusetts

2005 – Governor Schwarzenegger vetoes the bill that would have allowed same-sex marriage in California

2009 – President Obama signs Hate Crimes Prevention Act into law, expanding existing legislation to include sexuality among other protected characteristics

2016 – President Obama announces the first national monument to LGBTQI* rights

2017 – President Trump bans transgender people from serving in any capacity in the US Military

Sources: Hooker, 1957; Drescher, 2015.

Box 5.3 highlights some of the struggles, successes and losses encountered by the LGBTQI* community, shaping the way that they live their lives and the trajectories in which they are permitted to age. During these periods of social and political challenge, coming out caused great individual stress and anxiety in terms of the reactions of friends, family, co-workers and wider society. Although progress has been made, some young people in different areas of the world (including states in the US) find coming out to be just as traumatic and dangerous. These experiences, similar to the ones of the generation before them will continue through their lifecourse and in terms of receiving institutional support or care in later life, the 'second coming-out' to residents and staff when entering supported living is often traumatic and may push older LGBTQI* adults back into the closet (Wolfenson, 2017).

This 'recloseting' can occur for a number of reasons. First, due to trauma experienced earlier in life, the older person does not feel comfortable in openly coming out to those providing care for fear of impact on care, support and level of integration. Few long-term residential facilities have widely accessible or visible policies around LGBTQI* inclusion and care. Where most would argue that such characteristics are protected through human rights and equal opportunities, having lived through significant social, political and medical discrimination, it can be hard for older adults to open up to the potential trauma of coming out again. Second, it is not just the care staff who pose potential causes for concern.

Other residents have been through the same social and political environments and will have developed their own set of attitudes and opinions. Where care staff are not allowed to show prejudice, residents cannot be stopped from expressing cultural or religious beliefs that may repress sexual minorities. Older adults may fear social reprisals in terms of isolation, group ostracising or even physical attack. This is further compounded when fellow residents may be living with dementia and as such have impaired cognitive functioning or social cues, thus making discriminatory behaviours more likely. When considering an integrated health and social care approach, there is generally a lack of services specifically designed for older gay men and women. As an area of increasing research, evidence bases are being amassed to show the importance of specific policies and provision, thus pushing the agenda with policy makers. This minority group have the same social requirements in terms of socialisation, access to health services and provision of support but they have distinct requirements for delivery (Bauer et al, 2013).

An overview of minority ageing

The opening of the chapter outlined that the focus would be on gender identity and sexuality. However, it would be remiss not to mention other aspects of diversity that will impact the trajectories experienced by older adults. Many of the social categorisation processes for other diverse groups remain the same, although in different applied contexts. As another, and globally recognised minority grouping, ethnicity leads to major differences in the experience of ageing. For instance, migrants are particularly vulnerable in old age (Ahmed and Hall, 2016). Some ethnic groups have much lower life expectancies than the general population. For instance, members of the Travelling community living in Ireland and African Americans in the US both have life expectancies which are several decades below the average. When looking at international comparisons, it becomes clear that there is a significant relationship between chronological age and well-being which is highly correlated with place (Hubbard et al, 2014). This is most clearly demonstrated by the fact that average life expectancy in the UK is 81.3 years, in the US it is 78.7 years, while in Somalia it is 55 years. In this case, the gap is so large, that the experience of being old in Somalia may be unrecognisable to a British pensioner or an American senior.

Migration can be a major factor in well-being where you look at attachment to place as well as the presence of a social support network. Similarly to the LGBTQI* community, in this instance, a family of choice can become a substitute, providing the care, support and social structure that may otherwise be missing. It is not, however, just the sense of self that is important but also the reciprocation and accommodation from the host country. As has been demonstrated in the latter part of the 2010s in Europe and across America, there is an anti-immigration nationalism that threatens the assimilation and acceptance of migrants (Postelnicescu, 2016). When looking at intersectional disadvantage, older migrants may thus face multiple discrimination. Due to their age, they may be seen as dependants who are not contributing to society, and due to their reduced social integration, language acquisition may be slower or less apparent, creating an additional barrier to inclusion.

Diversity and dementia

When looking at health as a measure of diversity, dementia is an interesting lens to apply. Many will assume that dementia is a natural part of ageing but this is inaccurate. Although it is the age-related illness feared by many, less than 14 per cent of people aged 71 and over will develop dementia (Plassman et al, 2007). That said, over 46 million people live with dementia worldwide, more than the whole population of Spain (WHO, 2019). This number is estimated to increase to 131.5 million by 2050. At the time of writing, 58 per cent of people with dementia live in low- and middle-income countries; by 2050, this will rise to 68 per cent (Alzheimer's Disease International, 2015). The fastest growth in the older population is taking place in China, India, and their south Asian and western Pacific neighbours and so it follows that dementia poses an increasing challenge in these countries. These are regions where health and social care systems often provide limited or no support to people living with dementia, or to their families. This means that there is often no formal diagnosis. Even if there is, there is little support to enable the person with dementia, or indeed their family, to age well. This represents a huge global challenge, not least overcoming the associated stigma. Especially for those in countries where, socially and medically, little research is being done, stigma can be rife. Stigma can lead to older adults being hidden away within a family unit, isolated from the community to shield the family from the stigma of mental health issues within the bloodline and potentially affecting the likelihood of younger family members being married. This stigma and lack of knowledge can result in lack of diagnosis or late diagnosis. Both of these can lead to a worsening of symptoms or the hastening of disease progression.

We can also consider how culture can impact assumptions, highlighting the diversity in backgrounds and cultural assumptions. Cognitive testing for dementia in the form of standardised tests is built on cultural assumptions and norms. Research highlighted in Box 5.4 highlights some of the issues faced in estimating dementia rates, diagnosing dementia and the subsequent issues of treatment.

Box 5.4: Adapting cognitive assessments for minority ethnic groups

At the University of Manchester in the UK, researchers have a study called *Dementia in Ethnic Minorities*, looking at how dementia screening tools have been developed and how they are applicable for those ethnic minorities, even those immigrants residing in Western countries where scales have been developed. The study looked at the scores obtained by a range of people and also did item testing for cultural sensitivity. What they found was certainly interesting with regard to how diagnosing older people from non-white and minority ethnic backgrounds is conducted.

The researchers analysed existing scales, highlighting that they have been developed for Western cultures but are being used far more widely than this. The study investigated whether asking members of Black and minority ethnic populations with symptoms of cognitive impairment and low levels of English language questions that pertain to current British political leaders or cultural references such as when the Queen celebrated her Golden Jubilee has proven to be difficult for some adults outside the cultures for which the tests had been constructed. The Manchester team found:

- High numbers of false positives were reported, where older adults were scoring low, not because they had dementia but because the questions they were asked had little or no cultural or everyday relevance to them.
- False negatives were identified, where clinicians were attributing poorer scores on cultural sensitivity issues rather than dementia without the consideration of both.
- Incomplete tests were found in older adults who simply couldn't complete the test as it made no sense to them, so no final score could be obtained for diagnosis.

The research findings suggest that translation of tests into English language is not enough. Each of the tests needs to be made culturally sensitive, checking items with those healthy adults in different cultures to ensure item relevance and allow substitution where necessary. This of course brings up the issue of validation, but surely this is worth the additional effort for the health and well-being of those the tests currently discriminate against?

If the language and items more accurately reflect the life history and cultural backgrounds of the people being assessed, then the correct diagnosis and treatments can be implemented and the accurate prevalence established, not to mention the health and well-being of older adults irrespective of their ethnicity (Giebel et al, 2019).

Psychologists have identified how facets of personality are important in understanding the way in which we age, especially when looking across cultures. McCrae and Costa (1987) proposed a five-factor model of personality they believed to be appropriate across cultures. These are measured using an inventory questionnaire where answers are scored against the factors below. The factors, frequently referred to as 'OCEAN', are:

- **Openness to experience**: how adventurous people are, how eager they are to try new things and their willingness to learn.
- **Conscientiousness**: how thoughtful a person is and their ability to control their impulses.
- **Extraversion**: the level of sociability and expressiveness, an individual's desire to be outgoing and engage with others.
- **Agreeableness**: measuring prosocial behaviours such as altruism and trust, this item measures a person's ability and willingness to cooperate with others.

- **Neuroticism**: this is a composite measure for feelings and emotions such as anxiety, anger, frustration, jealousy, guilt and loneliness.

Looking more generally at ageing around the world, in a review of the literature, Hong et al (2019) reported that cultures high in self-expression reported more favourable ageing trajectories for new learning and life satisfaction, whereas those cultures high in secular-rational values reported more negative views of new learning in advanced age. In those cultures stereotyped as low in neuroticism, there were more favourable perceptions of age trajectories in new learning, general knowledge, received respect, family authority, and life satisfaction. Overall, perceptions about age trajectories in new learning were also more favourable in cultures that viewed their typical member as high on openness and ratings of societal views of ageing were more positive in cultures who view their typical member as open, agreeable, and low in neuroticism. Compared to Western countries, those in Eastern countries report more positive societal views of ageing but less favourable perceptions of age-related changes in wisdom. These East-West differences remained true even when values, national stereotypes, and education levels are added as culture-level predictors (Officer et al, 2016). However, when the proportion of older adults in the population were added, East-West differences were rendered insignificant. This illustrates that there are many factors which influence how older people are seen and consequently the way that they experience ageing (Officer et al, 2016).

New ageing populations

With constantly improving healthcare, social care and support services, there are people alive today who, in previous generations, would not have reached old age. It is these people we refer to as a new ageing population. This is increasing the population diversity where people are either ageing with, or being diagnosed and living with, a number of conditions and as we age. People with Down's syndrome and cystic fibrosis represent just two of the genetic conditions where people are living substantially longer than in previous generations, adding not only to the known care needs of the condition, but also adding in 'comorbidities' associated with age. One of the most prominent health advancements in a relatively short period of two or three decades is the situation of those people living with HIV. This population of adults were not expected to live long lives when they were diagnosed but, due to advances in medical research, investment and campaigning, are now living well into later life. There are complications, however, with the intersections of age, HIV stigma, comorbidities from medication, and also often homophobia. Box 5.5 details those living with HIV as a new ageing population and outlines some of the challenges being faced. When taking a wider global context, it is of note that according to the UNAIDS data (2019), Africa has over 20.6 million people who are living with HIV, many of whom would not identify as LGBTQI*. This is indeed a truly global challenge spanning all communities.

Box 5.5: A brief synopsis of HIV and the homosexual community

HIV was discovered in 1983 and at the time was seen as a death sentence. It was the virus that caused AIDS, for which there was no cure and which would inevitably develop after infection with HIV. As early as 1985, clinical trials for antiretroviral therapy (ART) started but it wasn't until over a decade earlier that effective treatments were developed and made available. In the early 2000s complications such as lipodystrophy, bone and kidney toxicity were identified, causing other health concerns in those who were receiving treatment. Newer treatments have minimised the levels of toxicity of the drugs and have also increased their efficacy not only as treatment but also as a pre-exposure prevention measure. In 2017 there were 36.9 million people globally who were living with HIV and about 1.8 million new infections (UNAIDS, 2019). Of those total cases, 1.1 million were in the US, with nearly 20 per cent of those newly diagnosed being over 50 (Center for Disease Control, 2018). There are many reasons that this could be the case. Most notably these include: lack of access to safe sex resources (such as condoms); lack of knowledge about transmission and the need for condoms; assumption of asexuality by family and medical professionals (Bulford and Singh, 2012) and lack of access to testing and preventative services.

So, there are two types of older people living with HIV: those who were diagnosed, had initial treatment that was high in toxicity, have survived beyond expectation and are living with health complications; and those who are diagnosed over the age of 50, for whom health care prevention information and services are not targeted. Before effective treatments, people struggled with uncertainty and tried to assert control over their lives. Many people living with HIV in the first decade of its discovery sought to ensure that their disease did not define their lives, and struggled to accomplish professional goals in their few remaining years despite their HIV status. Because of the stigma associated with the disease, many chose to surround themselves primarily with others who were HIV positive. Disclosing status was and still is something that remains very personal, largely due to the stigma and misunderstanding associated with the virus.

As people age with the HIV virus there are different health issues that can arise based on time of diagnosis, treatment, general health and so on, which can include HIV Associated Neurocognitive Disorders (HAND), affecting patients in a similar way to 'regular' dementia associated with ageing. Although comorbid health concerns may be different for these people, many of the social challenges faced remain the same. The stigma associated with ageing and HIV often leads to social avoidance, with 71 per cent of older HIV positive adults reporting the dual stigma (Emlet, 2006a) and to reduced social networks and increased social isolation (Emlet, 2006b). The levels of depression reported for HIV positive men over 50 years go up to 53 per cent (Cahill et al, 2010, as cited in Cahill and Valadéz, 2013). Combining these stigma-related issues goes part of the way to explain why this group are also more likely to be homeless, adding to the risk of medication non-compliance and other health risk factors as well as increasing the risk of transmission.

These challenges can be faced by increasing awareness, decreasing stigma and increasing the education of healthcare professionals to advance the medications and reduce the stigma. Treatments are enabling this group to become a new ageing population, but social prejudice is preventing them from accessing a positive trajectory.

A final thought

Diversity in ageing is exactly as the word suggests ... diverse. This chapter has centred on sexuality but considered the intersectionality of class, race, culture and ethnicity. Prejudice, discrimination and stereotyping have been shown to be just as important within this context as within the ageism sphere discussed in Chapter 2. Diversity is variety, and variety leads to formation of majority and minority grouping, which in turn leads to stereotyping and stigma. We have identified these factors as challenging an individual's optimised trajectory of ageing, not least those who belong to the new ageing populations. It is important to consider the individual when addressing the topic of diversity, taking account of transecting factors influencing both cumulative and intersectional disadvantage.

REVIEW EXERCISE 5

This exercise works either as a solo exercise or, as a group. Look up the websites of major charities for older people. How many of them make a conscious effort to understand and communicate the diversity of the older population? Where they use images of older people, how many are from the majority ethnic group? Are there any references to older migrants? Is the information available in more than one language? How is gender represented in their work?

Alongside this, look up websites supporting Black, ethnic and minority groups. How many provide support for older adults?

Compare the two provisions and look at any disparity for a group discussion. For example, do they discuss gender inequality or the relative poverty of older migrants? Create a mind map outlining the key issues, their connectivity where appropriate, and the missing links. HINT: To create a mind map, take a blank page, write Diversity in a speech bubble in the middle of the page, then add bubbles with words and thoughts as they occur to you in a sort of free word association from diversity. Draw arrows between ideas which are interconnected. Use different colours to make those connections clearer to you or to anyone you share your mind map with. Mind maps are a great way of realising what you know about a topic or the opinions you hold. The trick is to get to the point where your mind map has more knowledge and information, and fewer bubbles that are just conjecture or opinion.

Aren't gender differences neutralised by age?

(Gender)

> Women have another option. They can aspire to be wise, not merely nice; to be competent, not merely helpful; to be strong, not merely graceful... They can let themselves age naturally and without embarrassment, actively protesting and disobeying the conventions that stem from this society's double standard about aging. (Sontag, 1972: 38)

Introduction

In her many witty, insightful essays on life as an American woman, the late Nora Ephron offers some of the most quotable lines about each stage of the lifecourse. Her book *Heartburn* (1983) is a classic treatise on how women survive divorce. Her most famous film, *When Harry Met Sally* (1989) has become a 20th-century classic on heterosexual relationships. She sadly died at the age of 71 in 2012. In the final years of her life she published a number of humorous essays on being an older woman in America. Her words cut to the core of how gender and age intersect through the changing shape of the female body: 'Anything you think is wrong with your body at the age of thirty-five you will be nostalgic for at the age of forty-five' (Ephron, 2008: 1268).

We use the words of two second wave feminists, Sontag and Ephron, to open this chapter on gender as it is structured around critical questions asked by feminists who are interested in, or affected by, old age. Once we have laid out some differences in how men and women age, we use the concept of 'intersectionality' to look at reported experiences of ageing by men and women, critically examining how femininity and masculinity might interact with ageism and age-based social norms. Here, we draw on a rich literature on older women, specifically on the interaction of ageism and feminism and how women experience 'the double standard of aging' (Sontag, 1972). Next, we analyse the burgeoning literature on masculinity and ageing which is focused on how men can resist ageism. In terms of vignettes, in this chapter, we mine a rich seam of the literature on old age – books written by feminists who are now ageing. Authors who have produced seminal feminist works – such as Betty Friedan and Simone de Beauvoir – have gone on, in later life, to write about ageism and their experience of 'encore' discrimination, the experience of a age discrimination after a lifetime of dealing with sexism. The chapter concludes by assessing how critical studies of old age might better engage not just with gender differences, but with the influence of patriarchal constructs such as 'hegemonic masculinity' on how men and women age. The issue of gender and embodiment is the subject of some rich studies in cultural gerontology, and so will be dealt with in more detail in Chapter 9. In terms of this chapter, it is worth noting the important work of Julia Twigg (2004) whose research has demonstrated the social role played by the human body and the importance of recognising how ageing is embodied, particularly in 'deep old age'. First, we look at gender differences in terms of health, life expectancy, income and social activity in old age.

Why do women live longer than men?

The messages we hear about gender inequality in old age can be confusing. Possibly the question we are asked most often by students is, 'How can you talk about gender inequality in old age when women live longer than men?' This is a fair question. At the time of writing, women's life expectancy in the UK is 83 years and men's 79 (ONS, 2018: 2). In response, we often give our students the same answer that Gunhild Hagestad gave to hers: 'Women are sicker, but men die quicker'. This might seem rather trite, but it is, in fact, basically true. To put it in more gerontological language, we will quote Hogberg (2018: 236): 'While across the world women have lower mortality rates and a higher average life expectancy, they simultaneously have higher levels of morbidity.' In plain English, this means that women, in general, are more likely to report chronic and disabling conditions than men in old age (Rieker and Bird, 2005). An important driver of this inequality is the fact that men are more likely to die at a relatively young age through accidental deaths, suicide or military service. For instance, in the US, causes of male deaths between the ages of 25–44 years recorded 41 per cent as unintentional injury and 15 per cent as suicide. For older age cohorts, such as the 55–64 category, these unintentional injury and suicide numbers reduce to 6.2 per cent and 2.6 per cent respectively (Center for Disease Control, 2015). Men are also less likely to report their symptoms to a doctor or health professional when they do fall ill. All of these accumulated disadvantages may be conspiring to make men less likely to make a full recovery from infection with COVID-19. Early observational studies from China suggest that Chinese men's higher rates of diabetes and hypertension, as well as the fact that 80 per cent of Chinese men smoke, may have contributed to them being more likely to die from COVID-19 (Zhou et al, 2020).

On the other hand, the question still arises as to whether women's less healthy old age is related to their greater likelihood of reporting their illness and of course, whether this means they are more likely to survive whatever illness befalls them. Another argument is that women's higher levels of oestrogen act to protect them from killer viruses or other illnesses. This, in turn, may explain why they go on to live longer. Researchers are unclear on whether this gender gap in health and life expectancy in old age is influenced by women's tendency to recover from serious illness for physiological reasons, or because they report illness more willingly. Certainly, women's more critical self-assessment of their health in old age plays an important role in constructing the narrative that women's later life is less healthful than men's. Women are also more likely to step down from activities that herald a loss of independence (such as driving) based on ill health (Barrett et al, 2018: 2125). More gender disaggregated studies are needed (particularly studies focused on men's ageing and health) if we are to decouple the role of self-reporting from our knowledge of health in old age. For now, it seems safe to assume that women's extended life expectancy comes with a price, and that price is often a combination of poor health, loneliness and poverty.

In short, women live longer, but with more chronic, painful conditions in later life. In any case, the gender gap in life expectancy is narrowing. The Office for National Statistics in the UK report that, over the past 30 years, both men and women are living an average of just under eight years longer. For instance, in 1980 female life expectancy was 76.8 versus a male life expectancy of 70.81. These figures had increased to 82.93 for women and 79.25 for men by 2016. However, between 2016 and 2018 statisticians report that, while the gap between male and female life expectancy is narrowing, the trend towards increasing life expectancy has also been slowing down, and in some areas, coming to a halt (ONS, 2019b). A variety of inconclusive explanations have been offered for this, but one possible reason is the ongoing failure of governments to provide adequate social care for vulnerable older people.

How do pension and care policies affect women and men?

There are important gender differences in terms of socio-economic status in old age. Even though they live longer, women are also much more likely to live on inadequate pensions, often as a result of their reliance on a husband's pension, which stops once they are widowed (Evandrou and Glaser, 2003). An important issue giving rise to women's lower income in old age is the fact that most paid and unpaid care work is undertaken by women (Falkingham and Rake, 2001; O'Neill and Jepsen, 2019). This means that women are less likely to have a full and complete social insurance record, leading to partial and inadequate pension payments after retirement age. In recent years there has also been lively debate in the UK about the plight of the 'WASPIs' (Women Against State Pension Inequality; https://www.waspi.co.uk/). WASPIs are women who are adversely affected by the way the UK Pensions Act (1995) has been implemented, and subsequently amended. The reasoning behind the original Act, which worked to gradually equalise retirement age between men and women, is not a problem for the WASPIs, who were prepared to accept retirement at the same age as men, at that time, 65. The difficulty lies in later amendments to the legislation (in the Pensions Act 2011) leading to sudden and unexpected changes to pension entitlements, made at such a late stage in these women's careers that there wasn't enough time for them to make alternative provision, and sometimes forcing them to work for years longer than they had anticipated or planned for. Given what we have learned about the core role of social policies in allowing human beings to be 'planful and competent' (Elder, 1999: 247), this seems to be a particularly virulent example of policies working against people's best efforts to age successfully. The problems encountered by the WASPI women are testament to the critique of neoliberalism offered by Macnicol (2015: 52), who makes the key point that policy makers are happy to 'make the assumption that individuals have considerable control over their own lives'. Very often, this is not the case. These women may have been banned from earning their own income earlier in life because of social norms and cultural expectations around women's natural role as mothers or unpaid carers. In fact, the general rolling back of the welfare state we referred to earlier in the book has made planning for one's old age increasingly difficult. This situation has been exacerbated since the financial crash of 2008. Since then we have seen a variety of neoliberal policies such as the raising of retirement age. All of these changes have gender impacts, in most cases to the disadvantage of older women (Duvvury et al, 2018).

There is ample evidence of how the major policies for older people have particular effects on women across the gerontology and policy literatures. For instance, Hogberg (2018) argues that having a decent state pension system and provision of free eldercare would have a doubly positive impact on women. Just in terms of free eldercare, women are more likely to be widowed and to have higher levels of morbidity and are therefore more likely to need care. In 2002, the Office for National Statistics in the UK reported that the centenarian population had eight women to every man. By 2017, more men were surviving and there were five women to every man (ONS, 2019b). Even though this gender gap is decreasing, the majority of the frailest and oldest people living in ageing societies are female. Women are more likely to need eldercare and/or to provide it for others. This means that the provision of free and high-quality eldercare would have advantages for women as both providers and recipients of care, as most informal and unpaid care work is undertaken by them (O'Neill and Jepsen, 2019). Related to this, a fact often missed in popular accounts of the rising cost of our ageing population, is that many older people are cared for by a spouse, partner or adult offspring who is also aged 60 or more. For example, it is increasingly common to have a 90-year-old woman cared for by her 65-year-old daughter. Caring and/or being cared for will be issues of vital importance for future generations of women in ageing societies. Falling birth rates and the rising number of people who have never married and do not become parents will further complicate this picture (Timonen and Doyle, 2014). There is a growing awareness of the changing dynamics of family care and the need to acknowledge that some carers are sandwiched between conflicting needs of young children and older parents, all of whom need some kind of help and support. The Office for National Statistics in the UK reports that the majority of these sandwich carers are older women; 72 per cent are aged between 50 and 64, and 68 per cent of them are female (ONS, 2019a).

There are important gender differences in terms of how men and women spend their time in old age. Finkel et al's (2018) study of ageing in Sweden over a 17-year period found that men and women both stay physically, socially and cognitively active and engaged well into their 70s. However, they did note some gender differences. Women score more highly in social engagement while men were marginally more likely to remain physically active. A rapid decline in all activities is only observed towards the end of life, in the period increasingly referred to as 'the fourth age' (Finkel et al, 2018). It is certainly worth mentioning that future researchers will be more concerned with helping men to stay more socially connected and engaged in their communities, not least because we now know that cognitive health is adversely affected by social isolation (Burholt, 2016). In the next section we look at how some of the issues affecting older people are the result of the interaction of sexism, ageism and the differential effects these forms of discrimination have on men and women in later life.

Intersectionality: men, women and ageism

'Intersectionality' is a term that is often used by feminists to describe our attempts to move on from the 'add women and stir' approach to understanding how gender interacts with other forms of inequality such as race, ethnicity, disability or age (Carney, 2017). To add women and stir means to keep the same system, but allow women in. This contrasts with a more systematic change of the system from patriarchal to more egalitarian structures and principles, which deal with race, age and class as well as gender and other forms of inequality. For instance, we might choose to examine how ageism affects men versus how it affects women (as opposed to older people in general). By taking this approach we can start to see how ageism operates, not just on the basis of age, but also how it intersects with sexism. This intersection of ageism with sexism is classically recognised as the 'double standard of aging' where 'aging enhances a man but progressively destroys a woman' (Sontag, 1972). Nowadays, there is evidence that ageism can destroy both men and women, with Hurd Clarke and others finding evidence that men also 'disappear' into old age, fearing loss of independence and virility through age-related disease (Hurd Clarke and Lefkowich, 2018). In some instances, the experience of ageism is, arguably, especially devastating for some older men because they may be falling from the height of male privilege. There is some evidence (which we will examine in the section on masculinity and ageing) which suggests that older men may refuse to acknowledge apparent examples of ageism. For now, it is worth examining how feminists have discussed the intersection of ageism and sexism as it is experienced by older women, specifically through the experience of life after menopause.

Serrao (2015) makes the case that women are doubly disadvantaged in old age because they have already accumulated disadvantages throughout the lifecourse. We know from our earlier description of gender differences that there is evidence that women are poorer and sicker in old age. We also know that this is often the result of women's caring responsibilities and other gender-based disadvantages from earlier in the lifecourse. For instance, there are physical consequences of pregnancies and births that manifest in old age (Bichard et al, 2012). In some cases, these physical issues are then used to denigrate older women who 'smell' as a result of pregnancy incontinence or are bent over by osteoporosis. Women's experience of double jeopardy in old age is laid bare in the writing of feminists such as de Beauvoir (1972) and Friedan (1993: 36) who are deeply negative about the encore discrimination they experience in old age, leading Friedan to say that age discrimination was so familiar to her that she felt as if she had 'been here before'. Friedan (1993) expresses her dismay at 'menopause mania' – the obsession with women's loss of reproductive sexuality. She expresses frustration with the failure of female doctors and scientists to adequately challenge the medical model: 'They still conduct their studies and treatment within the framework of that medical model: menopause, age, as disease' (Friedan, 1993: 484).

Many female authors describe the process of disappearing after menopause, no longer feeling worthy as either an object of sexual desire or a holder of valid views and opinions (de Beauvoir, 1972; Ephron, 2008). The construction of the older woman as a non-person is repeated in various motifs such as zombies, which is critiqued through the writing of older women (see Lively, 2013). Another common complaint is from older women who object to being seen as socially separated from younger women. The younger woman lives in fear of her older self, and, by implication, the older woman, who she discounts as a potential friend or lover on the basis of age (Rich, 1983, cited in Segal, 2014).

For other feminist writers, the intersection of ageism with sexism is harmful, not for existential reasons, but for its more practical implications for older women. Arber and Timonen (2012) edited a volume on grandparenting, which acknowledges that, in many ageing societies, women who have already borne the burden of childbirth and childrearing are now expected to do it all again as grandmothers.

Box 6.1: Assumptions about who provides care in old age

Carney remembers an instance, early in her academic career, of hearing a presentation from a young Spanish scholar, delivered in English, the presenter's second language. The presentation was translated from the Spanish '*Cuidado de los hijos mayors para padres*' as 'How sons take care of their elderly parents in Spain'. There was much excitement among the Irish audience at the surprise research finding that men carry the burden of eldercare in Spain. The audience were disabused of this misconception before the end of the seminar when it was revealed that the presenter had literally translated '*hijos*' the collective noun for a sibling group as 'sons' throughout the presentation. This evidence is anecdotal. But the surprise and excitement of the audience is a useful demonstration of how taken for granted gender norms are. We were thrilled and excited about the idea of sons caring for their parents because of the extreme novelty of the idea. The anecdote also demonstrates how gender inequality and ageism intersect across the lifecourse.

Women experience oppression under patriarchy throughout their lives, beginning with lower expectations at school, pressure to marry and procreate, and to assume responsibility for childrearing and kin-keeping. These roles continue throughout the lifecourse, and women never retire from these social roles. It is the tenacity of patriarchal norms to reinvent themselves and survive many attempts at reform by various waves of feminism that prompts such a strong focus on the idea of intersectionality. By thinking about sexism and its intersection with other forms of oppression it becomes easier for us to name and challenge discrimination and inequality. A good example of this kind of work is that of Carroll Estes (1979; Estes et al, 2003) whose 30-year career in the political economy of ageing culminated with a call for 'stage three feminism' based on 'a care movement' that recognises the reciprocity of care and how individuals have family rights to care and to be cared for. There are many reasons why this excellent idea has not taken off, not least the success of the active ageing policy agenda whose focus on individual agency is more in tune with neoliberal politics than the solidarity-based agenda put forward by feminists like Estes.

Studying women versus using a feminist framework

Before we move onto the testimony of ageing feminists, it is worth drawing a distinction between 'studying women and using feminist frameworks' (Hooyman et al, 2002: 4). As we will demonstrate in the section on masculinity, it is possible to use a feminist framework without studying women. Likewise, it is possible to study women without being a feminist. Feminist gerontology tends to use gender as a lens through which to understand human ageing. We admire the work of Calasanti (2007) as an example of this kind of approach. In critiquing the anti-ageing industry, Calasanti is feminist in her exploration of the tension that exists for women struggling to age 'gracefully' within the limited confines of an anti-ageing culture (Calasanti, 2007). There are, of course, multiple tensions within feminist literature. There is the well-publicised debates between trans women and cis women about who has the necessary biology to justifiably claim oppression on the basis of sex (see Westbrook and Schilt, 2014). There is also an observable but less publicised split between younger and older women within the feminist movement, with many younger feminists failing to see how reminiscing about the 1970s is going to help them to narrow the gender pay gap or stamp out internet trolling and sexual shaming on social media. What we do know is that the generation of women who can now be classed as 'older' (the baby boomers and radicals of the 1960s), who are the *grandes dames* of the 1970s Women's Liberation Movement, are now writing about their own ageing. To be more precise, they are writing about experiencing ageism in terms borrowed from their earlier experiences of sexism. We will explore these issues of intersections between ageism and sexism more in the next section, which draws on the work of ageing feminists.

Ageing feminists

Some of the best, most readable, entertaining and useful writing on the issues of gender and ageing is being written by older women. To be accurate, these are female authors, many of whom have written about female oppression throughout their lives and who are now choosing to write about the ageing process, their experience of ageism and, specifically, their experience of sexism and ageism, a heady cocktail of discrimination in old age. Some of the most notable authors have already been mentioned; Simone de Beauvoir's (1972) *La Vieillesse* (*Old Age*) was perhaps the original piece in this genre of second wave feminists writing about old age. De Beauvoir started a trend. By 1993 Betty Friedan, author of *The Feminine Mystique,* had written a powerful polemic calling for the inclusion of older people in the narrative of later life called *The Fountain of Age* (Friedan, 1993). This work has grown into an exciting branch of feminist literature. Notable works include numerous pugnacious and irresistibly radical books such as *Declining to Decline* and *Agewise* by literary critic Gullette (1997; 2013) and *This Chair Rocks* by Applewhite (2016). The field is not dominated by Americans though; memoirs by British authors such as Diana Athill's *Somewhere Towards the End* (2008) and Lynne Segal's *Out of Time* (2013) were bestsellers. All of these books contain the core element of feminist writing: the belief that to experience discrimination is the result of structural inequality, not of personal failure. In short, these books apply the notion that 'the personal is political' to old age. The real contribution of this genre is put simply by Elaine Showalter in her introduction to Segal's book (Segal, 2013: xiv): 'What really matters is neither the sociology nor the biology of ageing' but the narrative of the self, 'the stories we tell ourselves' of how to 'be our age as we age'. Ultimately, as we age, the central question is still 'How are we to live our lives?'

It is this quest – clearly stated by the second wave feminist consciousness-raising, that everyone should be free to live their own life – that now applies to old age, and makes this work influential. In many ways, it has encouraged the increasing prominence of humanistic approaches to understanding ageing now often referred to as 'cultural gerontology' (Twigg and Martin, 2015), which has its philosophical and political roots in the work of these women and is the subject of Chapter 9. These authors have also played an important role in moving the debate from a rather sterile and depressing neoliberal obsession with the 'grey burden' and 'the cost of social care' to more ontological questions such as 'what does it mean to live a long life?'.

While there have been some excellent books by older men about the experience of ageing (Blythe, 2005; Wolpert, 2011), for the most part older women have led the field in exploring the experience of understanding ageism as a form of institutionalised discrimination. For example, Gullette's (2007: 195) argument that 'we acutely lack an anti-decline movement' demonstrates how overtly political these writings are. Friedan's dismay (1993) at the fact that even gerontologists are forced to retire demonstrate these women's recognition of old age as a residual category and their experience as a political problem. Research into older men's lives suggests that this insight is less common among older men (Jackson, 2016). For now, let's admit that we are not comparing like for like but agree that it is worth looking into research on older men and their experience of ageism.

Masculinity: sometimes it is hard to be a man ...

An important element of understanding gender and ageing is to engage with the concept of masculinity. Too often, gender studies is the de facto study of women, women's rights, women's experiences and the issue of sexism as it is used against women. This is to be expected and encouraged, given the many hundreds of years that women have been rendered silent and absent from history. However, there is merit to examining the gender regime from the perspective of older men.

There are three broad strands of literature that relate to ageing and masculinity. At its broadest level we have gender studies which focus on men. In this vein, researchers examine gender regimes and how women and men navigate social roles within these regimes. This work has its roots in gender studies and is sociological in origin. A key concept in the field is 'hegemonic masculinity', defined by Coles and Vassarotti (2012: 32) as 'those men's practices that perpetuate the dominance of men over women as well as creating hierarchy of masculinities that privileges those men in positions of power and wealth and subordinates others'. The key point about hegemonic masculinity seems to be that it subjugates other versions of manliness or types of men who cannot, or refuse to, subscribe to its norms. For example, a classic way of maintaining the power of this form of masculinity is to denigrate gay men as 'women' or 'sissies'.

Some writers in the field have started to think about how these conceptions of masculinity might work (or not) for older men. In a comprehensive overview of the field, Thompson and Langendoerfer (2016) reviewed 98 studies of older men in a paper ambitiously titled 'Older Men's Blueprint for "Being a Man"'. They find that the norms of male behaviour expected under a regime of hegemonic masculinity make no allowance for ageing. Men are still expected to perform according to established stereotypes, despite their physical health and social networks being altered by the process of ageing and the institution of retirement. This literature has not engaged with ageism in the same way as much as the feminist gerontology literature has. Thompson and Langendoerfer (2016: 137) conclude that researchers must fill this gap. What is needed is 'narrative studies ... that focus on the identity talk of older men as older men, how they go about managing their subordinate status in ageist societies, and what strategies of resistance ... are adopted'. To some extent, this work has been started by feminist gerontologists who have chosen to concentrate their studies on the private lives of older men.

Research by Hurd Clarke and colleagues (2014; Hurd Clarke and Lefkowich, 2018) as well as van den Hoonaard (2009) are based on interviews with older men, and in van den Hoonaard's case, older widowers. An interesting finding in both sets of studies is that female researchers find themselves belittled by the older men they are interviewing: 'The men's tones of voice – whether didactic or aggressive – were those of a dominant man talking to a subordinate, younger woman' (van den Hoonaard, 2009). The researchers are female, and have a certain set of expectations of what gender relations entail. Perhaps the men's tone reflects the narrowness of defined gender roles, which are constrained and prescriptive? In one case, the men were being interviewed about their experience of becoming widowed. Even the most aggressively macho responses suggest an attempt to maintain dominance (a socially learned role) not only over the interviewer, but, more importantly, over their own emotions, which threatened to betray them. It is worth quoting Jacob (J), an interviewee who van den Hoonard (I) (2009: 270) found particularly offensive:

J: The average male becomes a female when their wife kicks the bucket.
I: What does that mean?
J: You understand English?
I: Yes, but …
J: American males that lose their wives at my age are all fucked up. They don't do anything. They sit and die … and that's it, you understand it? I can't say it any other way, they die.

(van den Hoonaard, 2009: 270)

This quotation would seem to support the evidence that older men are likely to experience loneliness, social isolation and depression (Perren et al, 2003: 70). Jacob's is a firsthand account of how men's lives are changed by ageing, and particularly if they experience one of the most common experiences of later life, spousal bereavement. It should be noted that in another study van den Hoonaard (1997: 542) found that widows reported similar levels of dislocation and isolation after the death of a husband. The impact of what Hagestad has called 'the dying off of one's co-biographers' (that is, people who were born around the same time as you) is an intrinsic part of the experience of living through your sixties and beyond (Hagestad and Settersten, 2017). It is expertly described by Nora Ephron (2008) in 'Considering the Alternative', an essay on facing death:

When you cross into your sixties, your odds of dying – or of merely getting horribly sick on the way to dying – spike. Death is a sniper. It strikes people you love, people you like, people you know, it's everywhere. You could be next … And meanwhile, your friends die, and you're left not just bereft, not just grieving, not just guilty, but utterly helpless. There is nothing you can do. Everybody dies. (Ephron, 2008: 1295)

Male or female, widowhood and bereavement generally are an unacknowledged rite of passage into old age. Men and women deal with it differently. Nevertheless, when it comes to ageing and masculinity the difficulty lies in the men's lack of a narrative of resistance. Hurd Clarke and Lefkowich (2018) found that older men were still judging themselves by the standards of hegemonic masculinity, 'identifying the hallmarks of manhood, namely physical strength, leadership and sexuality'. Hurd Clarke and Korotchenko (2016) investigated experiences of ageism with the same group of Canadian men (aged 65–89 years). They found that men tended to deny ageism existed, or to claim that, while it did exist, it did not apply to them. They seemed unwilling to accept their own ageing, referring to old people as another category. It is worth admitting that many feminists do this, referring to 'women' as 'they' as if the author does not herself share the same gender or have similar experiences of oppression and diminutive social status. Feminists may not be as far advanced as we had hoped. The lack of progress in terms of intersectional or gender-neutral categories is evidenced in our language. We still use phrases like 'older male carer' when referring to men who care for their ailing wives in the final years of life. Significantly, the institution of retirement and institutionalised ageism mean that many men are relegated to the private sphere of home and family in old age. More investigation is needed into how men cope with this increasingly domesticated, and to some extent feminised, old age (Ribeiro and Paul, 2008).

A final thought

In this chapter we have taken a broad sweep across the vast, interdisciplinary literature on gender and ageing. We found that gender identities, both masculine and feminine, 'are the product of narratives and practices' (Ashe and Harland, 2014: 748). We examined significant differences between men and women in terms of life expectancy and health, income and gender roles. In the context of ageing, this is complicated by physiological changes and losses. However, one of the biggest and as yet unrealised threats to men's ageing well is ageism. Some men appear to be particularly ill equipped to oppose ageism, given its direct affront to the pillars of masculinity: youth, virility and the ability to provide material resources. We found a range of approaches to studying men and masculinities. Men's studies tend to focus on men to the exclusion of women (Ashe and Harland, 2014). This is a major problem when it comes to ageing, as many of the problems men experience are closely related to their marital status. Women's kin-keeping and caregiving roles mean that men can be rendered vulnerable without a close female relative to remind them to go to the doctor, for instance. Equally, they may need someone to care for them, or they may struggle with self-identity and worth when catapulted into unexpected roles such as 'older male carer.' It would seem that more progress would be made if gerontologists began to consciously set out to study older men and older women, not just older people. The chapter concludes by arguing that critical studies of femininity and masculinity in old age could then set out to investigate 'intersectional identities which are shaped not just by gender but also by factors such as ethnicity, social class, sexuality, age and disability' (Ashe and Harland, 2014: 749).

In the section on masculinity we discussed how men's lives change as they age. They are barred from the workplace, which means they spend much more time in the private sphere, which in turn, even with the massive changes in women's roles in the past 30 years, is still a female-dominated space. Women are also widely recognised in the literature as the 'kin-keepers'. Data bear this out, with more women than men taking leadership roles in how family relationships, particularly with grown-up offspring, are managed (Devine and Carney, 2017). When we study men we tend to forget this basic fact of gender relations: men's actions affect women. This seems obvious. On the other hand, what women do affects men.

The point is that, as we age, this relational category of gender still operates. In particular, the balance of power might switch and change or be passed back and forth between spouses depending on who is ill, and who is able to maintain independence at any given moment. When couples age together, they tend to take care of one another. Men's roles and activities move from the workplace and community into the home, family and in particular their primary, marital relationship (Jackson, 2016). We need critical studies of men, masculinities and gender inequality to begin to understand how ageist norms and stereotypes work hand in hand with masculine norms to marginalise men in old age. This process of relegating men to the private sphere is surely as harmful and limiting as the exclusion of women from the public sphere throughout the lifecourse. We need to address the structural barriers to men's ageing well. The role of hegemonic masculinity as harmful to both men and women must be recognised in this context.

REVIEW EXERCISE 6

Group: Split into two groups and prepare an argument for and against the motion: 'Older women have never had it so good'. Use examples from the readings of Friedan and de Beauvoir, or from Twigg and Martin to make your case.

Solo: Looking at increased longevity, record a 2-minute video presentation on how gender affects a person's lifecourse trajectory at *one* of three critical transition points: onset of adolescence, becoming a parent, and transitioning to retirement.

Why do older people have it so good?

(The myth of intergenerational conflict)

We owe all children a Planet Earth as wonderful as the one we have enjoyed. (Norwegian Grandparents Climate Change Campaign, nd)

Introduction

In this chapter we tackle a complex but important topic in the study of ageing societies: solidarity between generations. 'Solidarity between generations' is the idea that people born in different periods and into separate birth cohorts support one another in order for the whole of society to thrive. This solidarity is a central fulcrum on which much of our social cooperation hinges. Everything from the financing of pensions and childcare, to caring for children and older people is dependent on people who occupy different life stages helping and supporting one another. This solidarity operates within families and at societal level. Within families, parents who are raising children are practising solidarity between generations. At societal levels, people who are currently working to support the education, health and welfare of the very young and the very old are practising solidarity between generations too.

Despite the significance of this form of social cooperation, solidarity between generations is not without its problems. In this chapter, we will take you through each of these debates, providing a critical analysis of how they affect the core principle of solidarity between generations. There are major scholarly debates around what constitutes a generation. Likewise, solidarity is not a concept we can take for granted. Social and political life in the 21st century seems destined to erode forms of solidarity and we examine how the 'individualisation of the social' is impacting on intergenerational solidarity (Beck, 1992). We then break the concept down into its constituent parts, asking 'What is a generation?' and 'How does solidarity between generations work?'. We do this by first consulting the 'big thinkers in the sociology of generation' whose work includes concerns for future generations. These ideas are developed by discussing the notion of solidarity through a number of vignettes. These vignettes draw on research from Ireland, the current debate on climate change, a critique of the populist myth of generational conflict, and finally through a brief review of the literature on grandparenting. The chapter concludes by making the case for solidarity between generations as one of the key means of maintaining social, economic and political security and stability as this century unfolds.

There are a number of challenges in this area, not least, the presence of a virulent and unsubstantiated literature on 'intergenerational inequity'. For example, in *A Generation of Sociopaths: How The Baby Boomers Betrayed America*, Gibney (2017) claims that all of the problems currently facing Americans, everything from a crisis in healthcare to public highways in bad repair, are the result of the selfish actions of baby boomers. Gibney's is the latest in a virulent breed of popular books and reports which claim that many of the problems of austerity and neoliberalism, including the poverty and inequality which have resulted from cutting back public services and deregulating markets, are the fault of the generation born more or less between 1944 and 1964, the 'baby boomers'. Other texts belonging to this genre include *Jilted Generation* (Howker and Malik, 2010) and *The Pinch: How the Baby Boomers Stole Their Children's Future and Why They Should Give It Back* (Willetts, 2010; David Willetts is a British Conservative politician and founder of think tank, The Resolution Foundation). All of these books use age, and particularly the concept of generation, to explain away much of what is wrong with the world. Indeed, generation is seen, not just as the basic unit of organisation in society, but as the basis on which injustice is done. This approach has a long pedigree, dating back to when pensions were introduced in the early 20th century. Its recent resurgence runs neatly alongside the birth and meteoric rise of neoliberalism under the leadership of Prime Minister Margaret Thatcher in the UK and President Ronald Reagan in the US. The rise and rise of these unfounded claims that baby boomers are generationally advantaged have been referred to as 'New Ageism' by scholars of the political economy of ageing (Walker, 2012: 814). New Ageism will be discussed in one of the vignettes at the end of the chapter.

The reason that ideologues can command control of our perception of generation lies in the nature of generation as a concept, which is notoriously difficult to get some analytical purchase on. Think about it, if someone asked you: 'You're studying ageing, what does 'generation' mean?' You might struggle to give a definitive answer. This question is difficult to answer because the concept 'generation' operates on a number of different levels.

What is a 'generation'?

We all find it easy enough to understand the idea of family generations – that you and your siblings and first cousins are one generation, while your parents and aunts and uncles are the next generation up. Meanwhile, your children and your siblings' children are one generation down. They occupy a space that is two steps down the generational ladder from your parents, their grandparents. However, generation becomes much more difficult to understand when you move outside the family and attempt to talk about generations at societal level. Indeed, this is so difficult that some gerontologists argue that it is not much use talking about generations in any meaningful sense outside the family. Compelling examples of where the confusion lies can be found in popular culture and everyday discourse.

We are all familiar with the references to 'generation' that we read about in newspaper headlines and in reports published by think tanks and charities. Those reports might refer to the 'baby boomers' or to 'Generation X' or 'millennials'. In fact, none of these stereotypes of people born in the same decade or decades are particularly meaningful or useful for understanding anything about social life or policy. On the contrary, in many cases, stereotypes confuse us about intragenerational inequality by hiding the fact that some older people live in poverty, as do some younger people. To compare and contrast generations means we are trying to perform two very difficult conceptual exercises at once. First, we are trying to understand social change as it unfolds. Second, we are trying to map that onto the passage of time, as one generation gives way to the next in an infinite 'mortal life cycle' (Bengtson et al, 1983). With the death of each generation, memories are often lost and problems can reoccur as humans repeat the same mistakes again and again.

Box 7.1: Defining a generation

'Generation' is the term used to refer to a birth cohort or group of birth cohorts who are recognised as having some common attributes and experiences by virtue of the time into which they were born.

Solidarity between generations refers to the support that one birth cohort or group of birth cohorts provides to another. Also referred to as intergenerational solidarity this support can include anything and everything from financial aid to care for the very young or very old. At societal level, it refers to support for transfers between generations such as pensions and child benefit.

Nevertheless, when we combine generation with solidarity into the singular, dynamic concept of 'intergenerational solidarity' or 'solidarity between generations' we do produce a useful concept which describes many of the policies and practices which are the foundation stone of our welfare state. It is worth pinning down what gerontologists have argued makes up solidarity between generations, an important means of maintaining social cohesion, support for redistributive policies and family caring practices. We will examine this in some detail later in the chapter. For now, let's look at the heritage of generation as a concept which has excited and inspired scholars of history and sociology for some decades.

Anyone in pursuit of a meaningful definition of generation eventually finds it is necessary to return to Mannheim's *The Problem of Generations*, first published in 1927 (Mannheim, 1993). Mannheim clearly articulates the central problem in defining generations: when does one generation end and the next begin? 'Even more difficult is it to find the natural beginning of the generation series, because birth and death in society as a whole follow continuously one upon the other, and full intervals exist only in the individual family where there is a definite period before children attain marriageable status' (Mannheim, 1993: 24). The persistence of this problem explains why the investigation of intergenerational solidarity in the family has analytically progressed, whereas examinations of the same phenomenon at the societal level have struggled to move beyond conjecture (Binstock, 2010; Carney, 2018).

Mannheim makes a number of insightful observations, many of which are still valid today. First, he makes the case for the idea of generation as a necessary construct for understanding social and intellectual movements. This quality of the concept, to connect social change and the passage of time, is later identified by Bengtson et al (1983): 'The concept of generation thus serves as the crucial link between time and social structure and is important in understanding the progress of historical events and the course of social change' (Bengtson et al, 1983: 48). We will decode some of what Bengtson and his colleagues lay out in that article later. For now, it is worth noting Mannheim's 'fundamental facts in relation to generation. (See Box 7.2.)

Box 7.2: Decoding Mannheim's 'fundamental facts in relation to generation'

Mannheim's definition
'New participants in the cultural process are emerging, whilst former participants in that process are continually disappearing. Members of any one generation can participate only in a temporally limited section of the historical process, and it is therefore necessary continually to transmit the accumulated cultural heritage; the transition from generation to generation is a continuous process' (Mannheim, 1993: 35).

Mannheim's definition decoded
Babies are born, old people die off. Our life experience is a product of our times. In the grand scheme of things, history will forget us. In little things, we will have made our mark. The cycle repeats for as long as humans occupy this Earth.

Mannheim's work clearly stands the test of time. Though it might be a little hard to digest, as you read through this chapter and come to understand the concept of solidarity between generations you will realise how useful his conceptual schema is. Here, he offers what is close to a definition of generation: 'Individuals who belong to the same generation, who share the same year of birth, are endowed, to that extent, with a common location in the historical dimension of the social process' (Mannheim, 1993: 35). In short, you cannot help when you are born and the events occurring when you are born mean you are given a certain 'social location' which shapes and influences your understanding of the world for as long as you occupy this Earth.

In essence, Mannheim is rightly credited with attaching age groups to a 'social location', often referred to as his 'historical consciousness perspective' on generation (Bengtson et al, 1983; Nugin, 2010). He also makes clear what exactly 'theories of generation' have so far tried to achieve: '... to establish a direct correlation between waves of decisive year classes of birth – set at intervals of 30 years, and conceived in a purely naturalistic, quantifying spirit – on the one hand, and waves of cultural changes on the other' (Mannheim, 1993: 52). This brings us to the first stumbling block in understanding the implications of solidarity between generations for public policy. Should policy makers concentrate on promoting intergenerational solidarity or solidarity between groups at different stages of the lifecourse? How does generation intersect with class and other inequalities? What about birth cohorts? Should gerontology scholars focus on birth cohort and forget about generation?

As we attempt to answer some of these questions, we will be drawing on Mannheim's conceptual schema, using the idea of social location to draw out the difference between birth cohorts and generations. Mannheim's insistence that the cycle of generational change repeats on a loop is borne out in our critique of the short-sighted inter-generational equity debate, towards the end of the chapter. Further political implications of this debate are elaborated in Chapter 8. It is worth taking a little detour here to unpack the differences between a birth cohort and a generation (see Box 7.3).

Box 7.3: Birth cohort versus generation

As outlined in Chapter 1, a birth cohort is a group of people born within a particular time period, usually a five- or ten-year period. This contrasts with a generation, which generally refers to a group of birth cohorts who are born in the same 'social location' (so their life experience is qualitatively affected by the period of their birth). If an age group can be legitimately presented as a distinctive generation, it has to have some defining characteristic or 'social location'. A generation is a group of people who have been through some seismic cultural change which distinguishes them from an age cohort; see, for instance, Nugin's (2010) study of the defining generations of Estonians, those who were born immediately after the fall of Communism. As Mannheim says: 'Whether a new generation style emerges every year, every 30, every 100 years, or whether it emerges rhythmically at all, depends entirely on the trigger action of the social and cultural process' (Mannheim, 1993: 53). In essence, it takes a war, a famine or a revolution to produce the kind of social change which allows us to differentiate one generation from the next. So, it is not when one is born, but how one is socialised or affected by significant social and cultural processes that makes one a member of a defining generation. The fact that the baby boomers are an unusually large birth cohort, and are defined by the period in which they were born (after World War II) is one of the bases on which popular culture makes a claim that they are a 'generation'.

All of this concern with defining generation may seem to be straying from the central focus of the chapter, which is to investigate intergenerational solidarity. In fact, intergenerational solidarity is clearly identified as one of five themes in generational research in Bengtson et al's (1983) state-of-the-discipline article 'Time, Aging, and the Continuity of Social Structure: Themes and Issues in Generational Analysis'. This article describes a number of key points that help us to define a generation, which we have rephrased for ease of understanding. Defining aspects of a generation include:

- differences in expectations and standards of behaviour between age groups;
- the transmission of views and attitudes from older people to younger cohorts and the feedback as young people interact with elders;
- the idea that there are observable differences between young people today and young people in the past;
- the idea that differences between age groups might give rise to age-based conflict.

We also like the work of Rick Moody on this issue. Moody's overview of the history of the idea of justice between generations makes a very useful connection between the temporal and socio-political context to generation (Moody, 2007). While Moody refers specifically to decades, he also links age groups to particular time periods, or events that characterise a time period (such as the Great Depression, the Great War, World War II, the financial crisis of 2007–08). The real question for scholars of ageing is how a particular event might contribute to shaping one generation in as much as it might completely change the course of history for another, in practice: 'Elders make decisions but young people make the sacrifices' (Moody, 2007).

That's generation – now what about solidarity?

To recap, solidarity between generations refers to the set of human relations between birth cohorts that allows redistribution of material, emotional, social and economic resources. These same processes of exchange are also referred to as intergenerational solidarity. The most obvious form of intergenerational solidarity is when a parent provides support for their baby. This starts during pregnancy and continues for 20 years or more. The social expectation that parents will care for their own children is so deeply ingrained that it has become a basic form of social organisation. Parental responsibility is expected in all societies across the world, though it may be experienced in different ways, depending on access to income, resources, the local culture and the status of women. For the most part, we accept that as a parent we must care for our children, just as our parents cared for us when we were young. In countries where Confucianism shapes cultural norms, the concept of filial piety places similar responsibilities on adults towards their frail parents (Sung, 2018).

There have been major changes in how families are structured over the past 50 years. We know from Chapter 1 that one of the biggest drivers of population ageing is the falling total fertility rate. This means that women are having fewer children. We also know that people are living longer. This means that the practice of intergenerational solidarity is deeply affected. In ageing societies, there are fewer children to care for, but also more older adults potentially needing care. The family as a basic unit for intergenerational exchange is slowly transforming.

So, solidarity between generations at the family level is fairly straightforward to understand. It is when this individual experience is translated to the societal level that it gets infinitely more complicated. The set of social policies, the financing of pensions and the organisation of healthcare is based on expectations that a certain number of people will be in work. These people are expected to pay for the education of the current generation of children and to allow their taxes to be spent on pensions for people who already made their contribution earlier in the lifecourse. It is this tacit agreement between generations that provides the solidarity to establish something as transformative as the welfare state. Solidarity between generations is one of those important social resources that we are seldom aware of, but which we completely depend on to function in the social world. Certainly, policy makers are utterly dependent on this agreement if they are to run the health service, pay for public roads or expect children to arrive at school clean, fed and ready to learn.

Lessons from other crises

Changing generations (Ireland under austerity)

Borrowing from Mannheim's conceptual scheme again, another way to look at solidarity between generations is to think of the Earth, one's country or community being in the hands of each generation for only a few decades. There is a social contract between each cohort of individuals to act as custodians for whatever is good about the world (clean air and water, an absence of war, and access to healthcare when needed) and to endeavour to improve conditions for generations coming up behind them. This social contract is a useful way of understanding the breadth of the concept of solidarity between generations and how it permeates every aspect of life.

When working on a project to investigate solidarity between generations in Ireland, Carney and her colleagues found it useful to think about generational solidarity and relations as an important means of exchanging resources between birth cohorts. So, in The Changing Generations project, we examined solidarity between generations by finding men and women aged between 18 and 101 from across the social spectrum, including migrants, homeless people and the wealthiest in Irish society. The researchers interviewed 100 people living in Ireland in-depth, asking them to tell us about their life stage and how their age might influence their lived experience. The results revealed much about how intergenerational solidarity is a key means of exchanging social, emotional and material resources between groups (Timonen et al, 2013). In another article from the study, Conlon et al (2014) found that women supported one another according to their means, but always within the family. So, women from lower socio-economic status (SES) groups provided small loans or contributed some food or groceries, while women from higher SES groups made large payments to provide long-term care for older relatives. In many instances, grandparents were providing free childcare which allowed women of working age to earn a salary. From one perspective, this is unremarkable; it is normal for families to help one another out. From another perspective, the level of solidarity we witnessed, particularly, family solidarity *is* remarkable, because it occurred in the context of extreme hardship and under an austerity programme imposed on people living in Ireland by cross-national bodies following the financial crash of 2007–08. Indeed, the level of family solidarity observed was so high that it prompted the publication of an article attempting to explain why Ireland's austerity programme was leading to 'coping' rather than 'protesting' strategies among its population (Carney et al, 2014).

This attributed the solidarity in the Irish population to the high level of family solidarity, which, when combined with the emigration of younger birth cohorts, gave shape to a peaceable transition out of extreme poverty, national indebtedness and eventually a return to the global markets in 2015.

You might be wondering, what has any of this got to do with ageing and older people? The focus on Ireland is a useful vignette in demonstrating the strength of solidarity between generations, particularly in how family solidarity translates at the societal level. It is the capacity of this form of solidarity to be maintained within families, even when a population is under pressure to think and act in an individualistic manner during a programme of austerity, that makes it so remarkable. This vignette from Ireland allows us to see how intergenerational solidarity at the family and societal levels interact.

Climate change and the concept of stewardship

'If you still say we are wasting valuable lesson time, then let me remind you that our political leaders have wasted decades through denial and inaction' (Greta Thunberg, 16-year-old climate activist, 2019).

The idea that each generation only borrows the Earth, also known as 'stewardship', so eloquently expressed by Greta Thunberg (2019) in *No One is Too Small to Make a Difference*, is not new. The concept of 'stewardship' is the focal point of Partridge's oft-cited *Responsibilities to Future Generations* (Partridge, 1981). In that volume, which seems timely in the era of climate change Armageddon, a range of philosophers contribute chapters on everything from technology to environment, the rights of unborn future generations, food security and nuclear power. Most notable is Callahan's famous contribution 'What obligations do we have to future generations?'. Callahan (in Partridge, 1981: 84) makes a strong case for being cognisant of the significance of intergenerational transmission: 'There is no way to break the chain of obligation which is passed from one generation to another; it is the very condition of there being successor generations.'

The concept of stewardship of the world's resources implies that the future is not a trajectory but offers an infinite number of possibilities. We can redeem ourselves through future generations. Whatever ills have taken place can be cleaned up by the next generation; crimes of the past must be remembered but not repeated. A case in point is the EU whose earliest incarnation as the European Coal and Steel Community was viewed as a pragmatic means of fostering interdependence between previous foes. Economic cooperation was the solution that the post-war generation offered to make up for the damaging consequences of Nazism and World War II in Europe. The assumption that a generation of people will assume collective responsibility for the impact of their actions on the future generations is a core aspect of intergenerational solidarity at the societal level. You will see in Chapter 8 that some commentators use this very frame to blame the older generation for leading the UK out of the EU, through a form of direct democracy called a referendum in 2016. This is an immensely challenging and contested area of research into generations.

Neoliberalism and the myth of generational conflict

There are some commentators and politicians who have a less positive view of solidarity between generations. For these people, driven by an ideological commitment to the destruction of welfare and solidarity in favour of the market and individualism, generational interactions appear marred by inequity. Taking a rather short-term view on generational relations and committed to an ahistorical interpretation of the present, commentators like David Willetts wish to pit generations against one another (Macnicol, 2015). By staging a 'phoney war' between generations (National Pensioners' Convention, 2016), Willetts and other Right-wing commentators wish to remove support for pensions and healthcare for this generation of older people (the 'baby boomers'). While they single out the baby boomers in order to make their case, they are careful to keep obscure the long-term impact of what they propose, which is to reach a new status quo where the state avoids having to carry the cost for future generations of older people's welfare. Gerontologists have reacted to this attack in a number of different ways. Some, such as Alan Walker (2012: 815), have cited it as the 'New Ageism', pointing out that Willetts' rhetoric has antecedents in a movement called Americans for Intergenerational Equity which 'was eventually exposed as a front for a neoconservative campaign against the welfare state, which used generational equity as politically expedient cover, and it disappeared without trace at the end of the Reagan era'. Others, including Carney et al (2014), have pleaded for policy makers to take a long view on intergenerational relations and to preserve solidarity at all costs. Commentators like Willetts present themselves as 'experts' on the area of intergenerational relations. However, the research they disseminate rarely includes findings counter to their ideological narrative that older people have too many rights and benefits.

In a direct critique of Willetts' phoney war, Carney completed an analysis of the representation of older people as responsible for the Brexit vote in the UK. The results of her analysis demonstrated that Willetts' Resolution Foundation was successfully flooding mainstream media with 'evidence' of intergenerational equity by managing to publish one press release in 19 stories in 15 different newspapers in a matter of weeks. 'Every one of these articles led with a headline "Millennials earned £8000 less than the previous generation", and concluded that the issue of intergenerational inequality was now more important than other forms of social inequality' (Carney, 2018: 6). By cleverly arguing that the baby boomers are stealing from the young, Willetts (2010), Gibney (2017) and others successfully erode solidarity between generations. Their core aim is to remove citizenship rights to pensions and healthcare in old age on the basis of 'cost'. The logical implication of their work is that future generations will actually miss out on pensions and healthcare in old age themselves. As Mannheim has shown, the human lifecycle repeats and, if you vote to remove benefits for older people, you cannot expect to enjoy those benefits when you reach old age. The logical conclusion of the intergenerational equity movement is to make people poor in old age. Moreover, there is nothing in their research or claims which guarantees that money saved by not spending on older people will be returned to the young (Macnicol, 2015; Walker, 2012).

There is also evidence of spurious arguments about intergenerational equity seeping into research on young people and the financial crisis since 2008. The argument goes that young people are coming of age in a world that offers greater individual freedom in terms of expression and identity, but very little social or economic security. This is to be expected of a neoliberal political economy. A good example is a report by Kate Alexander Shaw (2017: 1), who argues that the UK has an 'economic context structured around the primacy of market forces, which demands that young people sink or swim as an individual economic unit'. While there is nothing wrong with what Alexander Shaw is saying, this statement gives the impression that only young people are subject to this regime. In fact, everyone is subject to the same regimen, and those worst off are those with the lowest level of education, no savings or even debt. The premise that Alexander Shaw is depending on is that age is somehow the root cause of intergenerational equity. This neglects a central premise of Mannheim's: the fact that every birth cohort comes of age in a certain set of circumstances when the world is a certain way. For some this means leaving home to go to war (for instance, men born in Europe around 1900). For others, it means growing up under the shadow of imminent nuclear war (children born in the 1970s) and for still others it means coming of age just as a long period of economic stability and growth comes to an end (such as children born around 2000). What is particularly virulent about the most recent iteration of the intergenerational equity argument, which has been put forward since 2008, is the practice of blaming the most unfortunate for their lower social status which is at the very heart of neoliberal politics. So, rather than offer the context of growing up in a harsh recession, neoliberal politics chooses to identify the current generation of young people as 'the worst off in history' (Gardiner, 2016).

In truth, every generation's experience is different. We come of age under a set of geopolitical, economic and social circumstances, all of which are beyond our control. This is what Mannheim was trying to show through the concept of 'social location'. For example, while millennials may have little economic security they have much more freedom in terms identity, sexual orientation, gender fluidity, international travel, freedom to marry, divorce or have a family with whom and whenever according to their personal preference. And there is one defining characteristic of the generation who came of age around the turn of the century: millennials have grandparents who are healthier, live longer and are more involved in their grandchildren's lives than any previous generations.

Grandparenting

The chapter will conclude by returning to intergenerational solidarity at the family level, making reference to the growing literature on grandparenting (Herlofson and Hagestad, in Arber and Timonen, 2012), and its increasing importance in the lives of current and future generations of children as well as the survival of society (Hayslip et al, 2019). We will explore the role of grandparenting in the hidden economy and the contributions made by older people in terms of volunteering and supporting younger generations through unpaid caregiving (Marhánková, 2015).

This section acts as something of a counterbalance to previous discussion of the alleged conflict between generations. In fact, the idea of a war between generations fizzles out completely when you consider the Generations United (2015) report that almost 6 million children are in the care of their grandparents in the US (cited in Hayslip et al, 2019). Similarly high rates of activity in grandparenting are found around the globe. Even in well-established Nordic welfare states, grandparents lead an intergenerational movement called Norwegian Grandparents Climate Change Campaign whose tagline opened the chapter: 'We owe all children a Planet Earth as wonderful as the one we have enjoyed' is expressly intergenerational (https://www.besteforeldreaksjonen.no/about-the-grandparents-climate-campaign/). The idea of an intergenerational war becomes even more ridiculous when you read the results of research on custodial grandparents in countries as diverse as China and the US. In countries with high rates of migration from rural to urban areas such as China and South Africa, grandparents take on the parental role (De Wet, 2019; Kim, 2019). Baker and Silverstein (in Arber and Timonen, 2012) demonstrate that grandparents fall into a range of categories, from 'child savers' when parents have become addicted to drugs to 'family savers' when illness affects dual income families in Nordic states. In the US, there are over 2.5 million grandparents, mainly African American women, who are effectively parenting their children's children. The relative strength of grandparent–grandchild bonds is evidenced by social workers who have reported on the grief that is experienced by grandparents who lose contact with their grandchildren through divorce or migration (Gair, 2017).

In countries where there is no state-funded childcare provision, Meyer (in Arber and Timonen, 2012: 71) finds that grandmothers are 'highly prized day care providers because the quality is often high, the cost of often very low, and the flexibility is often maximal'. The upshot of these trends, which have a long history in the US, is that many people have a strong sense of duty to be a 'good grandparent' given that their own grandparents might have had an important role in their upbringing. In a recent review of the literature, Hayslip et al (2019: 158) found that the growing number of custodial grandparents leads to complex new family forms and the need for further research into the psychological and social dynamics of 'grandfamilies'. The link between close relationships with grandparents and more positive views of older people is well documented in the literature (Flamion et al, 2019). However, the cost of providing care to one's grandchildren is often high. For the women in Meyer's study of 'grandmas at work', providing care for grandchildren was often on top of a commitment to paid work and their own home duties. Nevertheless, they presented the role as a fulfilling and important aspect of their lives: 'Being a grandma is the best job in the world. Love them, spoil them, and say goodbye' (Deanne, cited in Meyer, in Arber and Timonen, 2012: 77). The cost on grandparents of caring for grandchildren in terms of loss of time, social interaction and health has been documented in a range of studies (Sheppard and Monden, 2019; Marhánková, 2019). The use of grandparents as cheap or free childcare providers is most common in countries with weak or residual welfare states. The gender implications of this trend, given that grandmothers are likely to be carrying the bulk of this responsibility, is not to be overlooked.

A final thought

This chapter has reviewed the literature on solidarity between generations, revealing two distinct strands of scholarship. There is a strong empirical tradition investigating intergenerational transfers and the solidarity between generations as it is expressed between individuals and within families (Saraceno, 2008). The second tradition rests around the questions that intergenerational justice poses for the provision of public goods. This second vein is better described as a debate than a research area, as it is full of normative discussions of topical issues in healthcare and taxation, broadly relating to the distribution of resources at the macro level, typified by populist books on intergenerational inequity or justice referred to earlier. As neoliberalism has slowly destroyed alternatives to the market, this branch of the literature has become dominated by Right-wing think tanks whose work has moved from a discourse of solidarity between generations to one focused on perceived generational inequity.

REVIEW EXERCISE 7

Group: Discuss the benefits of intergenerational solidarity for both older people and younger people, and the barriers to increasing levels of solidarity. Identify one strategy for reducing intergenerational conflict and create a press release designed to reflect the benefits and successes of the programme.

Solo: Write a 600-word article for a newspaper outlining three main benefits of solidarity between generations in the context of the coronavirus pandemic. Hint: use Carney's (2020) article in *The Conversation* to help you address the benefits. Don't forget to include challenges posed by the requirement for family generations to remain physically distant during the lockdown that was used to contain the spread of the virus. What does this experience show us about the human tendency to live in intergenerational, family groups?

8

Why do older people vote, while younger people protest?

(Politics of ageing)

You stole our future from us! (Placard displayed by two young women at a rally following UK vote to Leave the European Union on 23 June 2016)

Introduction

In this chapter we will argue that research on ageing has failed to adequately take account of the role of political institutions and decision making in precipitating and responding to demographic change. In comparison with other areas of research such as care for older people or dementia, the political implications of demographic ageing have been under-researched. In this chapter we make the case that politics matters (Stoker, 2006) when investigating our ageing population. There are two ways to look at the politics of ageing. On the one hand, there is the issue of political participation – who votes and whether this is affected by age. On the other hand, there is the macro-level question as to how political decision making might affect population ageing, an important aspect of political demography. We will devote equal attention to each side of the debate, aiming to increase your understanding of both. We will draw on the work of demographers such as Weiner and Teitelbaum (2001) who argue that political demography (the study of population as it relates to government and politics) is an urgent challenge for scholars of population ageing. Given that the outcome of democratic elections is heavily influenced by population change, we will ask whether an ageing population is likely to lead to a 'gerontocracy' (rule by the aged). Examples from 2016 electoral events in the UK and the US will be used to illustrate this argument. This discussion will be followed by a brief overview of the relationship between universal benefit payments made on the basis of age and their possible impact on the formation of age-based interest groups. The chapter will conclude by drawing these issues together.

The political roots of population ageing as a policy problem

For some decades now we have tended to view the changing of the world's population as akin to a crisis or unforeseen event – as something that is happening *to* us, rather than caused *by* us. The terms we use to describe demographic ageing are often presented in neutral terms such as 'The world's population is ageing' or 'The population aged 60 or above is growing at a rate of about 3 per cent per year' (United Nations, https://www.un.org/en/sections/issues-depth/ageing/). Alternatively, it is expressed in terms normally reserved for natural disaster. A very quick scout around the internet will find evidence of this, for instance an opinion piece by Forbes consultant Sanghi on the World Bank website published in May 2018:

> According to our calculations, Russia's working-age population is projected to drop from about 100 million in 2015 to 89 million by the year 2030. Moreover, the dependency ratio is expected to rise from 50 percent today to almost 58 percent by 2030. In other words, Russia's talent pool – as proxied by its working-age population – is shrinking, while the number of dependents is growing. (Sanghi, 2018)

You will know from earlier chapters that there are lots of problems with this statement. There is an implied ageism in the assumption that only people of working age can belong to Russia's 'talent pool'. This piece also demonstrates how so much of what is said about our ageing population is based on assumptions around what we deem as usual or appropriate behaviour for someone aged 65 or over. Before we move on, it is worth thinking more critically about what we mean by politics in the context of ageing societies.

Box 8.1: Defining politics

In basic terms, politics is the organisation of society by government, including the distribution of power and resources, the means of electing public representatives and ultimately the making of laws and policies. While politics will differ between countries, base elements include power, some form of representation or leadership and ultimately the distribution of resources between groups. Any political system needs to have a legitimate state to govern. This state will usually be territorial (that is, there must be some land for people to live in and recognise as a nation-state) and also have citizenship (that is, some means of binding together those living in the nation-state in a way which allows them to trust government). Taking these base elements of politics you can start to see how a change in the balance of the population from younger to older might have political consequences. It is also worth noting that some of the decisions made by politicians and by voters in choosing their leaders and their policies might have led to population change.

In the UK, there is a clear example of how politics has played a role in the ageing of our population. First, in the period following World War II, we had a baby boom. This is a typical demographic trend as populations often rush to replace themselves after the heavy losses of war. The politics of post-war Britain were collective and cohesive. The experience of living through six years of death and destruction from the heavy bombing of most major cities, including London and Coventry, and the disruptive effect of that period on the British class system improved the quality of trust and shared citizenship between Britons. The result was an era of consensual state-building, which began with the election of a Left-wing Labour majority government in 1945, under the leadership of Clement Attlee. When Attlee swept to power under the mandate to establish the NHS and other important socialist legislation, it was thought that the conservative House of Lords would block his efforts. They did not. This is why the period is referred to as the 'post war consensus' and many of the institutions established between 1945 and 1951, including the NHS and the welfare state, are still with us today. The NHS provides universal free healthcare at the point of access and on the basis of need rather than ability to pay. It is still a universally popular institution in public life in the UK. While nowadays both NHS and the welfare state are under-funded and under threat, the establishment of a state-funded support for every citizen from birth to death had many long-term implications; not least it created the conditions for decreased mortality and fertility, as it was a universal health service free at the point of use. Moreover, the NHS helped women to control fertility when contraceptive methods became more reliable. The babies born at that time are today's baby boomers and much of their health and longevity and, some argue, their relative financial security, is the result of the post-war consensus and the collectivist social policies that results from the political mood and leadership at the time. Much has changed in the intervening 50 years. In particular, the past 30 years have seen a sustained onslaught on this collectivist mentality through neoliberalism.

Social policy demands of the 21st century

Of course, it is easy to see all of this in hindsight. At the time that Attlee and his colleagues set up the welfare state their focus was on rebuilding the United Kingdom of Great Britain and Northern Ireland on a more egalitarian playing field following the ravages of war. They were not thinking about population ageing. Whatever your views on their achievements, like many policy-makers they did make mistakes, such as establishing the entire system on the basis of gender politics of the 1950s (see Lister, 2003). The benefits and services that arose from the welfare state worked on the assumption that the basic unit of society was the nuclear family headed by a working male who is married to a woman who will provide free labour in the home. So, unemployment benefits were for men, education was for children, and care for older people was something that women did as part of their unpaid domestic role. Think about it. Some of the biggest challenges for today's welfare state result from these assumptions. The crisis in social care and eldercare arises from the fact that women are no longer available to provide free home care for older relatives as they are employed outside the home. Likewise, women are vulnerable to poverty in old age because their domestic duties did not leave them with enough National Insurance contributions to provide for a decent pension (see Arber and Ginn, 1991).

Another issue is the fact that the NHS is primarily set up as a system to treat critically ill people. It was designed as a hospital-based service where General Practitioners (GPs, general locally based doctors) are the point of access for further treatments. While the NHS now provides many other healthcare services, at government level there is still an unwillingness to take on responsibility for other forms of care, particularly social care, even if that would allow the core care for critically ill patients to be done more efficiently and effectively. (For an extensive and informative discussion of the evolution of social care in the UK, see Gray and Birrell, 2013.)

The problem of whether social care in old age should be provided as a universal benefit is linked to the fact that healthcare in the UK is free at the point of access and is a basic right of social citizenship. While there is consensus that this right should stay in place, there is a need to reassess the difference between health and aged care and whether preventative measures such as home care for older people, which keeps them out of expensive and inappropriate hospital beds, is worth investing in given its contribution to the smooth running of the rest of the NHS (Lloyd, 2012). In any case, the health needs of the UK nation have changed. Nowadays we are more likely to live longer, but with chronic conditions such as diabetes or in recovery from previously killer diseases such as breast cancer. The basic point is that today's UK population is not just older, it is also qualitatively different in terms of its healthcare needs.

In conclusion, this example of the UK welfare state is only one of a number of examples where describing the change in the world's population from younger to older runs the risk of being both literal and simplistic. Alternatively, viewing population change as an issue caused by human activity with political causes and consequences is much more revealing. For instance, it may make more sense to look at population change in the round, rather than to focus on the issue of population ageing exclusively (see Harper, 2016). This approach makes perfect sense when you think that two of the three main drivers of population change – declining mortality, fertility and migration – are interlinked in ways that can reverse the trend of population ageing. Increasing life expectancy cannot be taken for granted, as it is influenced by politics and policy. For instance, research by Ho and Hendi (2018) found that life expectancy had declined in the UK (England and Wales) and the US in 2014–15 but continued to rise in other high-income countries. Ho and Hendi (2018) managed to trace the cause of this decline to drug overdose in the US. There is speculation that the UK decline in life expectancy is due to cutbacks to social care for older people. Social policy scholars will remark that the obvious solution is to tackle the use of illegal drugs among some of America's poorest citizens. Political will to bring down the numbers engaged in substance misuse could bring life expectancy back in line with other high-income countries.

When it comes to the second driver of population change, fertility, we do not know the extent to which delayed fertility might mean that replacement birth rates end up being higher than expected (Weiner and Teitelbaum, 2001: 5). Finally, the movement of young people from regions of poor employment prospects in the Global South to the regions with older populations and greater opportunities in the Global North could alter the demographic balance in countries such as Germany. Of course, the extent to which there is free movement of people or motivation for couples to have larger families might depend on whether governments support immigration or decide to provide family-friendly policies such as free childcare. In short, the ageing of the world's population and the population in your own country is affected by political decision making. This is why making population projections is so difficult.

Box 8.2: A note of caution: population projections are not forecasts

In their excellent book on political demography, Weiner and Teitelbaum (2001: 10) offer a number of examples of how population projections have made some inaccurate predictions. For instance, the Royal Institute of International Affairs in 1936 predicted that the UK population, then 45 million, would have reduced to 37.6 million by 1976. In fact, by 1976 the UK had a population of 57 million and by 2016 that population reached 66 million, its largest ever (ONS, 2017).

Why were they wrong?
Declining death rates and immigration outnumbering emigration has contributed to a steadily rising population. The predictions of the 1930s demographers were inaccurate for a range of countries. In the case of the UK, we might guess that their long-range forecasts were wrong because the NHS and the welfare state were but a twinkle in the eye of Beveridge and Attlee at that point. Added to this, the other major change in the second half of the 20th century, migration, is notoriously difficult to predict. It is hard to predict events which might prompt mass migration from a country or region, such as the outbreak of war or the election of a despot. Unfortunately, today's policy makers do not seem to have learned from the experience of the past and continue to present population projections as forecasts of future performance. Readers of this book, we recommend that you heed history rather than projections when assessing the future of ageing societies: 'If historical experience rather than formal demographic projections from the present is our guide, we would be well advised to expect the unexpected, anticipate the unpredictable, as a substantial influx and outflow takes place in some regions and among some countries, driven less by demographics than by political circumstances' (Weiner and Teitelbaum, 2001: 9).

Political demography: linking population change to government and politics

At the macro-level, much public debate about how demographic ageing may or may not lead to changed resource allocation has led some to identify an area of research as 'political demography' – the study of how politics shapes and is shaped by demographic change. The study of political demography has, regrettably, been neglected by researchers and has 'been ceded to political activists, pundits and journalists, leading often to exaggerated or garbled interpretation' (Teitelbaum, 2015). This neglect is starting to be addressed by demographers such as Toft: 'Population change needs to be considered as a political force in its own right' (Kaufmann and Toft [in Goldstone et al], 2012: 4). This is related to the broader claim, which is difficult to dispute, made by demographer Billari (2015: S11) that: 'Explaining population change means recognising the fact that human actions and interactions, embedded in a macro-level context, are driving demographic events.' Such thinking has not been the fashion, and the political implications of trends like declining fertility in established Western democracies versus surges in youth populations of largely Muslim countries have been ignored by both demographers and political scientists. More importantly for readers of this book, social gerontologists have been almost completely absent from this debate. The crucial point made by Teitelbaum (2015) and other researchers in this field (such as Spijker and MacInnes, 2013) is that public perception of any big demographic change as 'dangerous' or 'apocalyptic' can prompt politicians to make popular decisions at the cost of better, long-term policy planning.

In the absence of a reasoned, academic and evidence-based 'long view' (Coleman et al, 2015) on population change, we have seen pundits and even some politicians use population change as a lever to bend public opinion to suit their ends. For the purposes of this chapter, it is worth reviewing what demographers such as Teitelbaum (2015) identify as the politically significant drivers of population change. In particular, we will draw out the position of demographic ageing in the context of these broader changes. The main issues for demographers are population size, demographic ageing, baby booms and youth bulges, 'rapid' shifts in composition of populations according to ethnic, religious, racial, linguistic or national origin. Let's concentrate on the two most relevant factors here, the shifts in age structure of a population and the incidence of baby booms and youth bulges.

In Chapter 1 we provided some detail about how demographic ageing of a society is basically defined by a shift in age structure of the population from one where there is a predominance of children and young people to one with a growing percentage of older people. However, it is worth noting that even the oldest populations still have less than 30 per cent of their population aged 65 or over, as outlined in Table 1.1. One of the many reasons why this shift has a political implication is because of the way we have structured welfare states on the basis of a range of assumptions about health and longevity, which are now outdated. As set out in earlier chapters, the pension age of around 65 is predicated on previous generations not living much beyond 70. So, in order to continue to offer healthcare and social security to a population with a different, older age profile, hard political choices will have to be made. Teitelbaum (2015: S90) argues that the decisions that need to be made, such as shifting from an assumed retirement age of 65 to one of 70+, are political decisions as 'it is politics that will determine whether the structures of public pension and education systems can adjust to changing proportions of the population in younger and older "dependent" age groups'. A similar argument is made about the impact of what Teitelbaum (2015: S90) identifies as 'baby booms' and 'youth bulges'. A youth bulge refers to a situation when a large proportion of the population is made up of children and young adults (for example, as in Sub-Saharan Africa). In the next section, we delve deeper into the causes and consequences of a baby boom.

The baby boomers

In earlier chapters we considered the usefulness of the term 'baby boomer' and how it can be used in a pejorative sense to justify the reallocation of resources away from older people. For demographers, it has a technical meaning, as a 'baby boom' refers to a suddenly large growth in birth rates following a bust caused by external factors such as a war. For instance, the increase in birth rates following World War II is attributable to the whole baby boomer phenomenon so often discussed in public debate. The thing to remember is that the baby boomers are a particularly large birth cohort, which is why they have dominated newspaper headlines throughout their lives. Writing over 30 years ago, Light (1988: 1) surmised: 'At 75 million strong, the baby boomers packed the maternity wards as infants, the classrooms as children, and the campuses, employment lines, and mortgage markets as young adults.' Now that baby boomers have reached retirement age, they are identified as 'bed blockers' who are driving up the cost of health insurance or taking up too many hospital beds. The point is that it is the size of their birth cohort that has allowed baby boomers to be used as a political football throughout their lives.

The opposite is also true. When a country that normally had high fertility rates experiences a decline in fertility without decent economic growth, this can lead to a 'youth bulge', which refers to a large cohort of young people in the 15–29 age group who are coming of age but in the context of austerity. While this trend has been observed in parts of the Middle East, South Asia and some areas of Sub-Saharan Africa, it has yet to be studied in detail. Some researchers argue that these demographic conditions can lead to political instability. 'We argue that one of the impediments to liberal regime change transition is the political volatility and uncertainty associated with the presence of a large proportion of young adults in the population' (Cincotta and Doces [in Goldstone et al], 2012:

99). Certainly, we have seen some evidence of this in the form of the Arab Spring of 2011; however, it is important to note that any political instability will always have multiple causes, of which demographic change is just one, albeit a significant one. The corollary of this would be to argue that older societies are likely to be more politically stable, a claim substantiated by some demographers referring to Northern Ireland: '… population aging among Catholics coincided with violence gradually subsiding' (Leuprecht [in Goldstone et al], 2012: 237). Given the electoral upsets that we have seen in Europe and the US in recent years, the basis for that argument seems to have weakened. In fact, what is really needed is longitudinal research which allows us to take a long-term view on the political implications of demographic change.

Box 8.3: How to take a long-term view of population change

'Demographic change is generally gradual, incremental even ponderous. It takes place more "in the background" of day to day political concerns, usually stimulating little public attention until it has been underway for several decades' (Teitelbaum, 2015: S89).

It can be difficult to see the long-term implications of population change as these are incremental. To do so, it is worth thinking about population change in the same way as we have learned to think about climate change. The weather might change on a daily basis, and we hardly notice that. It is only when all the little increases in temperature or rainfall are recorded and examined across a 20-, 30- or 50-year timespan that we can begin to recognise the more significant portent of climate change. A similar phenomenon is at play when it comes to population change; mortality rates slowly decline, followed by birth rates, which leads to the ageing of the population. In both cases, it is difficult to anticipate the general direction of travel without making some projections, which we have already identified as typically troublesome.

A crucial point to note in terms of the politics of ageing is that government policies, varieties of citizenship and regime types all affect population change. In a globalised world, the framing of a population as 'youthful' or 'old' is important as 'demographic narratives' which emphasise threats and burdens rather than demographic dividends can encourage politicians to make short-term decisions which lead to sub-optimal policy outcomes in the long run. For a fuller explanation see Hendrixson and Hartmann, 2019.

Another result of the failure of academic researchers to think critically and reflect on demographic change has led to an increasing gap between evidence of the political implications of population change and public understanding of those changes. One common misunderstanding is the conflation of the fact that we are more likely to vote as we get older, with the assumption that we vote strategically, in our own interests (Carney, 2010). We will discuss this in the next section.

Are we heading towards an era of 'gerontocracy'?

When we first mention politics of ageing, one of the most often asked questions is whether the ageing of populations in democracies means that a 'gerontocracy' (rule by the aged) is inevitable. The short answer to this question is: No, there is no substantial evidence of older people voting strategically, as a bloc, in their own interests. However, there are major gaps in terms of our knowledge in this area. There are also lots of 'facts' that are false friends; they mislead. For instance, in most elections, the over 65s are the group most likely to vote. This does not mean they all vote the same way. There is also growing evidence that the reasons why people vote are influenced by age. However, scientists are trying to uncover whether differences between generations can be explained by period, cohort or age effects. 'Period effects' are due to a one-off occurrence related to some external factor, such as a war or an economic boom, that impacted on everyone living through that time. People of a certain age might be more likely to vote because of a particular policy or political change that affected their specific cohort. This is known as 'cohort effect'. For example, the birth cohort born in the 1940s, who came of age in the more politicised 1960s and 1970s, became known as the 'protest generation'. There is specific evidence that this cohort did protest during worldwide protests in 1968 calling for more liberal and progressive politics in terms of women's rights and civil and political rights more generally (Grasso et al, 2019). Finally, there is 'age effect'; this is where a person's physiological age is seen as potentially figuring in their electoral participation. For example, Wagner et al (2012) considered arguments that under 18s are too immature to vote responsibly, which would be an age effect. The challenge is to untangle how age, period and cohort effects interact to produce overall 'generational differences' (Wagner et al, 2012).

So, as you can see, the relationship between age and political participation is complex. Received wisdom is that older people vote, and the younger people protest. Wagner et al (2012) undertook research in Austria, where the voting age in nationwide elections is 16 years. Their findings showed that voters in the 16–18-year-old category were capable of being responsible voters but they may see non-electoral forms of political participation as more useful than voting. Similar trends are observable in the youth support for older figures on the Left, such as Bernie Sanders in the US Presidential election campaigns of 2016 and 2020 and Jeremy Corbyn in the UK general elections of 2017 and 2019. However, we will see from the example of Momentum in the UK (https://peoplesmomentum. com) elaborated in this chapter that older people are also quite capable of protest activity. Examples of this can be seen in groups such as Grey Panthers and the Red Hat Society. If we were to take a lifecourse perspective on political participation, one might argue that it is not that age changes one's political views, rather, that one's attitude towards political participation changes as one gets older, known as the 'life cycle effect' (Konzelmann et al, 2012). Two cases in point are the 2016 Brexit referendum in the UK and the Trump election in the US that same year. In both cases, critics blamed younger people's decision not to exercise their vote as a major factor in the results. Others appeared to blame older people for voting too much (Carney, 2018). Some political scientists now argue that perhaps everyone goes through a political awakening at some stage in life. The 'age conservatism hypothesis … states that older people are expected to show higher participation because they get acquainted and comfortable with the political system and the rules of the game …' (Konzelmann et al, 2012: 252). Ultimately that leads to increased turnouts at the polls among older age groups, though perhaps not for the oldest old (Konzelmann et al, 2012). The ebb and flow of turnout across the life cycle and between different sub-types of the population has prompted 30 democracies to introduce a system of compulsory voting. Australia, Belgium and much of Latin America operate compulsory voting systems, which at least balances the turnout across generations.

Certainly, we have seen a growth in a more diverse range of forms of political participation since 2016. Some insights as to why are offered by Melo and Stockemeer (2014), who undertook a study of how different age groups choose to participate politically. In general, across Europe older people are more likely to take part in conventional forms of political participation such as campaigning, joining a political party and, of course, voting. Meanwhile, young people are more likely to take part in unconventional forms of participation such as sit-ins, boycotts, sabotage, petitions, protests, demonstrations and marches. In the 21st century, and especially since 2016, these lines have become blurred. Social media and technological change have made it much easier to organise unconventional forms of political participation, particularly marches and protests. The increasingly divisive words of political leaders (often using those same social media platforms) have also provided stronger grounds for dissent. Melo and Stockemeer (2014: 39) conclude that the change in how people participate in politics is fundamental, even going so far as to argue that it is a transformation in norms of democratic participation, with younger people leading the way: 'Younger generations are leading the way in norm transformation, towards a more "engaged citizenship" (Dalton, 2008a: 28), which values non-electoral forms of political engagement' (Melo and Stockemeer, 2014: 39). Given that the vote is still the only way to directly impact on politics in democratic societies, it is hard to predict how this might affect future politics. For now, there is no evidence of a surge of political participation (a 'youthquake') in UK elections, which continue along well-rehearsed lines of lower turnout among 18–35-year-olds than any other age group (Fox, 2019). On the other hand, the school strikes and climate change protests of recent years are most certainly a youth protest from the leadership of Greta Thunberg to the many individual school children standing up for Mother Earth through street protests every Friday.

Binstock (2012) outlines a range of myths and realities regarding older voters. In this section, we discuss, update and tease out some of the subtleties of his argument.

- **Older people vote, but are still a small percentage of voters.** There is overwhelming evidence that the older you get, the more likely you are to vote (Bhatti and Hansen, 2012). However, we know from Chapter 1 that, even in countries with the oldest population (such as Italy or Japan), less than 30 per cent of the population is over 65. Bearing in mind our warnings about the dangers of making forecasts, some researchers are suggesting that many ageing societies have populations that are shrinking. In the case of Germany, it seems likely that voting turnout will decrease as the baby boomers die off and are replaced by smaller and less politically active birth cohorts (Konzelmann et al, 2012).

- **Older people tend to garner lots of attention from political parties when campaigning for elections**. Why do political parties tend to focus so much on older people when they represent less than 20 per cent of the general population in most democracies (see Table 1.1, Chapter 1)? Wouldn't they be better off focusing on policies and programmes which benefit people of working age, who appear to have much greater likelihood of swinging the election? Politicians are pretty sure that older people will vote, so they hedge their bets that policies for older people are worth writing into electoral manifestos. Politicians see older voters as an easily identifiable target population whom they know are sure to vote (Carney, 2010). The losers in this particular set up are young people (aged 18–29) who, by virtue of the fact that they have a reputation for not bothering to vote at all (Dalton, 2008b), are less likely to be the focus of electoral campaign efforts.

- **Historically, there is little indication that older people vote en bloc**. In his extensive study of older voters in Europe, Goerres (2009) concluded that older people are unlikely to vote en bloc (that is, strategically and in their own interests). In fact, the diversity of the older population, which we discussed in Chapter 5, really comes into play here and is well described by Binstock (2012: 410): 'There is little reason to expect that a birth cohort – diverse in economic and social status, labour force participation, gender, race, ethnicity, religion, education, health status, family status, residential locale, political party attachments, and other characteristics in society – would suddenly become homogenised in interests and political behaviour when it reaches old age.' Look back at Chapter 5 if you need more convincing on this point.

- **Levels of political participation tend to drop off after age 80**. Levels of political participation tend to fall off in deep old age (Bhatti and Hansen, 2012. When we talk about older voters, it is easy to ignore those older people at the oldest age, who may, for health or other reasons, be less likely to vote (Bosquet et al, 2015). The research in this area is underdeveloped. Research has not begun to discuss the ethical issues that arise in terms of whether residents of care homes have the opportunity to exercise their democratic rights.

- **Universal age-based benefits do promote interest group formation.** There is some evidence that state benefits can influence identity politics. For instance, in the UK anyone old enough to qualify for the state pension is often referred to as a pensioner. The main grassroots interest group of older people is called the National Pensioners' Convention (https://www.npcuk.org/).

It is worth asking yourself, though, have you ever heard the word 'pensioner' being used to describe very well-off or famous older people such as Cher (born 1946), Donald Trump (born 1946) or the Queen of the United Kingdom (born 1926)? The social construction of ageing infers that to be a pensioner generally means to be old and to be dependent on the state. Nevertheless, there are political impacts of universal age-based benefits such as the pension. Campbell's (2003) work in the US showed a clear link between the universalism of Medicare and Medicaid among older people in America to the recognised political influence of older people's interest groups such as AARP. However, she is at pains to point out that her data suggest that it is their reputation for political participation that leads politicians to believe that older people are strategic and self-interested voters, despite ample evidence that no such strategic voting takes place (Goerres, 2009).

Box 8.4: Millennials and baby boomers – intergenerational politics

Recent years have certainly seen baby boomers take their place as political leaders. In the UK we saw the rise of Jeremy Corbyn, a Left-wing radical of the British Labour Party who is so admired by younger voters for his radical 1960s politics. On the other hand, in the US we have the election of Donald Trump, a businessman whose politics reflects a disruptive and extreme version of neoliberalism. Trump was elected following a divisive and, some people argue, illegitimate, electoral battle with Hillary Clinton. At the time of the election in 2016 Trump was 70 and Clinton was 69. Bernie Sanders, the main rival to Hillary Clinton for the Democratic Party nomination was 75 years old at the time of the election. Both Sanders (born 1941) and Corbyn (born 1949) enjoyed huge support from youth movements (see https://peoplesmomentum.com/). At least in the case of Left-wing voters, there is clearly something happening here in terms of the passing on of political values and beliefs directly from the 1960s generation to the 2010s generation. The global recession, disillusionment with capitalism, weariness with austerity and globalisation seems to have led younger generations to bypass the divisive neoliberalism of their parents' generation, opting instead to support the more collectivist and activist politics of their grandparents. It is unclear whether this trend is a one-off or will continue for future generations.

A final thought

We hope that this chapter has shown you that the politics of ageing is important now and will be increasingly recognised as such in future research. The first half of the chapter introduced you to the possibility that political decision making has had some impact on the construction of population ageing as a policy problem. We outlined how this manifests at micro- and macro-levels whereby we see big demographic changes influencing politics through baby booms and youth bulges.

We looked at the preparedness of existing systems of citizenship to redistribute resources for a different, older demographic profile, drawing on the example of the UK welfare state and the post-war consensus. The second half of the chapter was dedicated to the topic of political demography: how political decision making might affect population ageing. We provided examples of how and why policy makers must take a long-term perspective on population ageing. We investigated the possibility of one supposed impact of population ageing: gerontocracy, or rule by the aged. We provided a number of examples to illustrate the fact that this is an unlikely outcome, not least because older people represent a very diverse and relatively small sub-set of the electorate. We concluded with some examples of how social media technology has radically altered political participation and campaigning, while also providing additional opportunities for younger people to vote, older people to protest and for both generations to work together to produce their preferred political outcome.

REVIEW EXERCISE 8

Group: As a group, bring together the main party manifestoes for a recent election. Taking turns, discuss how age is used or ignored by political parties in their election pledges. Using this, search for evidence for which pledges have been kept.

Solo: Complete the above task but instead of discussing, critically compare the promises made regarding children and older people. Note down differences, similarities and use to inform group discussion when next in class.

What does it mean to live a long life?

(Cultural gerontology)

... in given historical circumstances, superior powers create systems of inequality and inferiority that bleed into individual lives. The 'woman problem' turned out to be sexism, not the supposed nature of women. The 'Jewish problem' was and is anti–Semitism, not Jews. The 'Negro problem' is still squarely racism. Now the whole world is said to be facing the 'Graying Nation' problem: too many old people, sickly, unproductive, costly, selfish ... (Gullette, 2017: xviii)

Introduction

'Cultural gerontology' is the term used to describe the growing interest in using arts and humanities approaches, methods and theories to understand ageing societies. This change, often referred to as 'the cultural turn' is very much the defining approach for early 21st century studies of ageing. While arts, humanities and other disciplines are making seismic and permanent impacts on how we view, discuss and understand human ageing, it is not possible to cover everything that is developing in a constantly changing area of research and study. Instead, we have reviewed a wide range of relevant literature, put it with our own experience and knowledge of ageing and tried to sketch a landscape of the field. First, we show how cultural gerontology offers a critique of political economy approaches (especially structured dependency). Second, we use narrative, an important analytical approach of humanities scholars, to show how the cultural turn has introduced scholars and students of ageing to new theory and methods. In practice, cultural gerontology scholars use narrative as a key method in offering robust critiques of biomedical approaches to understanding ageing, in particular the 'decline narrative', a point well made by Gullette at the opening of the chapter (and in Gullette, 1997; 2007; 2013; 2017).

At its core, cultural gerontology has altered the questions that gerontologists ask, broadening out from empirical questions such as 'how long will we live?' towards questions that could be described as ethical or philosophical such as 'what does it mean to live a long life?' The latter question is most clearly associated with humanities (or humanistic) approaches to ageing, such as those put forward by Ruth Ray (2000) who explores the idea that our culture must learn to accommodate a whole new generation of older people. Thomas Cole's (1992) seminal work *The Journey of Life: A Cultural History of Aging in America* established a clear case for examining old age as an important stage of life, not just as a set of medical conditions to be cured or managed. As is often the case in cultural gerontology, scholarship is matched by equally eloquent polemics by activists such as Segal (2013) and Applewhite (2016). Standing out from the field is cultural critic Margaret Morganroth Gullette (2017), who challenges negative or simplistic representations of old age as a stage of life. She often speaks up for older people as a growing minority with rights that deserve to be defended. For instance, she has spoken out about the risk of medical ageism during the coronavirus pandemic leading to people being refused treatment on the basis of age (Gullette, 2020).

Any reader who has taken a course on research design and methods will know that posing different questions will encourage researchers to use a wider range of diverse methods and approaches to understand human ageing. The cultural turn has broadened the remit of ageing studies in this way. The expansion of social gerontology brought on by the cultural turn is best described by Twigg and Martin (2015: 3) who set out five broad themes of research in cultural gerontology: 'theory and methods; embodiment; identity and social relationships; consumption and leisure; and time and space'. Given the limitations of space in a single chapter, we will focus on embodiment, gender identity and social relationships to illustrate how cultural gerontology has 'expanded age studies' (Twigg and Martin, 2015). Some of the examples we use draw on narrative method to explore the meaning of living a long life.

The cultural turn did not happen overnight; rather these paradigmatic changes in academic research tend to simmer away, in this case over a 30-year period. We will begin in the middle of that period, at the turn of the century, with the publication of a book by two British academics – *Cultures of Ageing*.

Cultures of Ageing

For many scholars, a key text in enhancing the fortunes of cultural approaches to understanding ageing is Gilleard and Higgs' (2000) book, *Cultures of Ageing: Self, Citizen and the Body*. This book drove a wedge between the then dominant political economy approach and newer, postmodern perspectives on old age. The core purpose of the book was to challenge the idea that all older people belong to a single class identity of poor, vulnerable pensioners. To be fair, Gilleard and Higgs' (2000) work was of its time, given that disciplines across the humanities and social sciences were undergoing a postmodern revolution which involved the deconstruction and analysis of established categories and approaches to study (Powell and Gilbert, 2009). The authors thereby rejected Townsend's seminal (1981) theory of structured dependency. Gilleard and Higgs (2000) presented an image of the retired population as diverse – in sexual orientation, income, lifestyle and consumption. They suggested that retirement is now a rite of passage into 20 or so years of wealth and health rather than an impoverished and short period before the end of life. The issue of embodiment was linked to disease and decline; there are numerous arguments about the ageing body, AD and social death. Again, this is a typical task of the cultural turn, which was to re-embody old age (Gilleard and Higgs, 2000). We will discuss embodiment in more detail when we review work on hair and dress later in the chapter. The core point Gilleard and Higgs were making is that ageing is now a part of our culture and so should be situated 'as a central constituent in the cultures of our times' (Gilleard and Higgs, 2000). The book concludes that the cultural turn was inevitable in social gerontology.

Cultures of Ageing caused much debate within British social gerontology at the time of publication and is still controversial in the minds of some political economy of ageing theorists. With the benefit of 20 years' hindsight, much of what is written in *Cultures of Ageing* maps out what is now identified as cultural gerontology. Nowadays, we can also see that cultural gerontology is additional to, rather than an alternative to, political economy of ageing approaches. The book contains sections that resonate with the four non-theoretical themes outlined by Twigg and Martin (2015): embodiment; identity and social relationships; consumption and leisure; and time and space. In short, *Cultures of Ageing* stirred gerontologists out of preconceived generalisations about older people, such as the automatic assumption that older people are all dependent or frail. As the chapters on gender and diversity in this book suggest, this is an important and necessary shift in our thinking; everyone aged 60 or over is not the same, rather older people are just as 'splendidly various' (Lively, 2013: 20) as any other minority group.

The next task on this abridged tour of the cultural turn is to investigate what exactly we mean by 'culture'. When Gilleard and Higgs (2000) write about 'the cultures of our times' and Gullette (1997) argues that we are 'aged by culture', what do they mean? The answer is not always clear. This is because culture, like other contested concepts, means different things depending on who you ask and what you are talking about. Culture can mean everything other than hard science (physics, chemistry and biology). So, culture potentially includes the arts, language, literature and history. Or, culture can be more closely defined as the set of beliefs, values, practices and objects that define a particular way of life or approach to being. Culture can refer to 'systems of value' (Lancet Commission, 2014) when the subject matter is an organisation or institution. Rather unhelpfully, this means that culture can refer to anything from religion and food to popular music and language. For the purposes of this book, culture can be seen to refer to the practices we use when providing care for older people, the values we have in terms of condoning or countering ageism, the relationship between acute and long-term care systems. All of these practical manifestations are deeply connected to our larger cultural values about ageing and older people.

Box 9.1: Culture and health

Very often we see culture and health as two completely separate aspects of life. However, this is slowly changing as policy makers charged with keeping whole populations healthy realise that health is more than the absence of disease. To promote good health, a certain set of cultural practices (for instance, eating fruit and vegetables, not smoking, exercising) is needed. Important institutions at national and international levels, such as the United Nations Economic Commission for Europe (https://www.unece.org/mission.html) and the Lancet Commission in the UK, agree that medical science and culture, rather than being opposed, should be seen as mutually constitutive, particularly when it comes to health: 'all people have systems of value that are unexamined. Such systems are, at times, diffuse and often taken for granted, but are always dynamic and changing' (Lancet Commission, 2014: 1607). By way of example, the Lancet Commission reports that health systems can have cultures which put patients at risk. When it comes to apportioning blame for the deaths of vulnerable people in care, for example, it proves impossible to pinpoint a single culprit. Often, the deaths will have been caused by poor communication between departments, sloppy record keeping or failure to meet basic hygiene standards. The Commission comes to an inevitable conclusion: in cases of systemic failure in delivering healthcare 'the real villain was culture – culture caused these crimes of neglect to occur' (Lancet Commission, 2014: 1608).

The most obvious place where we can observe implications of cultural difference is between countries or regions of the world. Differences in climate, religion, language, law and access to resources influence how we speak, where we live, who we live with and what we eat and drink. Culture goes some way towards exploring large differences in the HDI and life expectancies between countries like Norway and Yemen, as outlined in Table 1.1. A good example of this is the practice of filial piety in Confucian cultures such as China and Korea, which means that adult offspring are responsible for care of their parents in a way that is similar to how parents might be expected to care for children in the Western world (Cong and Silverstein, 2019). In the Global North, which includes countries with many of the oldest populations of the world (bar Japan, which is the oldest), cultures tend to hold values which privilege scientific and medical conceptions of ageing, rather than humanistic values. Cole (1992) called this 'the scientific management' of ageing, which had previously been a stage of life rather than an illness to be cured. Cole (1992) traced this shift in the cultural significance of old age back to the work of G. Stanley Hall, a 19th-century psychologist who is *sometimes* referred to as the father of gerontology (see Box 9.2).

Senescence: The Last Half of Life is a distressingly bleak outlook on later life, whose negativity could, at least in part, be attributable to Hall's depression following the loss of his career: 'Now I am divorced from my world and there is nothing more to be said of me save the exact date of my death' (Hall, 1922: xi). And so, it seems sensible to assume that – in the fog of depression, and while dealing with an unacknowledged experience of structural ageism that is involuntary retirement – Hall set the tone for future studies of ageing to be 'scientifically managed'.

Box 9.2: G. Stanley Hall's concept of senescence

The life and work of G. Stanley Hall (1846–1924) is worth a closer look. Hall's work represents putative scientific, rather than humanistic, understanding of human ageing. Hall was a successful academic who, earlier in his career, published a much-lauded book called *Adolescence* (1904) which identified the period between childhood and adulthood as an important stage of human development. After his retirement from the position of President of Clark College in the US, he set about understanding later life with the same analytical zeal. The result of a combination of personal reflections on the experience of ageing and research into physicians' approaches to understanding old age was *Senescence: The Last Half of Life* published in 1922.

Cole (1992: XXV) saw Hall's approach as ultimately limiting our conception of old age as the complex, contradictory and spiritual aspects of old age were exorcised by the Victorians: 'Victorian images of aging … did not reflect its uncertain and paradoxical nature. In place of ambiguity and contingency, Victorians portrayed a rigid polarity of positive and negative stereotypes whose legacy would extend far into the twentieth century' (Cole, 1992: XXVI). From the 20th century onwards, stages of the human lifecourse began to be formally linked to physiology, or rather, to be more exact, old age became synonymous with decline. The work of early gerontologists (such as Metchinkoff, Nascher, and Manning Child) completed work in a similar vein around the same time (see Achenbaum and Bengtson, 1994). Old age, which had previously been conceived as a stage of life full of mystery or 'an existential problem now began to be viewed primarily as a scientific and technical problem' (Cole, 1992: 195). The stage was set for a century or more of methodical analysis of the deficits and problems of old age.

Human ageing: rational, scientific management of old age

As well as privileging the medical (and hence, inadvertently, the physiological), Western cultures tend to work on a system of core beliefs that research- or data-based evidence (rather than, say, religious beliefs) should inform policy making for older people. These rational, scientific, cultural values have been useful in providing funding for important medical research, much of which has contributed to extending life expectancy. However, the cultural privileging of physical health and vitality has come at the cost of devaluing those who lose youth and good health. We are left with something of a cultural vacuum when it comes to understanding what we should do with extra years of life, particularly if they involve exclusion from the workplace, chronic illness or bereavement. A good example of Western, rational scientific cultural values can be taken from the focus in the US on AD as a way of diagnosing decline. The problem with this approach will be unpacked in detail when we examine Gullette's decline narrative (2017) and the re-embodiment of old age (Twigg and Martin, 2015) later in the chapter. For now, the main point to understand is that the cultural turn arose as a critique of these approaches (laid out in Hall's *Senescence*) which caused humanities scholars such as Cole (1992) to conclude that, by the 1990s, years of extensive study of human ageing needed refocusing. Why had 20 years of study brought us no closer to answering Robert Butler's (1975) question *Why Survive?* The time had come to begin to understand what processes other than the physiological are experienced in old age. Cole (1992) made a convincing case for interdisciplinary studies of culture to begin this quest.

While is it perfectly possible to undertake a discipline-specific study of ageing, such as Pat Thane's (2005) excellent *The Long History of Old Age*, many impactful studies in cultural gerontology have worked across disciplines. Where two disciplines (say history and sociology) become deeply intertwined, multidisciplinarity evolves into interdisciplinarity, yielding rich and powerful evidence of the experience of human ageing.

Box 9.3: An example of interdisciplinarity: European Network in Aging Studies (ENAS)

A good example of interdisciplinarity is the European Network in Aging Studies (ENAS), a network of academics from across the arts, humanities and social gerontology who work together to better understand human ageing. The founding project of the network drew together researchers from fields as diverse as media and film, literature and art who worked together to study 'narratives of longevity' (see agingstudies.eu/page/Founding_Project).

Oro-Piqueras and Falcus (2018) argue that the basic interdisciplinarity underpinning cultural gerontology benefits both social scientists and humanities scholars and students. By working together in a way which allows researchers to learn each other's methods and approaches, researchers can produce deeper insights on some of the harder questions for ageing societies and policy. Narrative – the use of stories to understand human life – is one way in which scholars have worked across disciplines. Oro-Piqueras and Falcus (2018) offer an insightful overview of how the concept of 'narrative', central to English studies, fits well with studies of ageing because stories can be conceived of as movement through time. Box 9.4 explores the use of narrative by linguistics and stylistics scholar Jane Lugea to open up the lived experience of dementia to carers and others (Lugea et al, 2017).

Box 9.4: Dementia in culture

Lugea et al's 'Dementia in the Minds of Characters and Readers' (2017) uses a cognitive stylistics approach from English studies to reveal how the minds of characters with dementia are constructed in language. By analysing fictional accounts of living with dementia, such as the novels *Still Alice* and *The Corrections*, Lugea and her colleagues examine the metaphors, language and imagery that authors use to draw readers into the experience of living with dementia. Extracts from the books are analysed and explored, with each of these approaches identified. This process reveals that authors might use metaphor to symbolise the protagonist's feelings of loss, disorientation or anger. Next, the researchers use focus groups with volunteers, carers and people with dementia. Extracts from the novels allow the group to discuss how some of the issues explored might apply to them and what is the most empathetic response. By using stories, rather than real-life accounts of living with dementia, everyone feels they can speak more freely about the emotions, challenges and rewards of working and/or living with dementia.

Cultural critique of the 'narrative of decline'

While the focus of Lugea's approach is on language and linguistics, there is also a highly developed range of work on narrative which uses literary analysis to uncover cultural norms about ageing. The work of Gullette (1997; 2007; 2013), who we also mentioned for her pugnacious and defiant brand of critique in the chapter on gender, represents an impressive body of work critiquing society's approach to ageing over a 30-year period. In a series of increasingly irate books, from *Safe at Last in the Middle Years* (1988) and *Declining to Decline* (1997), her series has culminated in two award-winning books attacking ageism, or what Gullette calls 'the narrative of decline'. In *Agewise* (2013) and *Ending Ageism, or How Not to Shoot Old People* (2017), Gullette makes the case that ageism persists due to the lack of a counterculture, an 'anti-decline' movement. She argues that such a movement could counteract the overwhelming and unchecked cultural practice of viewing ageing as symptomatic of decline – a 'progress narrative' of ageing is needed. The cultural perspective allows Gullette to draw comparisons between what she is observing as the human experience of older people now with discriminatory practices against minorities in the past: '... in given historical circumstances, superior powers create systems of inequality and inferiority that bleed into individual lives. The 'woman problem' turned out to be sexism, not the supposed nature of women ... Now the whole world is said to be facing the 'Graying Nation' problem: too many old people, sickly, unproductive, costly, selfish ...' (Gullette, 2017: xviii).

A core contribution of Gullette's cultural critique is that it allows her to identify issues as diverse as dementia and birthdays as cultural practices which demonstrate how the whole is greater than the sum of its parts when it comes to constructing a grand narrative of decline. While the root of this narrative comes from a core belief that 'ageing equals physiological decline', through a mixture of personal anecdotes and publicly available statistics, Gullette exposes the societal tendency to reduce all old people to the status of 'potential dementia patients'

(Gullette, 2017: 162). For Gullette, it is the interaction of biological determinism and ageism through the cultural concept of decline that fuels the 'duty-to-die' discourse and 'shaming about growing old' (Gullette, 2017: 162). Her approach is quite a departure from the careful dissection of later life into separate categories (health, financial well-being, social isolation and so on that is common in social policy making. Gullette's contention that the 'problem' of old age is actually a political problem is a good example of how cultural gerontology develops our understanding of human ageing; cultural critiques offer useful ways of looking at, understanding and interpreting our ageing world. Next we will examine another way in which cultural gerontology has enriched our understanding of the lived experience of ageing: through examining material culture – the use of objects and artefacts – to investigate the meaning of living a long life.

Material culture: the 'Lively project'

Historians' interest in material culture – or how objects and artefacts inform our understanding of life in the past – has lately been adapted to help us understand contemporary life. Many material culture enthusiasts have been inspired by Edward de Waal's (2011) popular work *The Hare with Amber Eyes*, a beautiful book vividly describing the meaning and purpose of objects in human lives. In the UK, Neil MacGregor (2010), then director of the British Museum, published *A History of the World in 100 Objects*, which demonstrated how mundane items such as the credit card could provide telling insights for the times we live in. This popularisation of objects as evocative and revealing may have been what inspired author Penelope Lively (2013) to publish her memoir, *Ammonites and Leaping Fish: A Life in Time*. Lively is a Booker Prize winning novelist who, at the age of 80, decided to write her memoir. She gave the final chapter of her memoir the title, 'Six Things'. In this, she describes, in some detail and with illustrations, six things that she felt told the story of her life, concluding that: 'People's possessions speak of them: they are resonant and betraying and reflective' (Lively, 2013: 199). Equally, Lively is aware that these objects have a particular significance as her possessions, representing a kind of 'material memoir' (Lively, 2013: 200), which may be lost were they to become ownerless: 'I imagine them at a car boot sale, or an auction room, mute, anonymous, though perhaps each might be picked up, considered, thought to have some intrinsic merit, or not' (Lively, 2013: 200).

Inspired by Lively's exercise, Carney worked with colleagues Hannan, Hodge and others to develop a project which explored the potential of objects to communicate the experience of living a long life. The team recruited six older people (aged 61–80) who were willing to engage in a series of interviews and workshops designed to explore the meaning of six of their possessions in the context of living a long life. The end result was an exhibition called 'Something of Who I Am' which displayed the objects and Hodge's art work at a local arts centre. (More details of the project can be viewed at https://thelivelyproject. wordpress.com/about/.)

The Lively project was an interesting exploration of the potential of cultural gerontology for a number of reasons. First, it allowed the researchers to explore the lived experience of living a long life through objects, allowing them to 'narrate age through things' (Hannan et al, 2019). By interviewing participants about their objects, a narrative of the older person's life emerged. Hannan et al (2019) later published some of the findings as an article, concluding that, 'the study of objects as evidence necessitates a negotiation between the experiential and the intellectual, which is particularly intense where items have been in a person's possession for many years' (Hannan et al, 2019: 55). The researchers also noted a marked but interesting gender difference from our small sample of older men and women. The male participants seemed to find the objects a welcome means of demonstrating how interesting and exciting their lives had been. Objects included a motorbike, a Morse key, a treasured sea urchin from a family holiday. Their objects were tied to roles of racing driver, merchant shipman or father. The women used the objects to narrate the passage of time through various stages of their lives. In assessing the contribution of the cultural gerontology approach, the researchers concluded that participants 'narration of their own lifecourse was aided by speaking about their objects' (Hannan et al, 2019: 63).

The research team also observed that displaying older people's possessions in an exhibition produced a kind of 'glass case effect', whereby the social status of their lives and experiences were elevated by the act of being exhibited. From both the perspective of the younger researchers (aged in their thirties and forties) and feedback from those who visited the exhibition, Hannan et al (2019) concluded that for younger people, 'it was enlightening and engaging to be drawn into the world of the past through the objects' (Hannan et al, 2019: 63). In the project evaluation, some younger people remarked that the exhibition allowed them to see the older person in a new light, as someone interesting, who had completed important milestones, survived certain hardships or shown resilience, lasting friendship or had an impact on their community. In the case of the Lively project, Hannan et al used material objects to try to move public understanding of population ageing beyond simplistic reasoning of older people as a costly burden. Instead, the team sought to contribute to this broader aim of cultural approaches, which is to explore 'what it actually means to live a long life' (Hannan et al, 2019: 51). The material basis of the work is not too far removed from another important aspect of cultural gerontology, which is to take back ownership of the ageing body from medical science, what Twigg identifies as 'the re-embodiment of old age'.

The re-embodiment of old age

Cultural gerontologists have led the movement to re-embody old age. Twigg (2000; 2004; 2007; 2018) has been particularly prolific in this regard, reinserting the embodied experience of ageing back into general parlance in social gerontology. She explains that the absence of the body in studies of ageing, particularly while the political economy of ageing perspective was ascendant (up until the turn of the century) was understandable. At the time, the dominance of biomedical perspectives led many scholars to believe that inclusion of the body was a risky strategy. Political economy of ageing scholars, concerned with the welfare and interests of older people, worried that focusing on the body could be a 'retrogressive step' – reducing older people to the category of declining adults, and thereby supporting the narrative of decline (Twigg, 2004: 60). Twigg (2004: 61) made a convincing case that embodiment is a 'central part of the subject matter' of social gerontology. She has since followed up these claims with an impressive body of work examining ageing bodies. Studies began by looking at personal care (Twigg et al, 2011), dementia and dress (Twigg and Majima, 2014; Twigg and Buse, 2013), fashion and age for both women and men (Twigg, 2013), the significance of personal possessions such as handbags to older women in care homes (Buse and Twigg, 2014), and discussions of older women's bodies in magazines (Twigg, 2018). Gender is an important fulcrum of this work, which has led to a number of important insights that we can draw from our understanding of how we are 'aged by culture' (Gullette, 2004). There are a number of angles we could use to illustrate this, but our review of the literature reveals that the idea of invisibility of old age, and the role that cultural gerontology plays in making older women visible is a good place to start.

The invisible older woman

King's (2013: 65) *Discourses of Ageing in Fiction and Feminism* offers numerous examples of how women disappear as they age, particularly within second wave feminism. King (2013) claims that second wave feminisms (1970 onwards) slowly recognised class, race and other intersections with gender, but still lack 'any conception that ageism may also generate an imbalance'. Invisibility also emerges in Twigg's (2018) study of women's magazines, which are a fascinating site for the negotiation of 'age identities'. As part of this shift towards consumerism identified in Gilleard and Higgs (2000) earlier work, Twigg observes an increasing focus on older women as consumers of fashion, advice and products which are designed to make them feel and look good despite their advancing years. Twigg (2018: 341) offers empirical evidence of unconscious bias against their own readers among fashion editors, such as the fashion editor for *Saga*, a magazine for older women, who remarks: 'I want to shoot them all, these women who are really elderly and they've got puff sleeves. You know you can't do that over the age of 18'. Twigg reports a more sympathetic perspective from the same editor that older women should not disappear, but rather 'have the right to join in' (Twigg, 2018: 342). The issue of invisibility and embodiment are powerfully connected in Twigg's discussion of how 'age disrupts the visual field' or at least how fashion sees its visual field. She links the absence of older models from fashion shoots to the 'body perfectionism' of popular culture of the late 20th and early 21st century. Another fashion editor, this time from elite *Vogue* magazine, remarks: 'I don't think people want to look really at older women as a kind of exemplars of fashion and beauty' (Twigg, 2018: 343). Nevertheless, the same editor goes on to note that she does use older celebrities to make older readers feel included. An editor at less elitist *Woman & Home* seems more cognisant of the invisibility of older women: '... people feel ... that they kind of disappear off the radar once they get to a certain age' (Twigg, 2018: 344).

Calasanti and King (2018: 15) use an entirely different method and source of evidence to explore 'the dynamic nature of gender and aging bodies' – interviews with older men and women about their ageing bodies. While a number of themes develop from their analysis, a clear finding is the sense of disappearing into old age. This finding is more pronounced for female rather than male participants. Elizabeth, a 58-year-old married, heterosexual woman remarks: 'My cousin and I sometimes talk about how we have both become invisible' (Calasanti and King, 2018: 16). This lived experience of becoming invisible is embodied, particularly in the sense that participants link it to their loss of sexual appeal. Twigg's (2018) findings around the invisible older woman certainly support her calls for the re-embodiment of old age. Next, we will expand on this the ways cultural gerontologists study embodiment by taking a closer look at hair in old age.

Earlier, we used an example of the 'Grey tsunami' to draw attention to a tendency among economists to see older people as one, undifferentiated mass of wants and needs. While it might be unconscious, the reference to grey hair is a powerful means of grouping everyone of a certain age together into one homogenous category. Ward (in Twigg and Martin, 2015: 142) argues that 'grey hair thus links the individual to a broader and undifferentiated collective'. Of course, nowadays, many older people, especially women, dye their hair, which is an everyday anti-ageing practice, albeit one that is rarely seen in those terms. The ubiquitous nature of hair dyeing has led to a whole field of study of hair salons and the relationships between clients and hairdressers. In a timely and useful overview of the idea of grey hair as a cultural signifier of old age, Ward (in Twigg and Martin, 2015) draws on ethnographic research by Furman (1997) which studied the hair salon as a site of social resistance. By examining the hair grooming practices of older women, Furman (1997) found that, despite their youthful orientation, salons acted as a site where older women could gather and support one another, albeit against a backdrop of the salon, which epitomises the anti-ageing culture. Ward (in Twigg and Martin, 2015: 144) also found evidence of hairdressers encouraging older female clients to adopt 'age-appropriate' styles. Hurd Clarke and Korotchenko (2010: 1012) also undertook a small, qualitative study of older women's decisions about dyeing their hair. They found that the practice of hair care in old age was an important aspect of enacting gender norms, but also of 'negotiating and resisting ageist stereotypes and societal discourses concerning older women' (Hurd Clarke and Korotchenko, 2010: 1012). It is interesting to note that other researchers have found differences between different sub-categories of women; 'lesbians and women of colour were more likely to accept their grey hair, as they rejected the dominant cultural appearance standards' (Winterich cited in Hurd Clarke and Korotchenko, 2010: 1013).

Ward and Holland (2011) in their detailed and careful discussion of age discrimination through the RoAD (Research on Age Discrimination) project drew links between seemingly 'frivolous' issues such as hair colour and style to show how the lived experience of discrimination and social marginalisation is firmly tied to the bodies of older people (Ward and Holland, 2011: 288). For instance, certain hairstyles which are identified with a certain time period can be used to stereotype older people. In his discussion of hair and ageing, Ward (in Twigg and Martin, 2015: 144) argues that the permanent wave, a style that was cutting edge in the 1950s and 1960s is, in contemporary terms, is now identified as a 'pensioners' hairdo'.

It is not just hair cut or style, but also the level of grooming that makes hair a useful means of understanding cultural conceptions of old age. The apparent loss of the capacity to be well groomed and to keep up appearances is 'open to being used as an indicator of cognitive impairment' (Ward in Twigg and Martin, 2015: 145). This links closely to arguments made elsewhere that grooming and control over one's personal appearance is an important indicator of when one moves from the third to the fourth age, where transfer of control over one's own appearance to a carer occurs (Gilleard and Higgs, 2013). Ward and Campbell (2013) take this argument one step further by arguing that, within care homes, maintaining an appropriate appearance of clean and well cared for older people then becomes a signifier of good quality care, though now it is an output of the regulated care system, no longer an expression of character or taste of the individual themselves.

Ward and Holland's (2011) and Ward's (in Twigg and Martin, 2015) work are good examples of how powerful cultural gerontology approaches can be in demonstrating how everyday aspects of daily life are connected to policies and interventions for older people, particularly those designed to tackle age discrimination. Who would have thought that we could learn so much about the cultural confines of later life by examining something as seemingly ordinary as hair and grooming?

A final thought

This chapter provided an overview of how cultural gerontology has developed and how it can help us to understand the lived experience of old age. It focused on the main contributions of the cultural turn, outlining how humanities perspectives allow us to witness and interpret human ageing in all the colour, diversity and potential through which it is experienced. It is interesting to note that some of the authors who are most clearly identified with the cultural turn have actually been writing about ageing within their disciplines for many years before cultural gerontology became fashionable. Twigg and Martin (2014) aptly summarise the contribution of the re-embodiment of old age: the realisation that narrative, material culture and history inform our understanding of old age, and that lived experience is valid are all sources of evidence that cultural gerontology is 'an intellectual shift from structure associated with the political economy school … [that] has opened up the possibilities for more reflexive accounts that focus on identities and lived experience of old age.' By bringing the human experience back into the foreground of our understanding of what it means to live a long life, the cultural turn opens us up to new sources of evidence, approaches and theories.

REVIEW EXERCISE 9

What is it really like to be old?

Group: Write a 500-word critical reflection on what you think it would be like to reach 100 years old. This is just a personal reflection, not an essay! When completed, review with the group. See what differences there are between your personal reflections and discuss the presence of any age stereotypes that you may have in your lists.

Solo: Write a bullet point list on what you think it would be like to reach 100 years old. Search online for the reflections of an older adult on their own ageing process and note the similarities and differences between what you wrote and how they described the process of ageing, identifying which were stereotyped beliefs. HINT: Some really interesting personal perspectives are available in G. Stanley Hall's (1922) *Senescence: The Last Half of Life* and in Gullette's (2017) *Ending Ageism, or How Not to Shoot Older People*.

10

What are my next steps?

(Conclusions, reflections and actions)

Introduction

In this final chapter we would like to spend some time pulling together all of the arguments we have made, the evidence we have presented and the authors we have cited. We want *Critical Questions for Ageing Societies* to be a book that you come back to again and again in the course of your continuing studies in gerontology. For this reason, we have decided to revisit each chapter, drawing out key concepts and ideas for you to take forward in your future studies and research. Next, we would like to pull together the chapters into thematic subcategories which you can use to understand ageing. For each subcategory we will suggest some possible next steps for your work in these areas, perhaps through researching and writing an undergraduate or postgraduate dissertation. In this closing chapter, we will finish with a discussion of how your view on ageing societies is influenced not only by facts and figures, but by the kind of language and approach that you use to understand, explore and – ultimately – explain the ageing world.

Chapter overview

Now that you have finished this book, you will have acquired a wide range of facts and information about ageing and older people. Hopefully, the theoretical and conceptual frameworks that we have provided in each chapter mean that you can now process this information in a way which allows it to become knowledge. For instance, in Chapter 1 we showed you how to read, interpret, describe and construct a population pyramid. Population pyramids are visual representations of a given population and so they allow you to summarise what stage of the demographic transition any given society is at, the numbers of old people relative to children, the dependency ratio and gender balance. All of this information feeds into policy planning in terms of the number of school places a society might need or the range of family supports and eldercare strategies that should be put in place. We hope that those of you who enjoy working with statistics and graphical representations of our ageing world will use this chapter as a good introduction to what can be achieved once you begin to analyse populations quantitatively.

In Chapter 2 we took a more critical perspective, focusing in on ageism and how it affects the quality of life of older people. To some extent this chapter provides some of the answers as to why presenting government and policy makers with excellent social science data on the needs and wants of an ageing population does not always translate into perfectly formed policy programmes. Instead, we see the persistence of myths about demographic change and how these form a substantial barrier to making successful policies for ageing societies (Börsch-Supan, 2013). The problem of the gap between (1) public perception of what it means to have an older population; and (2) the research evidence made available by social scientists can be traced back to the attitudes held by the general population. If public attitudes towards older people are negative or even paternalistic, it is likely that policy makers will produce policies that fail to optimise the opportunities available to older people in society, often on the basis of paternalistic attitudes towards older people. We hope you find the Nash and Carney 'AIR' model of ageism (Acquisition, Internalisation and Reinforcement) outlined in Chapter 2 (see Figure 2.2) useful in understanding and explaining how ageist attitudes are acquired across the lifecourse. Models like this are essential in explaining ageism because they provide the tools of analysis which help you to translate lots of facts and information into knowledge. You will know that you are acquiring knowledge when you start to be able to spot ageism in everyday life. With any luck you will be beginning to find ageist stereotyping on TV at least mildly annoying. You might even be beginning to critique friends who make blasé comments about how old people own too much property and wealth. Or, you may be appalled by the use of arbitrary chronological age cut-off points to make policy during a crisis (Carney, 2020). If any of these experiences sound familiar then, congratulations, you are well on the way to becoming a critical gerontologist. If you were to combine some of the theory from Chapter 2 with some of the methods and approaches described in Chapter 9, on cultural gerontology, you could produce a really fascinating dissertation on ageist representations of older women in the media, in art history or indeed through material culture.

Whenever we are teaching students about ageing, retirement is an issue that arises early in our discussions. Very often students will express a desire to retire early, or at least refer to a relative who is enjoying their retirement. The idea of spending all day doing what you want without having to account for your time, but while still earning an income from a pension is attractive. However, in Chapter 3 you discovered that this expectation of 20 years of pleasant and comfortable retirement is under threat. It is with a heavy heart that we have to tell our students that they may be close to 80 years of age before they can afford to retire. The issue of pensions, and their consistent underfunding for many decades, is discussed in detail in Chapter 3. Like the population pyramids in Chapter 1 and our 'AIR' model of ageism in Chapter 2, in Chapter 3 we call on the dependency ratio to help us make sense of why many economists seem to panic at the sight of an extended population pyramid, particularly one that looks a bit wide around the middle (i.e. where there are too few people in the younger, working age category). Of course, we are critical of the dependency ratio as, like some concepts from the economists' toolkit, it is based on assumptions, some of which are dated.

For instance, the dependency ratio fails to take account of women's labour, the extension of working life and the fact that many people do not start earning until much later in life than their parents, and have fewer children as they start a family much later (Gratton and Scott, 2016). The other big theory discussed in Chapter 3 is 'active ageing'. Once the pet theory of social gerontologists and policy makers all over the world, in recent years that approach has fallen out of favour, mainly because it fails to take account of how inequality and poverty make it impossible for some people to age actively (Bülow and Söderqvist, 2014). As we introduce other useful conceptual tools, such as birth cohorts and the institutionalised lifecourse, we move on to more contemporary empirical studies of work and retirement. Here we find many interesting studies, from Canadian physicians who refuse to retire, to English pensioners who have decided to become apprentices in trades and occupations normally reserved for 16-year-olds. The future of work and retirement looks most uncertain, but also replete with potential for people to find a job they love or to rebalance work and life through phased retirement in later life. There is huge potential for students wishing to study work and retirement to investigate 'encore careers' where the over 60s find a whole new way to earn a living, and alternative pathways to retirement, in dissertations or further study.

In Chapter 4 we took a critical gerontology perspective on the question of care. By posing a student's question, 'Who will care for me in old age?', we were able to open an important debate about the assumptions we make about declining health in old age. In an effort to bust the myth that old age must always be accompanied by disease, we undertook a detailed overview of the physiological changes that are normal in old age. Here, we made the distinction between the likelihood of needing some help in old age versus needing medical interventions for disease. There is an important ethical point underpinning this distinction – that none of us is truly independent through the lifecourse. Rather, we are all dependent at some time – think of how independent you were for the first five or ten years of your life. It is equally true that we will all take care of others, family members or friends, at some stage in our lives too. We use the work of Fineman (2005) and Kittay et al (2005), who are feminists with an interest in the ethics of care, to underline this point. The chapter then goes on to explain how eldercare is provided, the various differences between public and privately funded systems and the many complex issues that arise around carers' rights, the human rights of older people and questions around who is responsible for funding of care. We conclude with a detailed comparison of the UK and US long-term care systems, outlining how new models of funding and provision need to emerge if we are to meet need in the coming decades.

Picking up on some of the themes developed in Chapter 5 takes students into territory rarely explored in social gerontology textbooks. As the proportion of our populations aged 60 or over grows as a percentage of our general population, we also see an increase in diversity. This includes new ageing populations – people with disabilities or illnesses that would have meant they did not survive until old age in the past. Given that, by definition, a chapter on diversity is going to throw up a whole range of different issues from gender, race, ethnicity, income differences, sexual orientation, rural and urban, or migrants and indigenous people, we decided to focus on gay men as an interesting example of a community whose experience provides useful learning for all of us struggling with the challenges presented by a diverse ageing population. Of course, how this identity intersects with others is also of interest to scholars and students alike, and is often referred to as 'intersectionality'. In this chapter we also draw on the concept of social location, which is used by Mannheim to describe how people belong to a particular generation. The gay men who we are discussing in Chapter 5 provide an excellent example of the first generation of men to live through the decriminalisation of homosexuality and to go on to age with the potential of long-term legally recognised relationships or even gay marriages. There is so much further research needed in this area. Few researchers have asked the current generation of gay older people what it was like to live through such seismic changes to their civil rights and social status.

The diversity of our older population is one of the reasons why it provides scholars like us with so many fascinating research questions to investigate. Gay men are only one of a number of minorities. In fact, social gerontology has tended to be too focused on 'older people' as if they were one homogenous category of grey-haired people, all with the same needs and rights and access to the same resources. In fact, nothing could be further from the truth. We need future generations of researchers to delve deeper into the differences and identities which exist within our oldest birth cohorts.

Leading on from Chapter 5's focus on diversity, in Chapter 6 we introduce one of the most important forces shaping and changing our experiences of ageing – gender. While being unapologetically feminist in the sense that we lean on classic work such as de Beauvoir (1972) and Friedan (1993) to uncover what it means to age in the female body, we are also pragmatic and expansive in our approach to understanding and explaining the relationship between ageing and gender. There is no doubt that the disadvantages experienced by women are often exacerbated in old age, particularly women's tangential relationship with the labour market, specifically, secure and well-paid employment. Nevertheless, we do not shy away from the differences that exist between women and men. This springs directly from one of our students' most difficult questions – why do women live longer than men? In answering this question, we delve into gender relations and how women, wives in particular, play an important role in taking care of their spouses and children, and therefore, in narrowing the gap between male and female life expectancy. We also take a feminist lens to older men as we dig deeper into gender differences in terms of how men and women spend their time in old age. When taking a closer look at men, we examine how they may cope with widowhood and the general retraction from public life and work that accompanies old age in many cultures. We conclude that there is great merit in taking a feminist lens to older men's lives and in potentially opening the door for more critical investigations of gender relations for men and women in later life. For students wishing to develop their understanding of gender and ageing through dissertation research, a closer look at older men, patriarchy and hegemonic masculinity offer very fruitful lines of enquiry.

Relations between generations of all genders and ethnicities form the basis for Chapter 7, which investigates solidarity between generations. While this bond of mutual help and support across age cohorts is the main focus of the chapter, we begin by offering students a masterclass on the meaning of generation, a concept which is often used and abused in the popular media and public debate. Going back to the classic work of Mannheim, first published in 1927, the chapter takes students through the main factors that contribute towards indicating what generation a person belongs to. It becomes quickly apparent that defining a generation is difficult, particularly if you want to use those categories in the same analytical sense that you might use birth or age cohort. The distinction between generation and birth cohort is clearly drawn which leaves us on firm ground in terms of introducing the deeper question of solidarity between generations. Here, we draw on Carney's previous collaborative research on solidarity between generations during Ireland's austerity programme after the 2007–08 financial crash (Carney et al, 2014). While the study showed extremely high levels of family solidarity that included intergenerational exchange of material, cultural and social supports, this contrasts with media discussion of intergenerational inequity and conflict, which have little basis in research evidence.

In public debate in the UK and elsewhere, we see increasing reliance on partial facts from think tanks who wish to erode support for all sorts of cross-generational benefits such as pensions and healthcare. To illustrate this, we draw on stewardship and the need to preserve solidarity between generations in order to tackle huge global challenges such as climate change. While solidarity between generations is an aspect of social gerontology which has been relatively thoroughly investigated, there is room for more contemporary analysis of how the intergenerational equity debate has found new fuel in the general demise of collectivism since the financial crash of 2007-08. Future studies of how solidarity between generations is needed to combat climate change are certainly justified. Likewise, the role of intergenerational movements to protect civil and human rights for people of all ages is something that deserves deeper investigation in this era of uncivil politics and divisive populism. Having engaged in a serious critique of neoliberalism and its role in eroding solidarity between generations, we finish the chapter with a very clear example of how solidarity between generations is alive and well – through grandparenting.

The broader question of how political decision-making processes influence population change, and vice versa, is the subject of Chapter 8. We lay out the territory that has been covered in some detail, drawing on the work of demographers such as Weiner and Teitelbaum (2001) who laid out a series of research questions which must be urgently addressed in order to remove this area of research from pundits and commentators and place it in the relatively safer hands of social scientists. The role of the post-war consensus in providing political and societal agreement needed to underpin a broad-based welfare state such as the New Deal in the US and the NHS in the UK is discussed. Political demography is introduced as the most productive way of linking population change to government and politics analytically. This is elaborated through a series of concepts including youth bulges and baby booms in a way which gives these concepts the analytical weight that is often lacking in public debate of the 'baby boomers'.

The chapter takes students through the relationship between age and political participation, comparing how younger and older people engage with politics across the lifecourse. Of all the areas covered in this book, the politics of ageing is possibly the one most often ignored by social gerontologists. There are many reasons for this, not least that social gerontologists tend to emerge from sociology and not political science. Political science has, in many ways, more in common with economics than the other social sciences. It tends not to think of older people as a population worth studying seeing as they are well accounted for in the corridors of power and are the most active of all age groups when it comes to voting in democratic elections. The door is wide open for dissertation studies investigating why, despite the general maturity of politicians and voters, older people still tend to receive sub-standard policy such as the dismal situation with social care that has rumbled through UK politics for decades now, and is by no means settled in many other countries of the world.

The final substantive chapter of our book is concerned with the 'cultural turn', one of the most prolific and popular areas of social gerontology in recent years. In this chapter we draw on the creative and insightful work of Julia Twigg (2018), Wendy Martin (Twigg and Martin, 2015), Margaret M. Gullette (2007; 2013; 2018) and colleagues who have expanded age studies in ways which have greatly enhanced our ability to understand not just why people live longer, but why it is worth doing so. Theoretically, it can be difficult to concisely define cultural gerontology, which has strong links to history, narrative methods, literary criticism and postmodern sociology. We pin down this slippery beast by drawing on the writing of Gilleard and Higgs (2000) whose work has pushed forward new agendas for cultural gerontology for two decades. In doing so, we draw out the many different ways in which the cultural turn has helped to redraw the boundaries of gerontology, from understanding problems in the health service to tracing the significance of the work of early gerontologists such as G. Stanley Hall. By focusing on the cultural critique of the 'narrative of decline' and examining how material culture can help us to better understand the meaning of living a long life, we reveal how ageing is a human experience worth living through and old age is a stage of life worth reaching. Again, we draw on the work of feminists to investigate critical perspectives on hair, beauty, fashion and other narratives of the ageing experience. While this is an area that is alive with new or newly discovered studies, it is also ripe for development. Of particular interest in terms of dissertations and further study are research projects which fully embrace an interdisciplinary approach, thereby expanding both the import and audience for certain topics. So, you could use a narrative gerontology approach to investigate men's experience of ageing under patriarchy or use material culture to investigate how men spend their time in retirement. The trick to a good cultural gerontology project is to truly embrace the idea of using methods and approaches from arts and humanities to investigate critical questions for ageing societies.

Pulling it all together: themes and issues for further research

When you are charged with the task of writing an introductory textbook, you tend to spend a lot of time writing, rewriting, editing and refining. What seemed to be absolutely vital at the start of the project (for instance, a whole chapter on dementia) can be completely superseded by its end. In the case of *Critical Questions*, we were keen to stay true to our aim to answer students' questions, but also to make sure that our book offered a comprehensive overview for those studying the social dynamics of ageing and older people. If you have managed to read the book in its entirety you will probably have recognised certain commonalities between chapters, and how they seem to be addressing fairly similar challenges in ageing societies. This is because each chapter belongs to a broader subcategory of research and theory on ageing societies. Now that you have the basics, we can complicate things slightly by outlining how some chapters can be grouped together and how the issues that they cover belong to a particular line of research. Once you have identified a topic, you can then see how each subcategory idea leads to a suite of potential studies for future research projects, undergraduate dissertations or masters' theses.

Political economy of ageing

Work and retirement, politics of ageing and solidarity between generations all fit together under the broad umbrella of political economy. Across these issues there is an underlying concern with the distribution of resources between age groups and the relationship between demography and politics that are broadly conceived as the 'political economy of ageing'. Up until the late 1990s, around the time when research on the social aspects of ageing became an important part of mainstream gerontology, the political economy approach was hegemonic. If you read some classic textbooks and articles from the time, such as Peter Townsend (1981; 2006), Alan Walker (1981; 2012), or Carroll Estes and Chris Phillipson (2002), you will see how they have made powerful arguments about how structural issues such as the underfunding of pensions and healthcare led to long-term, endemic poverty for most older people. This approach was critiqued by postmodernists, who argued that not all older people are ill or dependent. These critiques marked the rise of cultural studies of ageing which seek to broaden the range of methods and approaches used to understand ageing societies, but also to argue against hegemonic theories of ageing which seek to offer the answer for all older people and their problems. As a result, scholarship on ageing is now much more diverse and interesting. However, one could argue that we have lost some of the political firepower that comes with the more collectivist approaches from political economy of ageing, although authors such as Phillipson have been back on the attack in recent times (see Phillipson, 2020).

Outside academia, the cultural turn means that it is hard to fathom how these arguments were ever hegemonic. Rather, we see an eviscerated political economy approach where the politics of generation is seen as a question of intergenerational inequity and the concept of solidarity between generations is replaced with liberal-individualist values. You can see how this seeps into our understanding of the institutionalised lifecourse, where school, work and retirement are defined periods of the lifecourse (Kohli, 1988). The idea of stable, paid work over a sustained period of your lifecourse, leading to a pension which is financed by a reliable group and government-backed schemes now seems old-fashioned. Nowadays, even highly skilled professionals can find themselves working in the gig economy, struggling to pay into private pension schemes. Well-financed, secure, defined benefit pension schemes linked to final salary seem like an impossible dream to those who struggle to pay the rent. From a political economy of ageing perspective, much of what seems to be natural, and the way things are, is actually the product of conscious policy making on behalf of governments. Governments are appointed on the basis of political participation, their policies underpin electoral success and people often choose political parties on the basis of how policies affect their current income rather than their future security. It is only through understanding how work and retirement have been affected by the hegemonic status of neoliberalism that we can begin to see how the intergenerational equity debate may have reduced public support for pensions. Future researchers in the field of gerontology will need to tackle big questions around the relationship between work and retirement and how that is reconciled with the fact that electoral cycles encourage short-term thinking amongst politicians while all of the big challenges facing ageing societies require longer term solutions. Political demography is, therefore, an area of research that is ripe for development.

Post-structuralist approaches to understanding ageing

While it might seem that Twigg's work on *Fashion and Age* (2013) and de Beauvoir's *La Vieillesse* (1972) are poles apart, in fact both are tackling the same challenge – the misrepresentation of older women through sexist and ageist stereotypes of old age. Moving beyond structural explanations for gender inequality, feminism and gender studies have provided an important philosophical basis and methodological innovation in our studies of later life. In this book, Chapters 6 on gender and 9 on cultural gerontology fit together well as they both discuss the post-structuralist approaches to understanding ageing through feminist and postmodern lenses. Both feminist scholarship and the cultural turn provide alternative and critical discussion points for scholars of ageing around lived experience. Ultimately, these approaches question what counts as evidence of knowledge of ageing. For feminists and humanities scholars, a biographical narrative account, diary entry or other personal narrative are considered as valid data and evidence. In both cases, asking new or different questions has led to major innovations in terms of approaches and methods to researching ageing. For dissertations and further research, there is potential here to undertake some very challenging and significant work around masculinity and material culture which expands the boundaries of age studies even further than the extent recognised by Twigg (2018) in her seminal work. Expanding out from fashion, why not examine gender and home ownership, the home lives of older men or the relationship between men and their cars, gadgets or gardens in old age?

Chapters 2 on ageism and Chapter 5 on diversity also belong to this post-structuralist section of the book. These chapters fit together as they share a critical and expansive attack on the many preconceptions and narrow viewpoints that have restricted our knowledge and understanding of the ageing world. For instance, it is an inability to see how ageist stereotyping narrows our perspective which has led to the exclusion of many minorities from consideration in the research and teaching of previous generations of gerontologists. It is crucial to avoid exclusive categories of ageing which restrict our work to heteronormative, non-disabled or white middle-class identities. To do so would be to provide partial evidence of our ageing populations, leading to ill-fitting policies and services for older people. One only has to look at recent work on people ageing with Down's syndrome to begin to understand how deficient is a version of gerontology that imagines a white, middle-class older woman as their typical subject of study (Finkelstein et al, 2019). In order to avoid similar omissions in the future, we must continue to expand the questions and frontiers of our research to include new ageing populations such as those reaching old age with intellectual disabilities. Further examples of ableism in gerontology were used throughout the book. We offered examples of this through the work of medical sociologists in Manchester, England, who are researching how tests for activities of daily living are ill-suited for British people of South-East Asian heritage, outlined in Chapter 5. Likewise, we consider diversity in terms of care for older people. When we consider health and care in Chapter 4 we draw on all of these issues. Many of the most common diseases of old age, such as cancer, are much harder to treat among populations with pre-existing conditions or disabilities like type 2 diabetes or high blood pressure. For gerontologists, the most important thing to understand is the accumulation of complexity that means older people experience health, illness and treatment in ways that are different to younger people.

By taking a more holistic approach to understanding how our bodies accumulate multiple health issues, we can all hope to enhance our quality of life in old age, limiting any suffering and pain to a shorter period immediately before death. In some cases, this means being more aware of the role of family carers in helping people with dementia to maintain their independence. In others, it may be in encouraging older people and their families to have difficult conversations about what life extending treatments they wish to have, well in advance of any medical emergency. For example, a person might decide not to be ventilated, as this can prolong life long after its quality has expired. Too often, decisions about medical interventions are made without any knowledge of what the person receiving the care would actually desire. This area of work is ripe for investigation. Interdisciplinary studies involving moral philosophers and ethicists, critical and social gerontologists, medical practitioners, nursing and hospice specialists are needed.

Language and the moral economy of ageing

This leads to the final section of this chapter, which is an important discussion on language throughout. We have sought to imbue this book with an approach which is unapologetically critical about pointing out and challenging ageist language and blanket stereotyping that unfortunately dominates many discussions of ageing and older people in the public realm today. It has become so important to be correct, and to say what is in line with popular views that sometimes we forget to argue for what is fair, or good or in the best interests of others, not just ourselves. We feel strongly that this stance is necessary as, at the time of writing, the language and tone of public discourse in our countries of residence, the UK and the US, have been downplayed to simplistic, reductionist and often inaccurate portrayals of many minority groups, including older people. A good example of how this politics of hate can be applied to older people is documented in Levy et al's (2014) study of Facebook as a site where negative stereotypes of ageing thrive. As we mentioned in the Preface, there are also many examples of over-generalisation of people on the basis of age in many governments' responses to the COVID-19 outbreak (British Society of Gerontology, 2020).

In Chapter 1 we highlighted the use of language as an important means of ascertaining levels of ageist stereotyping or, on the other hand, positive views on ageing. In this sense, we embrace the moral economy of ageing approach, put forward by Minkler and Estes (1991), which sought to make normative statements about what is appropriate language on moral as well as research grounds. This might seem like a very old-fashioned approach. Morality has long been associated with organised religion, which began to be decoupled from state apparatuses in majority Christian countries in Europe from the mid to late 20th century. In our minds, there is a still a place for morality in our lives, especially when it comes to making decisions for some of the oldest and most vulnerable members of our society. Moral philosophers and ethicists can play an important role in helping doctors, patients and ageing societies more generally to make decisions about what limitations should be placed on the use of life-prolonging medical interventions such as ventilators and intravenous feeding tubes (Gullette, 2020). There are always important ethical implications of using scientific advancement for the betterment of human lives. Quite often, the ethical questions arise when it is unclear whether the medical intervention is producing a health outcome that is desirable to the person receiving the treatment, their family and community or society as a whole.

Returning to the discussion of language, we draw on the work of other post-structuralists, who argued that discourse has a way of limiting or extending debates. In the book, we draw on the work of Gullette (2013; 2018), a literary critic who is something of a firebrand in this regard. One way of truly understanding how language has the power to change is to look back at some earlier examples of the terminology we used to use to refer to older people. 'The elderly' or 'dependent older people' are terms that are still used. This is before we even enter into popular usage, where it is possible to find people using terms such as 'coffin dodger', 'old codger', 'grumpy old man' or 'crone' to describe an older man or older woman. The language that we use to describe people tends to denote their value and status in our society. If we see people as old, smelly, past it or not worth bothering with, this is reflected in our language and feeds back into attitudes and behaviours. Therefore, tackling ageism and age discrimination requires us to tackle ageist language too.

As a scholar of ageing you are now equipped with more accurate, specific and egalitarian language to describe older people. You can use this language to make a positive change in your classroom, local community or country. Where possible, we would urge you to encourage your peers to use this language too. Much as language can imprison and disempower, it can have the opposite effect, providing all of us with words which better describe the human experience of living a long life.

11

Now that you know about ageing ...

(Additional questions and revision)

In this chapter we have devised a series of multiple-choice questions, designed to test your knowledge of ageing once you have read *Critical Questions for Ageing Societies* in its entirety. Each question arises directly from what you have learned in the relevant chapter. If you can answer more than 75 per cent of the questions correctly, you have studied well and are on the way to becoming a social gerontologist. Remember to flick back to the relevant chapter if you need to check an answer. The correct answers are listed at the end of the chapter.

QUESTIONS

Chapter 1: Demography

Multiple choice questions

1.1 Population ageing is:
    a. A situation when social policy is controlled by older people
    b. When everyone gets older everyday
    c. A phenomenon caused by climate change
    d. A consistent rise in the average age of the population due to decreased mortality, decreased fertility and other factors.

1.2 Japan has the highest life expectancy in the world, which is:
    a. 89 years
    b. 79 years
    c. 84 years
    d. 120 years.

1.3 Longitudinal studies of ageing are the gold standard of research because:
    a. They study the same people over a period of time and so can track changes in the ageing of a population
    b. They are comparable across different countries
    c. They provide appropriate evidence to support policy change
    d. All of the above.

1.4 Population pyramids display what type of data?
  a. Cross-sectional data for the number of males and females of different ages at a given time in a population
  b. Longitudinal data for the number of males and females of different ages at a given time
  c. The proportion of any given population expected to develop dementia
  d. The subjective wellbeing of men versus women in any given population.

1.5 The four drivers of population change are:
  a. Food, water, health and shelter
  b. Education, employment, emigration and equity
  c. Fertility, mortality, emigration and immigration
  d. Births, marriages, divorce, death.

Activity question

1.6 When applying the Demographic Transition Model to any given population, what might be some of the drivers for change between stages? Create a mind map to aid in your revision, using 'Population change' as your central phrase.

Chapter 2: Ageism and ageist stereotyping

Multiple choice questions

2.1 Ageism can be defined as:
  a. Prejudice and/or discrimination on the basis of a person's age
  b. Inclusion of person in a policy or programme irrespective of age
  c. Stereotyping based on socio-economic status
  d. The process by which older people discriminate against others.

2.2 When we describe an older person based on physical characteristics we associate with being old, this is referred to as:
  a. Exclusionary bias
  b. Stereotyping
  c. Cognitive priming
  d. Stimulus generalisation.

2.3 'Introspectively unidentified (or inaccurately identified) traces of past experience that mediate favourable or unfavourable feeling, thought or action toward social objects' is the definition of:
  a. Explicit attitude
  b. Bias

    c.   Implicit attitude
    d.   Stereotyping.

2.4 What makes ageism so different from other forms of prejudice or discrimination?
    a.   It is something that can be prevented by increased income
    b.   It is just in the minds of those people who report it and not measurable
    c.   It is confined to the Global West
    d.   It is building and reinforcing stereotypes against our future selves.

2.5 Which of the following is *not* a component part of an attitude?
    a.   Assertive
    b.   Cognitive
    c.   Conative
    d.   Affective.

Activity question

2.6 On no more than one A4 page, design an intervention to reduce ageism. This might be a series of public messages informing people of the dangers of ageist stereotyping, or an educational programme for schools. Explain the parts and explain why it would have the desired effect.

Chapter 3: Retirement, active ageing and working longer

Multiple choice questions

3.1 Which of the following do older adults bring to the workforce?
    a.   Experience
    b.   Flexibility
    c.   Life experience
    d.   All of the above.

3.2 Older adults remaining in the workforce take up the jobs of younger people trying to find employment:
    a.   True
    b.   False.

3.3 Retirement generally has a larger negative impact on the social network and social resources of:
    a.   Men
    b.   Women
    c.   Men and women equally
    d.   Neither men nor women.

3.4 Pensions were first introduced in the UK in what year:
    a.   1995
    b.   1908
    c.   1889
    d.   1946.

3.5 The concept of the 'dependency ratio' is used to describe:
    a.   The number of disabled people in society
    b.   The ratio of people who qualify for a pension versus those who do not
    c.   The balance between the number of people of working age versus those in retirement and those still in school or training
    d.   The number of older people who meet the standards of active ageing versus those who do not.

Activity question

3.6 Taking a country of your choice, list the supply and demand factors which affect older people in the workforce. Supply factors relate to the willingness of older workers to delay retirement and demand factors refer to the willingness of employers to employ older workers.

Chapter 4: Care and support in later life

Multiple choice questions

4.1 Who is considered to be a caregiver?
    a.   Those providing remote care
    b.   Families caring for someone living in an institution
    c.   Any close relation involved in care
    d.   All of the above.

4.2 How has caregiving been shown to impact the physical health of the caregiver?
    a.   Better immune system functioning
    b.   Decreased risk of musculoskeletal disorders
    c.   Increased cardiovascular risk
    d.   None of the above.

4.3 Being a primary carer without receiving suitable support can result in which of the following?
    a.   Decreased social support network or interaction
    b.   Increased risk of health issues
    c.   Increased relationship tension
    d.   All of the above.

4.4 The majority of older people in the US, the UK, Australia and across Europe are supported in some form of institution care setting or residential care facility:
   a.   True
   b.   False.

4.5 'Filial piety' can be defined as:
   a.   An awareness of repaying the burden borne by your parents and the desire to reciprocate the care they have given to you as a child
   b.   Women looking after their mother-in-law when unwell in later life
   c.   The first-born son taking financial responsibility for parents in later life
   d.   The feeling of family established in supported living environments such as residential care homes for older people.

Activity question

4.6 Yolande lives in her own three-storey house that she bought with her husband, who has recently passed away. She has a son who she is fairly close to, but he lives abroad so is unable to provide much hands-on support. Since her husband's passing, Yolande has spent more time reflecting on her life with him and less time with her friends. Most of them are still married and she doesn't want to impose herself upon them. While Yolande was making herself dinner she lost concentration and scalded her hand badly. Now she is left eating prepared food, sandwiches and cereal, as she doesn't have any support. She is also increasingly struggling to reach her bedroom on the third floor so frequently sleeps on the couch in the living room. This means that she isn't feeling rested and takes many more naps during the day. She is becoming increasingly forgetful and lethargic.

What would you identify as potential issues for Yolande, and what could be done to provide care and support for her? Think about the changes that have been noted, their causes and remedies.

Chapter 5: Diversity among the ageing population

Multiple choice questions

5.1 Older LGBTQI* adults are more likely than heterosexual older adults to live alone:
   a.   True
   b.   False.

5.2 Older people who belong to the LGBTQI* community are often described as experiencing 'intersectional' disadvantage. What does this mean?
   a.   Experiencing discrimination from each section of the community

b.   Experiencing disadvantage as a result of belonging to multiple disadvantage categories (for example, gender and age discrimination at once)

c.   Disadvantage caused by going back 'into the closet' to receive care

d.   Disadvantage caused by the transition between socially recognised groups.

5.3 Ageing as an LGBTQI* person means that you are:

a.   More likely to have strong family connections

b.   Less likely to face legal next of kin issues

c.   More likely to face discrimination from health and social care providers

d.   Less likely to require family support in old age.

5.4 'Having a level of social contact below the desired level or amount' can be defined as:

a.   Withdrawal

b.   Social isolation

c.   Loneliness

d.   Fatigue.

5.5 Which of the following is not an example of a 'new' ageing population?

a.   Older adults with Down's syndrome

b.   Older adults with HIV

c.   Older adults with cystic fibrosis

d.   Older adults with glaucoma.

Activity question

5.6 What are some of the challenges that may face a lesbian from a minority ethnic community as she ages? Try to think about all of the challenges faced and bullet point your responses. Give yourself no more than three minutes to brainstorm your answers.

Chapter 6: Gender

Multiple choice questions

6.1 'Cumulative disadvantage' is the concept that:

a.   Negative effects arise from patterns of inequality in wealth, status and opportunities across the lifecourse (for example, poor older widows are worse off than young rich widows)

b.   Disadvantaged communities stick together

c.   Adding up the negative events across a person's life gives them an 'at risk' score for dementia

    d.   Older adults accumulate negative traits across the later years of
        their life.

6.2 Women are more likely to live longer than men, but also report illness more regularly. Hence, the phrase, 'Women are sicker, men die quicker':
    a.   True
    b.   False.

6.3 The majority of the frailest and oldest people in ageing societies are female. How does this affect women?
    a.   It means that women are more likely to need eldercare in old age than men, who are often cared for by their wives
    b.   This means that women are lucky because they live longer than men
    c.   This means that men have a more active old age
    d.   Adult children are more likely to show more filial piety towards their fathers.

6.4 What are the strengths of a feminist analysis of later life?
    a.   Feminists allow us to see how sexism earlier in life can lead to unequal ageing between women and men
    b.   Feminists such as Calasanti offer enlightening critiques of how the anti-ageing industry sets impossible standards of physiological ageing
    c.   Feminism allows us to view the world from the perspective of older men and older women
    d.   All of the above.

6.5 Studies of ageing and masculinity have found that:
    a.   Men do not experience severe social exclusion following the death of a spouse
    b.   Men are still expected to perform according to established stereotypes, despite their physical health and social networks being altered by the process of ageing and the institution of retirement
    c.   All older people are basically the same; differences between men and women disappear as they age
    d.   Ageism does not affect older men.

Activity question

6.6 As both men and women age, they have different social roles, norms and expectations. Using an A3 piece of paper, draw a line down the middle with women on one side and men on the other. List the possible problems/advantages/opportunities that each gender might experience in old age. Who has better opportunities? Who has more problems? Which problems or opportunities affect both men and women?

Chapter 7: The myth of intergenerational conflict

Multiple choice questions

7.1 A generation can be defined as:
   a.   A birth cohort or group of birth cohorts, members of which are recognised as sharing a common social location associated with their time of birth
   b.   Every ten years or the start of a new decade
   c.   Purely the stages of family relationships (ie grandparent, parent, child)
   d.   An arbitrary social construct to group together people for stereotyping.

7.2 Pitting older people versus younger people (for example, when political commentators 'explain' voting patterns) is an example of:
   a.   Intergenerational solidarity
   b.   Intergenerational equity debate
   c.   Intergenerational cohesion
   d.   Intergenerational ambivalence.

7.3 One method of reducing ageism is:
   a.   Conforming to social norms
   b.   Ignoring stereotyping and not drawing attention to it
   c.   Increasing opportunities for intergenerational contact and communication
   d.   Segregating people by age.

7.4 Mannheim wrote the definitive text on generation, 'The problem of generations', in which year?
   a.   1999
   b.   1927
   c.   2003
   d.   1946.

7.5 Adults paying taxes to fund current retirees' pension and current children's education is an example of:
   a.   Conflict between generations
   b.   Generational exchange
   c.   Intergenerational solidarity
   d.   Social erosion.

Activity question

7.6 Design a policy that could increase intergenerational contact and, in turn, intergenerational solidarity. Explain the choices that you have made in terms of the challenge faced and how changes could made or helped to happen. Think about the role of existing social institutions such as the family in your plans.

Chapter 8: Politics of ageing

Multiple choice questions

8.1 Political demography is:
a. The study of voting in a given population
b. The study of population change in the context of government and politics
c. The study of how politicians age
d. The study of population change in democracies only.

8.2 It is a bad idea to use population projections as forecasts because we know from experience that some factors such as migration can be very difficult to accurately predict:
a. True
b. False.

8.3 Why is it important to be mindful of the role of human action in precipitating population change?
a. Because policies can affect human behaviour. For example, if war is declared between two countries this may prompt a surge in immigration from a particular region
b. Because human beings are unpredictable and self-interested
c. Because population change is predestined by history
d. Because population ageing is inevitable.

8.4 What is a 'baby boom'?
a. A surge in birth rates following a war or other event
b. A time period when a particularly troublesome birth cohort comes of age
c. An economic boom because of population change
d. A society where the rights of children are deemed more important than any other group.

8.5 Which of the following statements is false?
a. Older people vote, but still make up a small percentage of voters
b. Older people always vote for more conservative parties
c. Politicians pay attention to older people because they know they use their vote
d. There is little indication that older people vote *en bloc*.

Activity question

8.6 You are a group of young people who are seeking to get climate change on the political agenda. What arguments should you make to convince policy makers to take a 'long view' on issues such as climate change, population change and other global issues?

Chapter 9: Cultural gerontology

Multiple choice questions

9.1 Which of the following is *not* a focus within cultural gerontology?
   a.   Food
   b.   Clothing
   c.   Music
   d.   Dementia rates.

9.2 It is widely understood that _____ provides a strong underpinning for cultural gerontology. Which of the following fills the blank?
   a.   Feminism
   b.   Multiculturalism
   c.   Heterosexism
   d.   Philanthropy.

9.3 Cultural gerontology has been used as a framework to explain the _____ of women. Which of the following fills the blank?
   a.   Prominence
   b.   Invisibility
   c.   Lifecourse roles
   d.   Employment.

9.4 Using culture, arts, humanities and media to understand the meaning of ageing is often referred to as:
   a.   The zeitgeist
   b.   A psychodynamic perspective
   c.   The cultural turn
   d.   Political economy.

9.5 When a migrant moves to a new country, taking a cultural gerontological perspective suggests that which of the following would be important:
   a.   Clothing linked to cultural identity
   b.   Food from cultural celebrations in the country of origin
   c.   Social relationships within the community of people with shared cultures
   d.   All of the above.

Activity question

9.6 Select an item in your house that has meaning to you now and that you feel will have meaning to you in 40 years time. List the reasons why this object has meaning, thinking about the reasons behind this. Try to make sure that you reflect on the connections that this represents. For added fun, keep your list somewhere very safe and see if it holds true in 40 years!

ANSWERS

Chapter 1: Demography

Multiple choice questions

1.1 d
1.2 c
1.3 a
1.4 a
1.5 c

Activity question

1.6 The key words and concepts to include will be:

Fertility rate, Mortality rate, Sanitation, Personal hygiene, Health literacy, Vaccination, Healthcare, Gross Domestic Product, Per capita income, Household income, Corruption index, Environmental change (temperature or rainfall), Pollution, Food availability (processed or organic), Cultural expectation (filial piety), Technology, Infrastructure, Cultural norms, Transportation, Mobility

Be aware that this is not an exhaustive list and that each country will have specific drivers that you may want to consider.

Chapter 2: Ageism and ageist stereotyping

Multiple choice questions

2.1 a
2.2 b
2.3 c
2.4 d
2.5 a

Activity question

2.6 This is a wide scoped exercise designed to get you to think about the component part of an attitude as well as the two subsets. Your answer should reference the cognitive, conative, affective and evaluative aspects of attitudes and then should also address implicit and explicit ageism. Any proposed intervention should also look at intergenerational content and the role of skill-sharing as well as intrinsic motivation. There should also be some discussion of how often intergenerational contact should happen and for how long a period of time. Advanced answers would look at cultural and social norms, as well as self-presentation bias or social desirability in terms of measuring any changes to attitudes arising from the intervention.

Chapter 3: Retirement, active ageing and working longer

Multiple choice questions

3.1 d
3.2 b
3.3 a
3.4 b
3.5 c

Activity question

3.6 There will be specific examples of policy and cultural beliefs that will affect the factors which push or pull older people into and out of work based on the country that you choose. The following are examples of the minimum you should consider in your lists:

Supply:
No default retirement age; Supportive carer leave; Anti-ageism legislation; Flexible working practice; Training schemes; Cultural acceptance; Good health and social care; Lack of savings; Lack of pension system.

Demand:
Caring responsibilities; Discriminatory work policy; Age not being a protected status; No workplace flexibility; Youth focused access to training; Desire for increased social time; Grandparenting responsibilities; Ill health; Sufficient savings to enable comfortable retirement.

Your list should uncover how government or business can improve their levels of labour force participation among older workers.

Chapter 4: Care and support in later life

Multiple choice questions

4.1 d
4.2 c
4.3 d
4.4 b
4.5 a

Activity question

4.6 There are many facets to the vignette given but some of the key points that you may want to consider are:

- Yolande is a homeowner and so is likely to have to pay for all of her own care if she requires a formal care setting (dependent on the country).
- She has a three-storey home which may be too much to manage now and as such downsizing, or converting her home, may be an option
- Her son may be tempted to make decisions about supported living solutions as he cannot be there to help. This could give him peace of mind but would this be something that is right for Yolande?
- She is possibly lonely due to increasing social isolation (removing herself from social networks). A visitor or information about local groups could be what Yolande needs to help break this cycle. Additionally she may require short-term medication or counselling.
- She may require a cognitive screening for the forgetful episodes and loss of concentration.
- She could be offered short-term meal support so that she doesn't risk malnutrition.
- An occupational therapist could assess both the kitchen and living spaces to ensure Yolande was maximising her potential for an independent old age.

Chapter 5: Diversity among the ageing population

Multiple choice questions

5.1 a
5.2 b
5.3 c
5.4 c
5.5 d

Activity question

5.6 Depending on the context, you may have provided different examples. The following are the overarching issues that are true across environments: racial discrimination as a minority; barriers to practising cultural rituals; inability to maintain identity of cultural roots; homophobia; 'recloseting' in care, health or other professional settings; lack of recognition for partners; unequal pay opportunity; lack of retirement options due to cumulative disadvantage; behavioural stereotyping due to ascribed groups; assumptions of heteronormativity.

Chapter 6: Gender

Multiple choice questions

6.1 a
6.2 a
6.3 a
6.4 d
6.5 b

Activity question

6.6 There will be many options to choose from here, so it is not possible to give a model answer. However, the following are areas that need to be considered and reflected on within the context of your chosen area: social norms and values; historical context; current and past political and legislative impact; protections of rights; biological differences; intersectional and cumulative disadvantage; motivations and drivers for each gender within the contextual framework.

Chapter 7: The myth of intergenerational conflict

Multiple choice questions

7.1 a
7.2 b
7.3 c
7.4 b
7.5 c

Activity question

7.6 The best intergenerational interventions and activities start from a place of mutual respect between the generations. If there is skill-sharing between younger and older people then it has to be something that one wants to teach and the other wants to learn. The classic example is younger people teaching older people about Information Technology. For example, a younger person may teach an older person how to stay connected via social media and the older person may teach them a core life skill like budgeting, political participation such as voting, or more domestic skills like cooking or gardening. If both are seen as expert in their own right but also as novices in other areas, there is a level playing field that erases any age-related hierarchy. You should look at the social norms ascribed to each of the groups and design an intervention that challenges these, again breaking the barriers associated with ageism (in both directions).

Chapter 8: Politics of ageing

Multiple choice questions

8.1 b
8.2 a
8.3 a
8.4 a
8.5 b

Activity question

8.6 A number of arguments can be included here but the following are topics that should be addressed as fundamental concerns and topics to generate discussion: intergenerational solidarity; food security; global security; economic impacts of ecological change; voters' impact; costs of no preparation.

Chapter 9: Cultural gerontology

Multiple choice questions

9.1 d
9.2 a
9.3 b
9.4 c
9.5 d

Activity question

9.6 The items chosen will be very specific but the underpinning reasons will be surprisingly similar. The reflections should include some of the following:

• Social connectivity – who the item belonged to, was gifted by or was associated with

- Place – where the item was from or where you were when it became yours or entered your life
- The emotional associations – what emotions the item evokes and why (note: these may not always be positive)
- The purpose of the object – how it fits into your life now, and how its role may change as you grow older.

The key point is looking at the *meaning* of the object and not just its function. Understanding meaning is the basic fundamental to cultural gerontology.

Appendix 1:
Review exercise 1 – detailed instructions on constructing a population pyramid

Population pyramids are a fundamental tool for any gerontologist or demographer, or, indeed, anyone interested in understanding population change. Population pyramids enable the mapping of any given population by age and sex, presenting data in a graphical form that immediately makes accessible the comparisons between the numbers of children and older people or between men and women. On the horizontal axis (also called the x-axis), the proportion of the population is indicated in percentages. The vertical axis (also called the y-axis) is divided by age groups (0–4; 5–9 and so on), usually in 5-year intervals right up to 90+. In order to represent gender differences, the pyramid is then further split into male and female, with the left bars indicating the percentage of males within the population, and the right bars, the percentage of females.

The standard method for constructing a population pyramid is to input the data into MS Excel or a similar program which, provided you input the data correctly, will produce a very accurate pyramid. However, it is equally possible to create the pyramids manually using some graph paper, a ruler and some pencils of different colours. To do this, you will need the data for men and women as shown in 'Step 1' of the exercise guide below. You will then need to follow 'Step 2' and 'Step 3' to create the numbers needed to input. At this stage you can either manually plot the chart on graph paper or use a program such as Paint. Either way, use the gridlines to create the base of the pyramid, as shown below in Figure A1.1.

Label the horizontal axis 'Male' and 'Female', and assign age categories to the y-axis. Then select a colour for each side of the pyramid to represent males and females. You can also outline each of the bars for greater ease when reading off the exact numbers. HINT – Look at your data table (see completed table in Figure A1.5) before creating the horizontal X-axis as this will dictate the highest percentage that you need to include. In this exercise, the maximum is 7.4% (which is the percentage of men aged 30–35) so we stopped at 8.

The remainder of the exercise details how to complete the task using computer software. If you have Microsoft Excel, try doing it both ways, as it's a great skill to have!

This exercise will guide you through how to create a population pyramid. In the exercise we use Microsoft Excel version 16 but the steps remain consistent for other similar spreadsheet software. (Alternatively, if you calculate the numbers by hand, you can also draw the pyramid manually as outlined earlier.)

Figure A1.1: Chart to show manual population pyramid creation

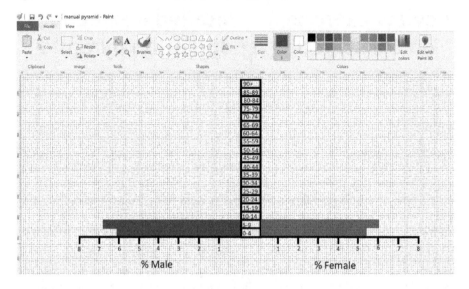

Below is a fictional data set for this example but you can use population data you have collected or downloaded, as long as you have the age groupings and the absolute numbers of males and females in each group. This could be a great way of learning more about the demographic profile of your country or region.

Step 1:
Set up the spreadsheet as shown below in Figure A1.2, ensuring that you accurately enter the figures and calculate a total for the male and female columns separately.

Figure A1.2: Table of population data split by age group and sex

	A	B	C	D
4				
5	Age Group	Male	Female	
6	0-4	86,042	81,861	
7	5-9	94,750	90,575	
8	10-14	100,975	95,001	
9	15-19	93,175	91,529	
10	20-24	84,382	91,536	
11	25-29	81,245	85,111	
12	30-34	95,552	102,758	
13	35-39	103,804	108,367	
14	40-44	95,603	99,878	
15	45-49	90,847	93,641	
16	50-54	103,267	105,079	
17	55-59	87,518	89,324	
18	60-64	75,175	77,749	
19	65-69	66,314	72,145	
20	70-74	51,237	68,458	
21	75-79	45,803	64,026	
22	80-84	26,294	46,079	
23	85-89	11,569	27,408	
24	90+	4,230	15,174	
25	Total	1,397,782	1,505,699	

Step 2:

Using the formula shown below on Figure A1.3, calculate the percentages for each cell of the age groups of men and women. It is important to remember to select the correct column total; otherwise, the calculation will be incorrect. HINT: You can check you have totalled each percentage column correctly by summing them and checking that each column adds up to exactly 100.

Figure A1.3: Table to illustrate population percentages by sex and age group

	A	B	C	D	E	F
4						
5	Age Group	Male	Female	%Male	%female	
6	0-4	86,042	81,861		=C6/C25*100	
7	5-9	94,750	90,575			
8	10-14	100,975	95,001			
9	15-19	93,175	91,529			
10	20-24	84,382	91,536			
11	25-29	81,245	85,111			
12	30-34	95,552	102,758			
13	35-39	103,804	108,367			
14	40-44	95,603	99,878			
15	45-49	90,847	93,641			
16	50-54	103,267	105,079			
17	55-59	87,518	89,324			
18	60-64	75,175	77,749			
19	65-69	66,314	72,145			
20	70-74	51,237	68,458			
21	75-79	45,803	64,026			
22	80-84	26,294	46,079			
23	85-89	11,569	27,408			
24	90+	4,230	15,174			
25	Total	1,397,782	1,505,699			
26						
27						

Step 3:

Create an additional column to the right of your existing data, give it the title 'Neg Male', or something similar, to represent the inverted data. This is to calculate the left side of your pyramid. It is convention that the male data are presented on the left and, in order to do this, you will need to use the formula shown in Figure A1.4 to multiply the male data column by minus 1. Repeat this for each cell of male data.

Figure A1.4: Table to illustrate inversion of male percentages

	A	B	C	D	E	F	G
4							
5	Age Group	Male	Female	%Male	%female	Neg Male	
6	0-4	86,042	81,861	6.155609	5.436744	=D6*-1	
7	5-9	94,750	90,575	6.778596	6.015479		
8	10-14	100,975	95,001	7.223945	6.309428		
9	15-19	93,175	91,529	6.665918	6.078838		
10	20-24	84,382	91,536	6.03685	6.079303		
11	25-29	81,245	85,111	5.812423	5.652591		
12	30-34	95,552	102,758	6.835973	6.824604		
13	35-39	103,804	108,367	7.426337	7.197122		
14	40-44	95,603	99,878	6.839622	6.633331		
15	45-49	90,847	93,641	6.499368	6.219105		
16	50-54	103,267	105,079	7.387919	6.978752		
17	55-59	87,518	89,324	6.261205	5.932394		
18	60-64	75,175	77,749	5.378163	5.163648		
19	65-69	66,314	72,145	4.744231	4.791462		
20	70-74	51,237	68,458	3.665593	4.546593		
21	75-79	45,803	64,026	3.276834	4.252244		
22	80-84	26,294	46,079	1.881123	3.060306		
23	85-89	11,569	27,408	0.827668	1.820284		
24	90+	4,230	15,174	0.302622	1.007771		
25	Total	1,397,782	1,505,699				

Step 4:

Now comes the fun bit … making the graph. This part may vary depending on your software package but select the horizontal 2-D bar chart, as demonstrated in Figure A1.5. It is possible the options will appear via a 'wizard' or automatic prompt but they will all be grouped using similar icons to those shown.

Figure A1.5: Screenshot to illustrate graph selection

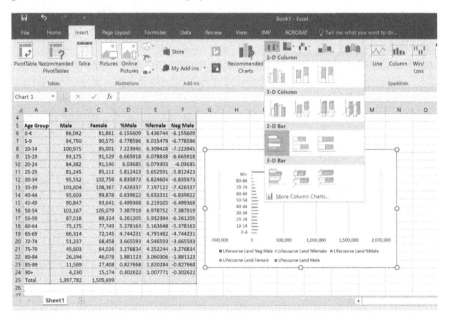

Step 5:

Click on 'Chart Filters' and then 'Select Data', and the following box will appear. This is where you start to input your data. Depending on your software, this section may already be populated. If it is, don't panic. Select all of the items and remove them until you have a blank display box as shown below in Figure A1.6. Then you need to select the data for the pyramid by clicking on the button indicated below by the arrow.

Figure A1.6: Screenshot indicating data selection

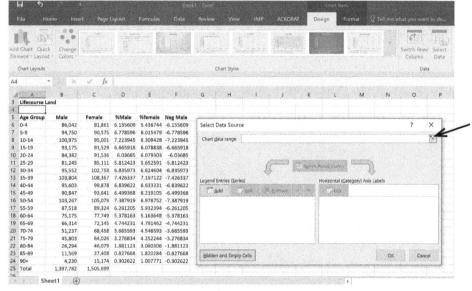

Step 6:

You will now see the 'Edit Series' box (Figure A1.7) that will appear upon completing 'Step 5'. Now you can manually type in 'Female' in the 'Series name' field before clicking on the button indicated by the arrow to select the 'Series values'.

Figure A1.7: Screenshot of series labelling

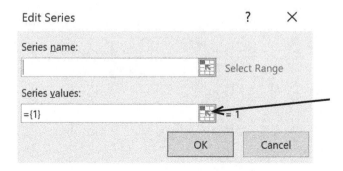

By clicking the 'Series values' button, you will return to the full spreadsheet, as illustrated in Figure A1.8. Now highlight/select the data in the '%Female' column, as shown below.

Figure A1.8: Screenshot of %Female data selection

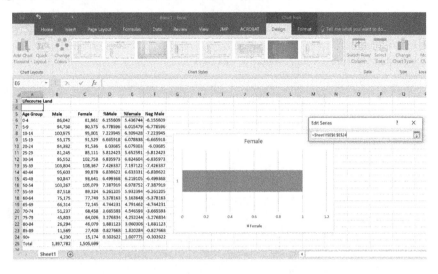

Step 7:
Repeat Step 6 for the 'Neg Male' column (as this is the data that you have converted to a negative value and is suitable for the pyramid) and click 'OK'. For the horizontal axis, click 'Edit' and select the age group labels. You will be left with a box that looks like Figure A1.9 below. Click 'OK' and proceed.

Figure A1.9: Screenshot of axis selection

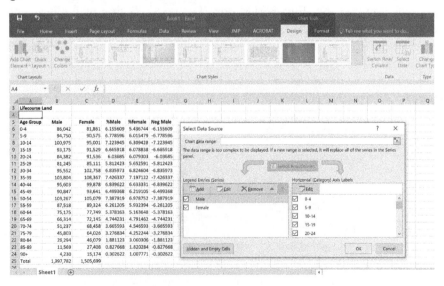

Step 8:

Now to bring it all together. You have a basic chart, but it doesn't look quite right. You need to edit the displays to make it look like a real population pyramid: this will make it much easier to see the differences between age groups. Double click on one side of the data bars as shown in Figure A1.10. You will be presented with the 'Series Options', where you will change the 'Series Overlap' to 100% and the 'Gap Width' to 0%. This will group the bars together. Now repeat this on the other set of data bars.

Figure A1.10: Screenshot formatting the data visualisation

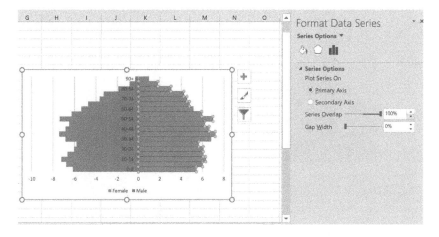

Step 9:

Double click on the age group axis that is running down the centre of your pyramid and the 'Format Axis' tab will appear. Change the value of the 'Label Position' to 'Low' as illustrated in Figure A1.11 and this will move the axis labels to the left of the pyramid.

Figure A1.11: Screenshot formatting the Y-axis

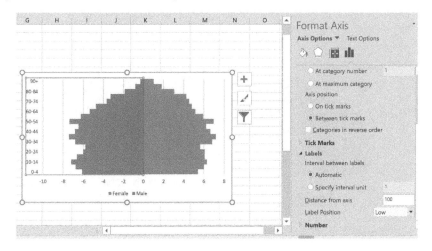

Step 10:
Select the data bars again to edit the 'Series Options', as demonstrated in Figure A1.12. Now add a 'Solid Line' border, changing the colour to black (or another colour, depending on your colour scheme) and ensure that the 'Transparency' is set to 0%. This will define the bars and enable you to see the different values for each age group.

Figure A1.12: Screenshot demarcating age group data bars

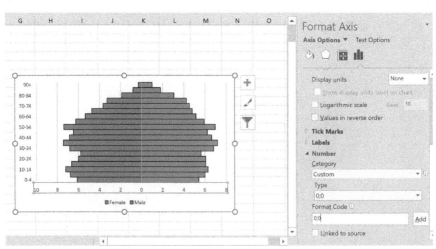

Step 11:
Double click on the X-axis along the bottom as illustrated in Figure A1.13. Within the 'Axis Options', change the 'Number' values by changing the 'Category' to 'Custom' and inputting '0;0' in the 'Format Code' field and click 'Add'. This will change the axis to reflect a centre point and equal values in each direction.

Figure A1.13: Screenshot formatting the X-axis

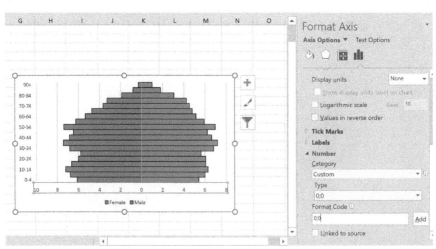

Step 12:

Now you have your completed population pyramid! You can add titles, change colours and alter the display, but your finished product should look something like that shown in Figure A1.14. If it doesn't, not to worry, go back and check your data input then repeat the steps from 'Step 4'.

Figure A1.14: Screenshot of completed population pyramid

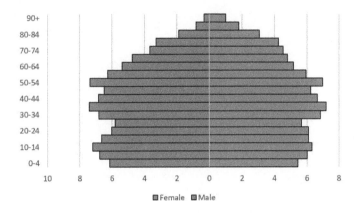

Appendix 2:
World Health Organization
liveability framework domains

In 2007, the World Health Organization (WHO) produced a publication called *Global Age-friendly Cities: A Guide*. This guide detailed eight domains that cities and communities around the world can focus on to reimagine their existing structures and services to better meet the needs of their ageing populations. This appendix offers an introductory guide to the WHO approach to help you understand the contexts in Chapter 4. For a full copy of the guide, you can search 'Global age-friendly cities: a guide' on the WHO website or follow the link below:

https://www.who.int/ageing/publications/age_friendly_cities_guide/en/
(accessed 20 April 2020)

The built environment

Outdoor space and buildings – This is more than just the buildings we inhabit. This is the space that we navigate and the space in which we interact. Public spaces where people gather are key spaces for engagement with friends, family and the wider community. This domain includes monitoring of green spaces, safe streets and sidewalks, and seating in spaces to open them up for those who may need to rest as well as for those who just want to enjoy the space. In terms of the built environment, this domain is about ensuring buildings and outside spaces are accessible using ramps, rails and elevators to minimise the stress of access and to ensure that spaces can be used and enjoyed by people of all ages.

Transportation – The car is not always king. What happens if you never learnt to drive? If you cannot afford a car? Or if changes in health mean that you can no longer drive? Cost effective, clean and accessible public transport that gets people where they want to go when they want to get there is key in ensuring a transportation network that people of all ages can –and will want to – use. Innovative solutions with trams, trains, buses, boats and even taxis should be considered to meet the diverse needs of all of ages.

Housing – Universal design, accessibility, futureproofing: all these terms are bandied about but need to be incorporated into thinking about housing from the cradle to the grave. Changes need to be made in individual home settings but only by embracing a conceptual change within housing design will any significant improvements be felt by the greatest number of people.

The social environment

Social participation – Social isolation and loneliness are widely regarded as the greatest social challenges facing today's population due to the individual and societal impacts they have. This is not something that is just an issue for older people but something that needs to be considered for all ages. Environments can be designed and used in ways to maximise accessibility and create natural gathering points to enhance socialisation. Designing spaces with affordable social activities is key to providing a more positive outlook and turning the tide on loneliness and social isolation.

Respect and social inclusion – As humans we want to feel needed and valued. Having intergenerational activities available is an effective way of challenging misconceptions about other age groups, fostering a relationship of sharing, and understanding what each has to offer.

Civic participation and employment – With the removal of the mandatory retirement age in many countries, working lives are changing. Does this have to be an all-or-nothing approach? What about flexible employment? What about volunteering? This domain looks at how communities and governments can come together to provide ways in which older adults can continue to work on either a paid or voluntary basis. This enables skills to be retained, knowledge to be passed on and for older adults to remain engaged in community life.

Communication and information – Everyone today has a smartphone, right? Everyone today watches the television, right? Wrong. The way in which we consume information is changing and changing quicker than ever before. Age-friendly communities understand that communication is multifaceted and, as such, information needs to be accessible through various outlets.

Community support and health services – At some point in their life, every person will need to access health and community services. It is important that care and support services are available in the community, but it is just as important that people know about and can access these services. This will include providing a range of opening times, locations and staff numbers to ensure that everyone can utilise the services they need as they need them.

Appendix 3:
Care Quality Commission
fundamental standards

The Care Quality Commission (CQC) is the independent regulator of health and social care in England, UK and is responsible for the regulation, monitoring and inspection of health and social care services. Further to ensuring standards of care, they have set out a series of fundamental standards that everybody has the right to expect, regardless of individual characteristics or group membership. Below is a summary of these standards to contextualise the information in the chapter. Full details of the CQC, its reports and its standards for professionals and consumers can be found on its website:

https://www.cqc.org.uk/
(accessed 21 April 2020)

Person centred care – Treatment must be demonstrably tailored to the needs *and* preferences of the resident. This is to ensure that there is no 'cookie-cutter' treatment, and indeed that treatment plans change and adapt as the needs of the older person change.

Dignity and respect – Each resident must be afforded dignity and respect at all times. This includes being treated as an equal regardless of race, ethnicity, sexuality or any other characteristic. The option of privacy whenever a resident wants or needs it as well as the support to engage with the community and to retain independence.

Consent – Both oral and documented consent must be given prior to the start or change of any treatment plan prior to handling or any other service being provided for the older person. This is integral and vital. It is key to ensuring safe care and it is central to note that (a) consent can be withdrawn at any point, and (b) consent must be obtained from the older person unless there is a designated person legally acting on their behalf.

Safeguarding from abuse – In essence this ensures that no older person suffers any form of abuse or improper treatment while under the care of any facility. This encompasses everything from placing inappropriate limitations on freedom through to applying physical restraints, degrading treatment, and neglect. This covers a wide range of aspects which can also be subjective so could be reported by a resident as impinging upon their freedoms.

Safety – The guarantee that residents will not be given unsafe treatment or care and not be placed at risk or in harm's way if there is any other possible course of action to prevent it. Risk assessments must be completed and recorded for all types of care provided, and should be updated as situations and equipment change. All staff must have regular skills updates and have obtained the relevant qualifications to deliver care.

Food and drink – Sufficient food and drink must be provided not just to sustain life but also to meet the needs and requirements of the older person. This would include changes to allow for dietary requirements and religious observations.

Premises and equipment – Equipment must be suitable, clean and in a safe working and well-maintained order to meet the requirements of the residents in the facility. Staff must be trained with the equipment and a log kept to show that maintenance has been carried out as required.

Complaints – In the circumstance that something goes wrong, there must be a formalised complaints procedure. This must include recording, assessing, investigating, resolving and escalating where necessary. All complaints, no matter the level of resolution, should be recorded and stored.

Good governance – Evidence plans on how all of the standards are going to be met and what standard operating procedures are in place for each type of care and process must be provided.

Staffing – There needs to be sufficient, qualified, competent and experienced staff to meet the needs of residents and the standards outlined. There must be detailed training documents, evidencing the training received, upcoming training and regular rotations of training to support staff in their work.

Fit and proper staff – Staff must undergo Criminal Records Bureau (CRB) checks as they are working with a vulnerable population. Recruitment procedures must be rigorous and well documented and the work history of staff must be checked prior to employment. This is enforced to try to minimise the incidences of elder abuse.

Duty of candour – In essence, processes need to be transparent, providing open, clear channels if something goes wrong and to have clear accountability.

Display ratings – All providers need to display the ratings that they have received from the CQC in their facility, on their website and, further, make sure that the full inspection report is available upon request.

References

AARP Public Policy Institute (2011) *Valuing the invaluable*, available at: https://assets.aarp.org/rgcenter/ppi/ltc/i51-caregiving.pdf.

Achenbaum, A. and Bengtson, V. (1994) 'Re-engaging the disengagement theory of aging: On the history and assessment of theory in gerontology', *The Gerontologist*. 34(6): 756–63.

Ahmed, A., and Hall, K. (2016) 'Negotiating the challenges of aging as a British migrant in Spain', *GeroPsych*, 29: 105–14.

Akar, G.C., and Ergul, S. (2008) 'The oral hygiene and denture status among residential home residents', *Clin Oral Investig*, 12: 61–5.

Alexander Shaw, K.A. (2017) *Baby boomers versus millennials: Rhetorical conflicts and interest construction in the new politics of inter-generational fairness*, Working Paper, available at: http://speri.dept.shef.ac.uk/wp-content/uploads/2018/11/Baby-Boomers-versus-Milennials-Kate-Alexander-Shaw.pdf.

Alley, D., Liebig, P., Pynoos, J., Banerjee, T., and Choi, I. (2007) 'Creating elder-friendly communities: preparations for an aging society', *Journal of Gerontological Social Work*, 49(1–2): 1–18.

Alzheimer's Association (2011) 'Alzheimer's disease facts and figures', *Alzheimer's & Dementia*, 7(2): 208–44.

Alzheimer's Association (2018) 'Alzheimer's disease facts and figures', *Alzheimer's & Dementia*, 14(3): 367–429.

Alzheimer's Disease International (2015) *World Alzheimer Report 2015: The global impact of dementia, an analysis of prevalence, incidence, cost and trends*, available at alz.co.uk/research/WorldAlzheimersReport2015.pdf.

Alzheimer's Disease International (2019) *Dementia statistics*, available at: https://www.alz.co.uk/research/statistics.

American Society on Aging (nd) 'Diversity', available at asaging.org/diversity.

Amirkhanyan, A.A., and Wolf, D.A. (2003) 'Caregiver stress and non-caregiver stress: Exploring the pathways of psychiatric morbidity', *The Gerontologist*, (43): 817–27.

Anand, S., and Sen, A. (1994) *Human development index: Methodology and measurement*, New York: Human Development Report Occasional Papers, available at: https://ora.ox.ac.uk/objects/uuid:98d15918-dca9-4df1-8653 60df6d0289dd/download_file?file_format=application/pdf&safe_filename=HDI_methodology.pdf&.

Applewhite, A. (2016) *This chair rocks: A manifesto against ageism*, Thorndike Press: Waterville.

Arber, S., and Ginn, J. (1991) *Gender and later life: A sociological analysis of resources and constraints*, London: SAGE.

Arber, S., and Timonen, V. (2012) *Contemporary grandparenting: Changing family relationships in global contexts*, Bristol: Policy Press.

Arza, C., and Johnson, P. (2006) 'The development of public pensions 1889 to 1990s', in Clark, G., Munnell, A., and Orszag, J. (eds) *The Oxford handbook of pensions and retirement*, 52, DOI: 10.1093/oxfordhb/9780199272464.003.0004.

Ashe, F., and Harland, K. (2014) 'Troubling masculinities: Changing patterns of violent masculinities in a society emerging from political conflict', *Studies in conflict and terrorism*, (37): 747–62.

Athill, D. (2008) *Somewhere towards the end*, London: Granta Books.

Baars, J., Dannefer, D., Phillipson, C., and Walker, A. (2006) *Aging, globalisation and inequality: The new critical gerontology*, Amityville, NY: Baywood.

Baker, L. and Silverstein, M. (2012) 'The well-being of grandparents caring for grandchildren in China and the United States', in Arber, S., and Timonen, V. (eds) *Contemporary grand-parenting: Changing family relationships in global contexts*, Bristol: Policy Press.

Banse, R., Seise, J., and Zerbes, N. (2001) 'Implicit attitudes towards homosexuality: Reliability, validity, and controllability of the IAT', *Zeitschrift für experimentelle psychologie*, (48): 145–60.

Bar-Anan, Y., Nosek, B.A., and Vianello, M. (2009) 'The sorting paired features task: A measure of association strengths', *Experimental Psychology*, (56): 329–43.

Barrett, A., Clayton, G. and Douglas, R. (2018) 'Explaining gender differences in self-regulated driving: What roles do health limitations and driving alternatives play?', *Ageing & Society*, (38): 2122–45.

Bauer, M., Featherstonhaugh, D., Tarzia, L., Nay, R., Wellman, D., and Beattie, E. (2013) '"I always look under the bed for a man": Needs and barriers to the expression of sexuality in residential aged care: The views of residents with and without dementia', *Psychology and Sexuality*, 4(3): 296–309 doi:10.1080/1941 9899.2012.713869.

Beck, U. (1992) *Risk society: Towards a new modernity*, Thousand Oaks, CA: Sage Publications.

Beck, U., and Beck-Gernsheim, E. (2003) *Individualisation: Institutionalized individualism and its social and political consequences*, London: Sage.

Bengtson, V.L., Furlong, M.J., and Laufer, R.S. (1983) 'Time, aging, and the continuity of social structure: themes and issues in generational analysis', *Journal of Social Issues*, (39): 45–71.

Bengtson, V., Elder, G., and Putney, N. (2005) 'The life course perspective on ageing: Linked lives, timing and history', in Johnston, M.L. (ed) *The Cambridge handbook of age and ageing* (2005), Cambridge: Cambridge University Press.

Besné, I., Descombes, C., and Breton, L. (2002) 'Effect of age and anatomical site on density of sensory innervation in human epidermis', *Arch Dermatol*, 138: 1445–50.

Betti, G.F., Georgiadis, F., Bettio, T., and Tinnios, P. (2015) *Unequal aging in Europe: Women's independence and pensions*, US: Palgrave Macmillan.

Bhatti, Y. and Hansen, K. (2012) 'The effect of generation and age on turnout to the European Parliament – How turnout will continue to decline in the future' *Electoral Studies*, 31(2): 262–72.

Bichard, J-A., Van den Heuvel, E.A., Jowitt, F., Gilhooly, M., Parker, S.G., Long, A., et al (2012) 'Tackling ageing continence through theory, tools and technology (TACT3)', *The International Journal of Aging and Society*, 1(2): 83–96.

Billari, F. (2015) 'Integrating macro- and micro-level approaches in the explanation of population change', *Population Studies*, 69(1): S11–S20, DOI:10.1080/003 24728.2015.1009712.

Binstock, R. (2012) 'Older voters and the 2010 US election: Implications for 2012 and beyond?', *The Gerontologist*, 52(3): 408–17.

Binstock, R.H. (2010) 'From compassionate ageism to intergenerational conflict?', *The Gerontologist*, 50(5): 574–85.

Birch, K. (2017) 'What is neoliberalism?', The Conversation, available at: http://theconversation.com/what-exactly-is-neoliberalism-84755.

Blythe, R. (2005) *The view in winter: Reflections on old age*, Norwich: Canterbury Press.

Bodley-Tickell, A.T., Olowokure, B., Bhaduri, S., White, D.J., Ross, J.D., Smith, G., Duggal, H.V., and Goold, P. (2008) 'Trends in sexually transmitted infections (other than HIV) in older people: Analysis of data from an enhanced surveillance system', *Sexually Transmitted Infections*, (84): 312–17.

Börsch-Supan, A. (2013) 'Myths, scientific evidence and economic policy in an ageing world', *Journal of Economics and Aging*, (1): 3–15.

Bosquet, A., El Massioui, F., and Mahé, I. (2015) 'Conditions for exercising residents' voting rights in long-term care residences: A prospective multicenter study, *Journal of Aging & Social Policy*, 27(1): 47–62, doi: 10.1080/08959420.2015.969090.

Bourdieu, P. (1986) 'Forms of capital', in Richardson, J.E. (ed) *Handbook of theory of research for the sociology of education*, London: Greenwood Press.

British Society of Gerontology (2020) 'Statement from the President and Members of the National Executive Committee of the British Society of Gerontology on COVID-19' at https://www.britishgerontology.org/DB/latest-news/press-release-from-british-society-of-gerontology-20-march-2020

Broad, K.D. (2017) 'Mechanisms and potential treatments for declining olfactory function and neurogenesis in the ageing brain', *Journal of Gerontology and Geriatrics*, 65(2): 93–100.

Bulford, S.J., and Singh, S. (2012) 'Qualitative exploration of sexual health in old age', *Sexually Transmitted Infections*, (88): 557.

Bülow, M., and Söderqvist, T. (2014) 'Successful ageing: A historical overview and critical analysis of a successful concept', *Journal of Aging Studies*, 31: 139–49.

Burholt, V. (2016) 'Transnational relationships and cultural identity of older migrants', *Journal of Gerontopsychology and Geriatric Psychiatry*, 29(2): 57–69.

Buse, C., and Twigg, J. (2014) 'Women with dementia and their handbags: Negotiating identity, privacy and "home" through material culture', *Journal of Aging Studies*, 30: 14–22.

Butler, R. (1969) 'Age-ism: Another form of bigotry', *The Gerontologist*, 9: 243–6.

Butler, R. (1975) *Why survive? Being old in America*, London: Harper & Row.

Butler, R. (2004) *The longevity revolution: the benefits and challenges of living a long life*, New York: Public Affairs.

Cahill, S., and Valadéz, R. (2013) 'Growing older with HIV/AIDS: New public health challenges', *American Journal of Public Health*, 103(3): 7–15 doi:10.2105/AJPH.2012.301161.

Calasanti, T. (2007) 'Bodacious Berry, Potency Wood and the aging monster: Gender and age relations in anti-aging ads', *Social Forces*, 86(1): 335–55.

Calasanti, T., and King, N. (2018) 'The dynamic nature of gender and aging bodies', *Journal of Aging Studies*, 45: 11–17.

Campbell, A.L. (2003) *How policies make citizens: Senior political activism and the American welfare state*, New Jersey: Princeton University Press.

Carney, G. (2020) 'Why young and old must pull together to survive this' *The Conversation* at theconversation.com/coronavirus-why-young-and-old-must-pull-together-to-survive-this-133973.

Carney, G. (2020) 'Coronavirus: Social gerontologist Dr. Gemma Carney on why arbitrary isolation for over 70s is wrong' at https://www.belfastlive.co.uk/news/belfast-news/coronavirus-social-gerontologist-dr-gemma-18033036

Carney, G.M. (2010) 'Citizenship and structured dependency: The implications of policy design for senior political power', *Ageing & Society*, 30(2): 229–51, doi.org/10.1017/S0144686X09990110.

Carney, G.M. (2017) 'Towards a gender politics of aging,' *Journal of Women & Aging*, 30(3): 242–58, doi: 10.1080/08952841.2017.1301163.

Carney, G.M. (2018) 'Brexit and the myth of generational conflict', Paper presented at the National Pensioners Convention Annual Conference, Blackpool, 12 June 2018.

Carney, G.M., and Gray, M. (2015) 'Unmasking the "elderly mystique": Why it is time to make the personal political in ageing research', *Journal of Aging Studies*, 35: 123–34, doi.org/10.1016/j.jaging.2015.08.007.

Carney, G.M., Scharf, T., Timonen, V. and Conlon, C. (2014) 'Blessed are the young for they shall inherit the national debt: Solidarity between generations and the Irish Crisis', *Critical Social Policy*, 34 (3): 312–32.

Carter, R. (2011) 'Written testimony of Rosalynn Carter before the Senate Special Committee on aging' at cartercenter.org/news/editorials_speeches/rosalynn-carter-committee-on-aging-testimony.html

Center for Disease Control (2015) *Data on causes of male deaths*, available at: https://www.cdc.gov/healthequity/lcod/men/2015/all-males/index.htm.

Center for Disease Control (2018) *Estimated HIV incidence and prevalence in the United States 2010–2016*, available at: https://www.cdc.gov/hiv/pdf/library/reports/surveillance/cdc-hiv-surveillance-supplemental-report-vol-24-1.pdf.

Central Statistics Office (2016) 'Ethnicity and cultural background', in *Census of Population 2016 – Profile 8 Irish Travellers, Ethnicity and Religion*, available at: https://www.cso.ie/en/releasesandpublications/ep/p-cp8iter/p8iter/p8e/#targetText=The%20fastest%20growing%20ethnic%20group,3%2C854%2C226%20(82.2%25)%20usual%20residents.

Chase, K. (2009) *The Victorians and Old Age*, New York: OUP.

Choi, J., McCargo, A., and Goodman, L. (2019) 'Three differences between black and white homeownership that add to the housing wealth gap', available at: https://www.urban.org/urban-wire/three-differences-between-black-and-white-homeownership-add-housing-wealth-gap.

Cincotta, R., and Doces, J. (2012) 'The age structure maturity thesis: The impact of the youth bulge on the advent and stability of liberal democracy', in Goldstone, J., Kaufmann, E. and Toft, M. (eds) *Political demography: How population changes are reshaping international security and national politics*, London: Paradigm Publishers.

Cole, T. (1984) 'The prophecy of senescence: G. Stanley Hall and the reconstruction of old age in America', *The Gerontologist*, 4(4): 360–6.

Cole, T. (1992) *The journey of life: A cultural history of aging in America*, Cambridge: Cambridge University Press.

Coleman, P., Basten, S. and Billari, F. (2015) 'Population ageing – the long view', *Population Studies*, 69(1): S1–S9.

Coles, T., and Vassarotti, T. (2012) 'Ageing and identity dilemmas for men', *Journal of Religion, Spirituality & Aging*, 24(1–2): 30–41.

Cong, Z., and Silverstein, M. (2019) 'A vignette study of older adults' preferences for intergenerational transfers in the context of competition between grandparents and grandchildren in rural China', *Journals of Gerontology B*, 74(3): 496–505.

Conlon, C., Timonen, V., Carney, G., and Scharf, T. (2014) 'Women (re)negotiating care across family generations: Intersections of gender and socioeconomic status', *Gender & Society*, 28(5): 729–51, doi.org/10.1177/0891243214536466.

Cooper, C., Selwood, A., and Livingston, G. (2009) 'Knowledge, detection, and reporting of abuse by health and social care professionals: A systematic review', *American Journal of Geriatric Psychiatry*, 17(10): 828–38.

Correia, C., Lopez, K.J., Wroblewski, K., Huisingh-Scheetz, M., Kern, D.W., Chen, R.C., Schumm L.P., Dale, W., McClintock, M.K., and Pinto, J.M. (2016) 'Global sensory impairment in older adults in the United States', *Journal of the American Geriatrics Society*, 62(2): 303–13.

Dalton, R.J. (2008a) *The good citizen: How a younger generation is reshaping American politics*, Washington DC: CQ Press.

Dalton, R. (2008b) 'Citizenship norms and the expansion of political participation', *Political Studies*, 56: 76–98.

Dawes, P., Emsley, R., Cruickshanks, K.J., Moore, D.R., Fortnum, H., Edmondson-Jones, M., McCormack, A., and Munro, K. (2015) 'Hearing loss and cognition: The role of hearing aids, social isolation and depression', *PLoS One* 10(3), doi: 10.1371/journal.pone.0119616.

De Beauvoir, S. (1972) *Old age*, London: Penguin.

De Waal, E. (2011) *The hare with amber eyes: A hidden inheritance*, London: Vintage Books.

De Wet, N. (2019) 'The association between mother's socio-economic status and non-orphan kinship care arrangements in South Africa', *Children and Youth Services Review*, 103: 79–86.

Decorps, J., Saumet, J.L., Sommer, P. et al (2014) 'Effect of ageing on tactile transduction processes', *Ageing Res Rev*, 13: 90–9.

Department of Housing and Urban Development (2016) *The 2016 Annual Homeless Assessment Report (AHAR) to Congress*, US Government. Washington DC.

Department for Work and Pensions (2019) *Benefit and pension rates 2019 to 2020*, available at: https://www.gov.uk/government/publications/benefit-and-pension-rates-2019-to-2020/proposed-benefit-and-pension-rates-2019-to-2020.

Devine, P., and Carney, G. (2017) 'Social connectedness: older people as members of their families and communities', in Cruise, S., and Kee, F. (eds) *Early key findings from a study of older people in Northern Ireland: The NICOLA study*, Belfast: Queen's University Belfast.

Dickinson, C.M., and Taylor, J. (2011) 'The effect of simulated visual impairment on speech-reading ability', *Ophthalmic Physiol. Opt.*, 31: 249–57, doi: 10.1111/j.1475-1313.2010.00810.x.

Dong, X., Simon, M., Mendes de Leon, C., Fulmer, T., Beck, T., Hebert, L., Dyer, C., Paveza, G., and Evans, D. (2011) 'Elder self-neglect and abuse and mortality risk in a community-dwelling population', *JAMA*, 302: 570.

Doty, P. (2010) 'The evolving balance of formal and informal, institutional and non-institutional long-term care for older Americans: A thirty-year perspective', *Public Policy & Aging Report*, 20, no.1.

Drescher, J. (2015) 'Out of DSM: Depathologizing homosexuality', *Behavioral sciences (Basel, Switzerland)*, 5(4), 565–75.

Duvvury, N., Ni Leime, A., and Callan, A. (2018) 'Erosion of pensions rights: Experiences of older women in Ireland', *European Journal of Cultural and Political Sociology*, 5(3): 266–94.

Ebbinghaus, B. (2015) 'The privatisation and marketization of pensions in Europe: A double transformation facing the crisis', *European Policy Analysis*, 1(1): 56–73.

Elder, G.H. (1999) *Children of the Great Depression: Social change in life experience 25th anniversary edition*, Abingdon: Routledge.

Emlet, C. (2006a) '"You're awfully old to have this disease": Experiences of stigma and ageism in adults 50 years and older living with HIV/AIDS', *The Gerontologist*, 46(6): 781–90.

Emlet, C. (2006b) 'An examination of the social networks and social isolation in older and younger adults living with HIV/AIDS', *Health & Social Work*, 31(4): 299–308.

Ephron, N. (1983) *Heartburn*, London: Hachette.

Ephron, N. (2008) *I feel bad about my neck and other thoughts on being a woman*, London: Black Swan.

Erber, J.T., and Szuchman, L.T. (2015) *Great myths of ageing*, Wiley-Blackwell.

Estes, C. (1979) *The aging enterprise: A critical examination of social policy and services for the aged*, London: Jossey-Bass.

Estes, C. and Phillipson, C. (2002) 'The globalization of capital, the welfare state and old age policy', *International Journal of Health Services*, 32(2): 279–97.

Estes, C., Biggs, S., and Phillipson, C. (2003) *Social theory, social policy and ageing*, Maidenhead: McGraw Hill

European Union (2019) 'Societal Challenges', available at: https://ec.europa.eu/programmes/horizon2020/en/h2020-section/societal-challenges.

Evandrou, M., and Glaser, K. (2003) 'Combining work and family life: The pension penalty of caring', *Ageing and Society*, 22: 583–601.

ExtraCare Charitable Trust Quality Team (2015) *Care satisfaction survey June 2015*, ExtraCare Charitable Trust, Coventry.

Falkingham, J., and Rake, K. (2001) 'Modelling the gender impact of British pension reforms', in Ginn, J., Street, D., and Arber, S. (eds), *Women, work and pensions: International issues and prospects*, Buckingham: Open University Press.

Family Caregiver Alliance (2015) *Caregiver statistics: Demographics*, available at: https://www.caregiver.org/caregiver-statistics-demographics.

Federal Interagency Forum on Aging-Related Statistics (2015) *Older Americans 2015: Key indicators of well-being: Federal interagency forum on aging-related statistics*, Washington, DC: US Government Printing Office.

Feldman, P.H., Oberlink, M.R., Simantov, E., and Gursen, M.D. (2004) *A tale of two older Americas: Community opportunities and challenges*, New York: Center for Home Care Policy and Research.

Feng, P., Huang, L., and Wang, H. (2014) 'Taste bud homeostasis in health, disease, and aging', *Chem Senses*, 39: 3–16.

Financial Times (2019) 'The squeeze on local authority funding needs to be eased', available at: https://www.ft.com/content/5801a0d2-23e8-11e9-b329-c7e6ceb5ffdf.

Fineman, M. (2005) *The autonomy myth: The theory of dependency*, New York: New Print Press.

Finkel, D., Andel, R., and Pedersen, N. (2018) 'Gender differences in longitudinal trajectories of change in physical, social and cognitive/sedentary leisure activities', *Journals of Gerontology L: Social Sciences*, 73(8): 1491–1500.

Finkelstein, A., Tenenbaum, A. and Bachner, Y. (2019) '"I will never be old": Adults with Down Syndrome and their parents talk about ageing-related challenges', *Ageing & Society*, 1–20 doi:10.1017/S0144686X190000266.

FitzGerald, C., and Hurst, S. (2017) 'Implicit bias in healthcare professionals: A systematic review', *BMC Medical Ethics*, 18(1): 19, doi:10.1186/s12910-017-0179-8.

Flamion, A., Missotten, P., Marquet, M., and Adam, S. (2019) 'Impact of contact with grandparents on children's and adolescent's views of the elderly', *Child Development*, 90(4): 1155–69.

Forbes (2019) 'Why isn't the black homeownership rate higher today than when the 1968 fair housing act became law?', available at: https://www.forbes.com/sites/johnwake/2019/05/16/heres-why-the-black-homeownership-rate-is-the-same-50-years-after-1968-fair-housing-act/#5be39f4430cd.

Foster, L. (2010) 'Towards a new political economy of pensions? The implications for women', *Critical Social Policy*, 30(1), 27–47.

Foster, L. (2018) 'Active ageing, pensions and retirement in the UK,' *Population Ageing*, 11: 117–32.

Foster, L., and Walker, A. (2013) 'Gender and active ageing in Europe', *European Journal of Ageing*, 10(1): 3–10.

Foster, L., and Walker, A. (2015) 'Active and successful ageing: A European policy perspective', *The Gerontologist*, 55(1): 83–90.

Fox, S. (2019) 'Labour's car crash result by age group', available at: https://www.brunel.ac.uk/news-and-events/news/articles/Labour's-car-crash-result-by-age-group.

Fraboni, M., Saltstone, R., and Hughes, S. (1990) 'The Fraboni scale of ageism (FSA): An attempt at a more precise measure of ageism', *Canadian Journal on Aging*, 9: 56–66.

Friedan, B. (1993) *The fountain of age*, London: Simon & Schuster.

Füllgrabe, C., and Rosen, S. (2016) 'Investigating the role of working memory in speech-in-noise identification for listeners with normal hearing', in van Dijk, P., Baskent, D., Gaudrain, E., de Kleine, E., Wagner, A., and Lanting, C. (eds) *Physiology, psychoacoustics and cognition in normal and impaired hearing*, Heidelberg: Springer: 29–36.

Furman, F. (1997) *Facing the mirror: Older women and beauty shop culture*, New York: Routledge.

Gair, S. (2017) 'Missing grandchildren: grandparents' lost contact and implications for social work', *Australian Social Work*, 70(3): 263–75.

Gardiner, L. (2016) 'Stagnation Generation: the case for renewing the intergenerational contract', Resolution Foundation, available at: https://www.resolutionfoundation.org/publications/stagnation-generation-the-case-for-renewing-the-intergenerational-contract/.

Generations United (2015) *The state of grandfamilies in America: 2014.* Available at: https://www.gu.org/resources/the-state-of-grandfamilies-in-america-2014/

Gibney, B.C. (2017) *A generation of sociopaths: How the baby boomers betrayed America*, New York: Hachette Books.

Giebel, C., Worden, A., Challis, D., Jolley, D., Bhui, K., Lambat, A., Kampanellou, E. and Purandare, N. (2019) 'Age, memory loss and perceptions of dementia in South Asian ethnic minorities', *Aging and Mental Health*, 23(2): 173–82.

Gilleard, C., and Higgs, P. (2000) *Cultures of ageing: Self, citizen and the body*, London. Routledge.

Gilleard, C., and Higgs, P. (2013) *Ageing, corporeality and embodiment*, London: Anthem Press.

Goerres, A. (2009) *The political participation of older people in Europe*, London: Palgrave Macmillan.

Gott, M., and Hinchliff, S. (2003) 'How important is sex in later life? The views of older people', *Social Science & Medicine*, 56: 1617–1628.

Golant, S.M. (2015) *Aging in the right place*, Baltimore, MD: Health Professions Press.

Government Accountability Office (2019) *Retirement security: Most households approaching retirement have low savings, an update*, available at: https://www.gao.gov/assets/700/697898.pdf.

Grabowski, D.C. (2007) 'Medicare and Medicaid: Conflicting incentives for long-term care', *The Milbank Quarterly*, 85(4): 579–610.

Grasso, M., Farrall, S., Gray, E., Hay, C. and Jennings, W. (2019) 'Socialization and generational political trajectories: An age, period and cohort analysis of political participation in Britain', *Journal of Elections, Public Opinion and Parties*, 29(2): 199–221, doi: 10.1080/17457289.2018.1476359.

Gratton, L. and Scott, A. (2016) *The 100 year life: Living and working in an age of longevity*, London: Bloomsbury.

Gray, A.M., and Birrell, D. (2013) *Transforming adult social care: Contemporary policy and practice*, Bristol: Policy Press.

Greenwald, A., and Banaji, M. (1995) 'Implicit social cognition: Attitudes, self-esteem and stereotypes', *Psychological Review*, 102(1): 4–27.

Greenwald, A., McGhee, D., and Schwartz, J. (1998) 'Measuring individual differences in implicit cognition: The implicit association test', *Journal of Personality and Social Psychology*, 74(6): 1464–80.

Grose, J.H., and Mamo, S.K. (2010) 'Processing of temporal fine structure as a function of age', *Ear Hear*, 31: 755–60, doi: 10.1097/AUD.0b013e3181e627e7.

Gullette, M. (1988) *Safe at last in the middle years: The invention of the midlife progress novel*, Berkeley: University of California Press.

Gullette, M. (1997) *Declining to decline: Cultural combat and the politics of the midlife*, Charlottesville, VA: University of Virginia.

Gullette, M. (2004) *Aged by culture*, Chicago, IL: University of Chicago Press.

Gullette, M. (2007) 'What exactly has age got to do with it? My life in critical age studies', *Journal of Aging Studies*, 22: 189–95.

Gullette, M. (2013) *Agewise: Fighting the New Ageism in America*, Chicago, IL: The University of Chicago Press.

Gullette, M. (2017) *Ending ageism, or, how not to shoot old people*, Chicago: Chicago University Press.

Gullette, M. (2020) 'Ageist "triage" is a crime against humanity' blogpost at lareviewofbooks.org/short-takes/ageist-triage-covid-19/

Hagestad, G. (2018) 'Interdependent lives and relationships in changing times: A life-course view of families and aging', in Settersten, R. (2018) *An invitation to the life course: Towards new understandings of later life*, New York: Routledge.

Hagestad, G. and Settersten, R. (2017) 'Aging: It's interpersonal – reflections from two lifecourse migrants', *The Gerontologist*, 57(1): 136–44.

Hall, G.S. (1904) *Adolescence*, New York: D. Appleton.

Hall, G.S. (1922) *Senescence: The last half of life*, available at: https://ia800602.us.archive.org/view_archive.php?archive=/8/items/olcovers569/olcovers569-L.zip&file=5697208-L.jpg&ext=.

Hannan, L., Carney, G., Devine, P., and Hodge, G. (2019) 'A view from old age: Women's lives as narrated through objects', *Life Writing*, 16(1): 51–67.

Harper, S. (2016) *How population change will transform our world*, Oxford: OUP.

Harris, K., Krygsman, S., Waschenko, J., and Laliberte-Rudman, D. (2018) 'Ageism and the older worker: A scoping review', *The Gerontologist*, 58(2): e1–e14.

Hawkes, K. (2003) 'Grandmothers and the evolution of human longevity', *American Journal of Human Biology*, 15: 380–400.

Hayslip, B., Fruhauf, C.A., and Dolvin-MacNab, M.L. (2019) 'Grandparents raising grandchildren: What have we learned over the past decade?', *The Gerontologist*, 59(3): e152–e163.

Hendrixson, A., and Hartmann, B. (2019) 'Threats and burdens: Challenging scarcity-driven narratives of "overpopulation"', *Geoforum*, 101: 250–9.

Herlofson, K., and Hagestad, G.O. (2012) 'Transformations in the role of grandparents across welfare states', in Arber, S., and Timonen, V. (eds) *Contemporary grandparenting: Changing family relationships in global contexts*, Bristol: Policy Press.

Hill, A. (2017) 'A world without retirement', *The Guardian*, 29 March 2017.

Ho, J., and Hendi, A.S. (2018) 'Recent trends in life expectancy across high income countries: Retrospective observational studies', *British Medical Journal*, 362: k2562.

Hobbes, T. (1651) *Leviathan*, Oxford: Clarendon Press, available at: http://files.libertyfund.org/files/869/0161_Bk.pdf (downloaded 29 August 2019).

Hogberg, B. (2018) 'Gender and health among older people: What is the role of social policies?', *International Journal of Social Welfare*, 27: 236–47.

Hong, J.H., Charles, S.T., Lee, S., and Lachman, M.E. (2019) 'Perceived changes in life satisfaction from the past, present and to the future: A comparison of US and Japan', *Psychology and Aging*, 34(3), 317–29.

Hooker, E. (1957) 'The adjustment of the male overt homosexual', *Journal of Projective Techniques*, 21: 18–31.

Hooyman, N., Browne, C., Ray, R., and Richardson, V. (2002) 'Feminist gerontology and the life course', *Gerontology and Geriatrics Education*, 22(4): 3–26, doi: 10.1300/J021v22n04 02.

Howker, E., and Malik, S. (2010) *Jilted generation: How Britain has bankrupted its youth*, London: Icon Books.

Hubbard, R., Goodwin, V., Llewellyn, D., Warmoth, K and Land, I. (2014) 'Frailty, financial resources and subjective well-being in later life', *Archives of Gerontology and Geriatrics*, 58(3): 364–9.

Hurd Clarke, L., and Korotchenko, A. (2010) 'Shades of grey: To dye or not to dye one's hair in later life', *Ageing & Society*, 30(6): 1011–26.

Hurd Clarke, L., and Korotchenko, A. (2016) 'I know it exists … but I haven't experienced it personally': Older Canadian men's perceptions of ageism as a distant social problem', *Ageing & Society*, 36(8): 1757–73.

Hurd Clarke, L., and Lefkowich, M. (2018) 'I don't really have any issue with masculinity': Older Canadian men's perceptions and experiences of embodied masculinity', *Journal of Aging Studies*, 45: 18–24.

Hurd Clarke, L., Bennett, E.V., and Liu, C. (2014) 'Aging and masculinity: Portrayals in men's magazines', *Journal of Aging Studies*, 31(4): 26–33.

Hurley, J. (2012) *Employment trends and policy for older workers in the recession*, http://www.eurofund.europa.eu/areas/populationandsociety/agemanagement.htm.

Iwamoto, T., Hanyu, H., and Umahara, T. (2013) 'Age-related changes of sensory system', *Japanese Journal of Clinical Medicine*, 71(10); 1720–5.

Jackson, D. (2016) *Exploring aging masculinities: The body, sexuality and social lives*, New York: Springer.

Jansen, A. (2018) 'Work-retirement cultures: A further piece of the puzzle to explain differences in the labour market participation of older people in Europe?', *Ageing & Society*, 38: 1527–55.

Kaneda, H., Maeshima, K., Goto, N., Kobayakawa, T., Ayabe-Kanamura, S., and Saito, S. (2000) 'Decline in taste and odor discrimination abilities with age, and relationship between gustation and olfaction', *Chem Senses*, 25: 331–7.

Katz, J., Peace, S., and Spurr, S. (2012) *Adult lives: A life course perspective*, Bristol: Policy Press.

Kaufmann, E., and Toft, M. (2012) 'Introduction', in Goldstone, J., Kaufmann, E., and Toft, M. (eds) *Political demography: How population changes are reshaping international security and national politics*, London: Paradigm Publishers.

Kim, S.W. (2019) 'Left behind children, teachers' perceptions of family-school relations in rural China', *Compare*, 49(4): 584–601.

King, J. (2013) *Discourses of ageing in fiction and feminism: The invisible woman*, Basingstoke: Palgrave Macmillan.

Kittay, E.F., Jennings, B., and Wasunna, A.A. (2005) 'Dependency, difference and the feminist ethic of long-term care', *The Journal of Political Philosophy*, 13(4): 443–69.

Kohli, M. (1985) 'Die Institutionalisierung des Lebenslaufs: Historische Befunde und theoretische Argumente' [The institutionalisation of the life course: Historical findings and theoretical arguments], *Kölner Zeitschrift für Soziologie und Sozialpsychologie*, 37: 1–29.

Kohli, M. (1988) 'Ageing as a challenge for sociological theory', *Ageing & Society*, 8: 367–94.

Kohli, M. (1999) 'Private and public transfers between generations: Linking the family and the state', *European Societies*, 1(1): 81–104.

Kohut, A. (2014) *The global divide on homosexuality: Greater acceptance in more secular and affluent countries*, Pew Research Center, available at: file:///C:/Users/3048783/Downloads/Pew-Global-Attitudes-Homosexuality-Report-REVISED-MAY-27-2014.pdf.

Konzelmann, L., Wagner, C., and Rattinger, H. (2012) 'Turnout in Germany in the course of time: Life cycle and cohort effects on electoral turnout from 1953 to 2049', *Electoral Studies*, 31: 250–61.

Lain, D. (2016) *Reconstructing retirement: Work and welfare in the UK and the USA*, Bristol: Policy Press.

Lalla, R.V., and D'Ambrosio, J.A. (2001) 'Dental management considerations for the patient with diabetes mellitus', *J Am Dent Assoc*, 132: 1425–32.

Lancet Commission (2014) 'David Napier: cultivating the role of culture in health', *The Lancet*, 384(9954): 1607–39, https://doi.org/10.1016/S0140-6736(14)61603-2.

Laslett, P. (1991) *A fresh map of life: The emergence of the third age*, Cambridge, MA: Harvard University Press.

Leonard, P., Fuller, A., and Unwin, L. (2017) 'A new start? Negotiations of age and chrononormativity by older apprentices in England', *Ageing & Society*, 38(8): 1667–92.

Leopold, T., and Skopek, J. (2016) 'Retirement and changes in housework: A panel study of dual earner couples', *The Gerontologist*, 73(4): 733–43.

Leuprecht, C. (2012) 'Deter or engage? The demographic structure of ethno-nationalist mobilization', in Goldstone, J., Kaufmann, E., and Duffy Toft, M. (eds) *Political demography: how population changes are reshaping international security and national politics*, Boulder: Paradigm.

Levy, B. (2009) 'Stereotype embodiment: A psychosocial approach to aging', *Current Directions in Psychological Science*, 18(6): 332–6.

Levy, B.R., Slade, M.D., Kunkel, S.R., and Kasl, S.V. (2002) 'Longevity increased by positive self-perceptions of aging', *Journal of Personality and Social Psychology*, 83(2): 261–70.

Levy, B., Chung, P., Bedford, T., and Navrazhina, K. (2014) 'Facebook as a site for negative age stereotypes', *The Gerontologist*, 54(2): 172–76.

Liew, T.M., and Lee, C.S. (2019) 'Reappraising the efficacy and acceptability of multicomponent interventions for caregiver depression in dementia: The utility of network meta-analysis', *The Gerontologist*, 59(4): e380–e392, doi. org/10.1093/geront/gny061.

Light, P.C. (1988) *Baby boomers*, New York: W.W. Norton.

Lister, R. (2003) *Citizenship: Feminist perspectives*, Basingstoke: Palgrave Macmillan.

Lively, P. (2013) *Ammonites and leaping fish: A life in time*, London: Penguin.

Lloyd, L. (2012) *Health and care in ageing societies: A new international approach*, Bristol: Policy Press.

Loretto, W., and White, P. (2006) 'Employers' attitudes, practices and policies towards older workers', *Human Resource Management Journal*, 16(3): 313–30.

Loretto, W., Vickerstaff, S., and White, P. (2007) *The future for older workers: New perspectives*, Bristol: Policy Press.

Lugea, J., Carney, G., and Devine, P. (2017) 'Dementia in the minds of characters and readers', presented at Dementia and Cultural Narratives Symposium, Aston University, UK.

Macnicol, J. (2015) *Neoliberalising old age*, Cambridge: Cambridge University Press.

Mannheim, K. (1993) 'The problem of generations', in Hardy, M.A. (eds) *Studying aging and social change: Conceptual and methodological issues*, London: SAGE.

Marhánková, J.H. (2015) 'The changing practices and meanings of grandparenthood. Reflections on the demographical trends and changing representations of ageing', *Sociology Compass*, 9(4): 309–19.

Marhánková, J.H. (2019) 'I want (to be) an active grandmother: Activity as a new normative framework of subjective meaning and expectation associated with the grandmother role', *Ageing and Society*, 39(8): 1667–90.

Marmot, M., and Wilkinson, R. (eds) (1999) *Social determinants of health*, Oxford University Press: Oxford.

Martin, J.I., and d'Augelli, A. (2009) 'Timed lives: Cohort and period effects in research on sexual orientation and gender identity', in Martin, J.I. and Meezan, W. (eds) *Handbook of research with gay, lesbian, bisexual and transgender populations*, New York: Routledge.

Mayer, K.U., and Müller, W. (1986) 'The state and the structure of the life course', in Sorensen, A.B., Weinert, F., and Sherrod, L.R. (eds), *Human development and the life course*, Hillsdale, NJ: Lawrence Erlbaum Associates: 217–45.

Mayer, K.U. (2009) 'New directions in life course research', *Annual Review of Sociology*, 35: 413–433

MacGregor, N. (2010) *A history of the world in 100 objects*, London: Penguin.

McCrae, R.R., and Costa, P.T., Jr. (1987) Validation of the five-factor model of personality across instruments and observers, *Journal of Personality and Social Psychology*, 52(1): 81–90.

McLaughlin, J.S., and Neumark, D. (2018) 'Barriers to later retirement for men: Physical challenges of work and increases in the full retirement age', *Research on Aging*, 40(3): 232–56.

Melo, D., and Stockemeer, D. (2014) 'Age and political participation in Germany, France and the UK: a comparative analysis', *European Politics*, 12: 33–53.

Meyer, M.H. (2012) 'Grandmothers juggling work and grandchildren in the United States', in Arber, S., and Timonen, V. (eds) *Contemporary grandparenting: Changing family relationships in global contexts*, Bristol: Policy Press.

Milgram, S. (1963) 'Behavioral study of obedience', *Journal of Abnormal and Social Psychology*, 67: 371–8.

Minkler, M. and Estes, C. (1991) *Critical perspectives on ageing: The political and moral economy of growing old*, New York: Baywood.

Moody, H.R. (2007) 'Justice between generations: The recent history of an idea', in Scharf, T., and Bernard, M. (eds) *Critical perspectives on ageing societies*, Bristol: Policy Press.

Moore, D.R., Edmondson-Jones, M., Dawes, P., Fortnum, H., McCormack, A., Pierzycki, R.H., and Munro, K.J. (2014) 'Relation between speech-in-noise threshold, hearing loss and cognition from 40–69 years of age', *PLoS One*, 9(9), doi: 10.1371/journal.pone.0107720.

Morland, P. (2019) *The human tide: How population shaped the modern world*, London: John Murray.

National Alliance for Caregiving and AARP (2009) *Caregiving in the US*, Washington DC: National Alliance for Caregiving.

National Archives (2015) 'Data on male life expectancy', available at: https:// webarchive.nationalarchives.gov.uk/20160105223326/

National Association of Home Builders (2019) *Homeownership rates by race and ethnicity*, available at: http://eyeonhousing.org/2019/03/homeownership-rates-by-race-and-ethnicity/.

National Council on Aging (2016) *Elder abuse facts*, available at: https://www.ncoa.org/public-policy-action/elder-justice/elder-abuse-facts/.

National Opinion Research Center (2014) *Long term care in America: Expectations and realities*, available at: http://www.longtermcarepoll.org/PDFs/LTC%20 2014/AP-NORC-Long-Term%20Care%20in%20America_FINAL%20WEB. pdf.

National Pensioners Convention (2016) *Intergenerational fairness – Work and Pensions Select Committee Inquiry: Submission from the National Pensioners Convention*, available at: https://www.npcuk.org/research-and-reports.

Navarro, V. (2008) 'Neoliberalism as a class ideology; or, the political causes of the growth of inequalities', *International Journal of Health Services*, 37(1): 47–62.

Norwegian Grandparents Climate Change Campaign (nd) 'About the grandparents campaign', available at: besteforelderaksjonen.no/about-the-grandparents-climate-campaign

Nosek, B., and Banaji, M. (2001) 'The go/no-go association task', *Social Cognition*, 19: 625–66.

Nosek, B., Greenwald, A. and Banaji, M. (2007) 'The implicit association test at age 7: A methodological and conceptual review', in Bargh, J.A. (ed) *Automatic Processes in Social Thinking and Behavior*, Psychology Press: 265–92.

Nugin, R. (2010) 'Social time as the basis of generational consciousness', *Trames-Journal of the Humanities and Social Sciences*, 14(4): 342–66.

O'Neill, M., and Jepsen, M. (2019) 'Women's desire for the kaleidoscope of authenticity, balance and challenge: A multi-method study of female health workers' careers', *Gender, Work & Organisation*, 1–21.

OECD (2017) 'Greece', in *Pensions at a glance 2017*, available at: oecd.org/els/ public-pensions/PAG2017-country-profile-Greece.pdf.

OECD (2019) 'How does Japan compare?' In *Pensions at a glance 2019*, available at: https://www.oecd.org/japan/PAG2017-JPN.pdf.

ONS (Office for National Statistics) (2013) *Inequality in disability free life expectancy by area deprivation: England 2000–2003 and 2007–10*, Newport: ONS, available at: https://www.ons.gov.uk/peoplepopulationandcommunity/healthandsocialcare/ healthandlifeexpectancies/bulletins/inequalityindisabilityfreelifeexpectancyby areadeprivationengland/2013-07-25.

ONS (2018) *Estimates of the very old, including centenarians, UK, 2002–2007*, Newport: ONS, available at: https://www.ons.gov.uk/peoplepopulationand community/birthsdeathsandmarriages/ageing/bulletins/estimatesoftheveryold includingcentenarians/previousReleases.

ONS (2019a) *More than one in four sandwich carers report symptoms of mental ill health*, Newport: ONS, available at: https://www.ons.gov.uk/peoplepopulationandco mmunity/healthandsocialcare/healthandwellbeing/articles/morethanoneinfou rsandwichcarersreportsymptomsofmentalillhealth/2019-01-14.

ONS (2019b) *National life tables, UK: 2016–2018*, available at: https://www. ons.gov.uk/peoplepopulationandcommunity/birthsdeathsandmarriages/ lifeexpectancies/bulletins/nationallifetablesunitedkingdom/2016to2018.

Office of Inspector General, Department of Health and Human Services (2013) *Medicaid fraud control units fiscal year 2013 annual report*, Washington DC: DoHHS.

Office of Inspector General, Department of Health and Human Services (2014) *Adverse events in skilled nursing facilities: National incidence among Medicare beneficiaries*, Washington DC: DoHHS.

Officer, A., Schneiders, M., Wu, D., Nash, P., Thiyagarajan, J., and Beard, J. (2016) 'Valuing older people: Time for a global campaign to combat ageism', *Bulletin of the World Health Organization*, 94: 710–710A.

Ogawa, T., Annear, M.J., Ikebe, K., and Maeda, Y. (2017) 'Taste–related sensations in old age', *Journal of Oral Rehabilitation*, 44(8); 626–35.

Orel, N.A. (2017) 'Families and support systems of LGBT elders', *Annual Review of Gerontology & Geriatrics*, 37(1): 89–109.

Oro-Piqueras, M., and Falcus, S. (2018) 'Approaches to old age: Perspectives from the 21st century', *European Journal of English Studies*, 22(1): 1–12.

Page, J.W., and Crognale, M.A. (2005) 'Differential aging of chromatic and achromatic visual pathways: Behavior and electrophysiology', *Vision Res*, 45: 1481–9, available at: doi: 10.1016/j.visres.2004.09.041.

Pahl, R. and Spencer, L. (2003) *Personal communities: Not simply families of 'fate' or 'choice'*, Working Papers of the Institute for Social and Economic Research, paper 2003–4 (March), Colchester: University of Essex.

Palmore, E. (1990) *Ageism: Positive and negative*, New York: Springer.

Pannor Silver, M. and Williams, S. (2018) 'Reluctance to Retire: A qualitative study on work identity, intergenerational conflict, and retirement in academic medicine' *The Gerontologist*, 58(2): 320–30.

Pannor Silver, M. (2019) 'The unbearable lightness of being retired' *Canadian Journal of Aging/La Revue canadienne du vieillissement*, 38(1): 21–34.

Partridge, E. (1981) *Responsibilities to future generations: Environmental ethics*, Buffalo, New York: Prometheus Books.

Paulhus, D.L., and Reid, D.B. (1991) 'Enhancement and denial in socially desirable responding', *Journal of Personality and Social Psychology*, 60: 307–17.

Payne, B.K., Cheng, C.M., Govorun, O., and Stewart, B.D. (2005) 'An inkblot for attitudes: Affect misattribution as implicit measurement', *Journal of Personality and Social Psychology*, 89(3): 277–93.

Pemberton, H., Thane, P., and Whiteside, N. (2006) *Britain's pensions crisis: History and policy*, British Academy Scholarship online, available at: https://britishacademy.universitypressscholarship.com/view/10.5871/ bacad/9780197263853.001.0001/upso-9780197263853.

Perren, K., Arber, S., and Davidson, K. (2003) 'Men's organisational affiliations in later life: The influence of social class and marital status on informal group membership', *Ageing & Society*, 23 (1): 69–82.

Pettigrew, T. (1979) 'The ultimate attribution error: Extending Allport's cognitive analysis of prejudice', *Personality and Social Psychology Bulletin*, 5: 461–76.

Phillipson, C. (2013) *Ageing*, London: Polity Press.

Phillipson, C. (2020) 'COVID-19 and the crisis in residential and nursing home care' at https://ageingissues.wordpress.com/2020/04/08/covid-19-and-the-crisis-in-residential-and-nursing-home-care/

Plassman, B.L., Langa, K.M., Fisher, G.G., Heeringa, S.G., Weir, D.R., Ofstedal, M.B., and Wallace, R.B. (2007) 'Prevalence of dementia in the United States: the aging, demographics, and memory study', *Neuroepidemiology*, 29(1–2): 125–32, doi:10.1159/000109998.

Platts, L., Corna, L., Worts, D., McDonough, P., Price, D., and Glaser, K. (2017) 'Returns to work after retirement: A prospective study of unretirement in the United Kingdom', *Ageing & Society*, 39(3): 439–64.

Polivka, L. (2012) 'The growing neo-liberal threat to the economic security of workers and retirees', *The Gerontologist*, 52(1): 133–44.

Postelnicescu, C. (2016) 'Europe's new identity: The refugee crisis and the rise of nationalism', *European Journal of Psychology*, 12(2): 203–9.

Powell, J. and Gilbert, T. (2009) *Aging and Identity: A dialogue with postmodernism*, New York: NOVA.

Price, D. (2007) 'Closing the gender gap in retirement income: What difference will recent UK pension reforms make?', *Journal of Social Policy*, 36(4): 562.

Prince, M., Wimo, A., Guerchet, M., Ali, G.C., Wu, Y.T. and Prina, M., (2015) 'The global impact of dementia', *World Alzheimer Report*, 1–82.

Rajan, R. (2010) *Fault lines: How hidden fractures still threaten the world economy*, Woodstock: Princeton University Press.

Ray, R. (2000) *Beyond nostalgia: Aging and life-story writing*, Charlottesville: University of Virginia Press.

Reber, A. (1995) *Dictionary of Psychology*, London: Penguin Reference.

Redden, E. (2019) 'Hungary officially ends gender studies programme', available at: https://www.insidehighered.com/quicktakes/2018/10/17/hungary-officially-ends-gender-studies-programs.

Reher, D. (2015) 'Baby booms, busts and population ageing in the developed world', *Population Studies*, 69(1): S57–S68.

Reinhard, S.C., Friss-Feinberg, L., Houser, A., Choula, R. and Evans, M. (2019) *Insight on the issues valuing the invaluable: 2019 update charting a path forward*, AARP Public Policy Institute.

Ribeiro, O., and Paul, C. (2008) 'Older male carers and the positive aspects of care', *Ageing & Society*, 28(2): 165–83.

Rich, C. (1983) 'Look me in the eye: old women, aging and ageism', in Segal, L. (2014) *Out of time: The pleasures and perils of ageing*, London: Verso.

Rieker, P., and Bird, C. (2005) 'Rethinking gender differences in health: Why we need to integrate social and biological perspectives, *Journals of Gerontology: Series B*, 60(2): 40–47.

Robert, K., and Allen, H. (2016) 'Perception and cognition in the ageing brain: A brief review of the short- and long-term links between perceptual and cognitive decline', *Frontiers in Aging Neuroscience*, 8: 89, doi=10.3389/fnagi.2016.00039.

Roth, D.L., Fredman, L., and Haley, W. (2015) 'Informal caregiving and its impact on health: A reappraisal from population-based studies', *The Gerontologist*, 55(2): 309–19, doi.org/10.1093/geront/gnu177.

Roth, D.L., Perkins, M., Wadley, V.G., Temple, E.M., and Haley, W.E. (2009) 'Family caregiving and emotional strain: Associations with quality of life in a large national sample of middle-aged and older adults', *Quality of Life Research*, 18: 679–88.

Rowe, J. and Kahn, R. (1987) 'Human aging; Usual and successful,' *Science*, 237(4311): 143–49.

Royal Voluntary Service (2011) *Gold age pensioners: Valuing the socio-economic contribution of older people in the UK*, Cardiff: WRVS, available at: www.royalvoluntaryservice.org.uk/Uploads/Documents/gold_age_report_2011.pdf.

Ruddock, K.H. (1965) 'The effect of age upon colour vision II. Changes with age in light transmission of the ocular media', *Vision Res*, 5: 47–58, doi: 10.1016/0042-6989(65)90074-x.

Sanghi, A. (2018) 'The single most under-rated trend affecting us', World Bank, available at: www.worldbank.org/en/news/opinion/2018/05/11/the-single-most-underrated-trend-affecting-us-especially-russia.

Saraceno, C. (2008) *Families, ageing and social policy: Intergenerational solidarity in European welfare states*, Cheltenham: Edward Elgar.

Sato, K., Endo, S., and Tomita, H. (2002) 'Sensitivity of three loci on the tongue and soft palate to four basic tastes in smokers and non-smokers', *Acta Otolaryngol Suppl*, 546: 74–82.

Schneider, B.A., and Pichora-Fuller, M.K. (2000) 'Implications of perceptual deterioration for cognitive aging research', in Craik, F.I.M., and Salthouse, A. 2nd edn (eds) *The handbook of aging and cognition*, London: Lawrence Erlbaum Associates: 155–219.

Schulz, R., and Eden, J. (eds) (2016) *Families caring for an aging America*, 8 November 2016, 2, Committee on Family Caregiving for Older Adults; Board on Health Care Services; Health and Medicine Division; National Academies of Sciences, Engineering, and Medicine, Washington, DC: National Academies Press (US).

Segal, L. (2013) *Out of time: The pleasures and perils of ageing*, London: Verso.

Serrao, S. (2015) *Population ageing and its gender dimensions: The direct and indirect impacts on women (A synthesis of literature with evidence from the Asia-Pacific region)*, available at: https://hr.un.org/sites/hr.un.org/files/Population%20ageing%20and%20its%20gender%20dimensions_0.pdf.

Sheppard, P. and Monden, C. (2019) 'Becoming a first-time grandparent and subjective well-being: A fixed effects approach', *Journal of Marriage and Family*, 81(4): 1016–26.

Snowden, R.J., and Kavanagh, E. (2006) 'Motion perception in the ageing visual system: Minimum motion, motion coherence and speed discrimination thresholds', *Perception*, 35: 9–24, doi: 10.1068/p5399.

Sontag, S. (1972) 'The double standard of aging', *Saturday Review of the Society*, 29–38, available at: http://www.unz.com/print/SaturdayRev-1972sep23-00029.

Spear, P.D. (1993) 'Neural bases of visual deficits during aging', *Vision Res*, 33: 2589–609, available at: doi: 10.1016/0042-6989(93)90218-l.

Spijker, J., and MacInnes, J. (2013) 'Population ageing: The timebomb that isn't?', *British Medical Journal*, 347, available at: www.bmj.com/content/347/bmj.f6598.

Stange, K.C. (2009) 'The problem of fragmentation and the need for integrative solutions', *Annals of Family Medicine*, 7(2): 100–103, available at: doi:10.1370/afm.971.

Stoker, G. (2006) *Why politics matters: Making democracy work*, London: Palgrave Macmillan.

Sung, S. (2018) 'Gender, work and care in policy and practice: Working mothers' experience of intergenerational exchange of care in South Korea', *Critical Social Policy*, 38(3): 589–608, doi.org/10.1177/0261018317746042.

Taylor-Gooby, P. (2016) 'The divisive welfare state', *Social Policy & Administration*, 50(6): 712–33.

Teitelbaum, M. (2015) 'Political demography: Powerful trends under-attended by demographic science', *Population Studies*, 69(1): S87–S95.

Thane, P. (2005) *The long history of old age*, London: Thames & Hudson.

Timonen, V. and Doyle, M. (2014) 'Life-long singlehood: intersections of the past and present', *Ageing & Society*, 34(10): 1749–70.

Timonen, V., Conlon, C., Scharf, T., and Carney, G. (2013) 'Family, state, class and solidarity: re-conceptualising intergenerational solidarity through the grounded theory approach', *European Journal of Ageing*, 10(3): 171–79. https://doi.org/10.1007/s10433-013-0272-x

The English Longitudinal Study of Ageing (ELSA) (https://www.elsa-project.ac.uk/).

The Irish Longitudinal Study of Ageing (TILDA) (https://tilda.tcd.ie/).

The Northern Ireland Cohort for the Longitudinal Study of Ageing (NICOLA) (https://www.qub.ac.uk/sites/NICOLA/).

The Retirement Project (2007) *Meeting the long-term needs of the baby boomers: How changing families will affect paid helpers*, available at: https://www.urban.org/UploadedPDF/311451_Meeting_Care.pdf.

The Survey of Health, Ageing and Retirement in Europe (SHARE) (http://www.share-project.org/).

Thompson, E.H., and Langendoerfer, K.B. (2016) 'Older men's blueprint for "being a man"', *Men and Masculinities*, 19(2): 119–47, doi: 10.1177/1097184X15606949.

Thunberg, G. (2019) *No one is too small to make a difference*, London: Penguin.

Tomita, H., and Yoshikawa, T. (2002) 'Drug-related taste disturbances', *Acta Otolaryngol Suppl*, 116–121.

Townsend, P. (1981) 'The structured dependency of the elderly: A creation of social policy', *Ageing & Society*, 1(1): 5–28.

Townsend, P. (2006) 'Policies for the aged in the 21st century: More structured dependency or the realisation of human rights?' *Ageing & Society*, 26: 161–79, doi:10.1017/S0144686X05004666.

Twigg, J. (2000) *Bathing: The body and community care*, London: Routledge.

Twigg, J. (2004) 'The body, gender and age: Feminist insights in social gerontology', *Journal of Aging Studies*, 18: 59–73.

Twigg, J. (2007) 'Clothing, age and the body: A critical review', *Ageing & Society*, 27: 285–305.

Twigg, J. (2013) *Fashion and age: Dress, the body and later life*, London: Bloomsbury.

Twigg, J. (2018) 'Fashion, the media and age: How women's magazines use fashion to negotiate age identities', *European Journal of Cultural Studies*, available at: http://dx.doi.org/10.1177/1367549417708432.

Twigg, J., and Buse, C. (2013) 'Dress, dementia and the embodiment of identity', *Dementia*, 12(3): 326–36.

Twigg, J., and Majima, S. (2014) 'Consumption and the constitution of age: Expenditure patterns of clothing, hair and cosmetics among the post war "baby boomers"', *Journal of Aging Studies*, 30: 23–32, available at: http://dx.doi.org/10.1016/j.jaging.2014.03.003.

Twigg, J., and Martin, W. (2014) 'The challenge of cultural gerontology', *The Gerontologist*, 55: 353–9, available at: http://dx.doi.org/10.1093/geront/gnu061.

Twigg, J., and Martin, W. (2015) *Routledge handbook of cultural gerontology*, London: Routledge.

Twigg, J., Wolkowitz, C., Cohen, R., and Nettleton, S. (2011) 'Conceptualising body work in health and social care', *Sociology of Health & Illness*, 33: 171–88, available at: http://dx.doi.org/10.1111/j.1467-9566.2010.01323.x.

UK Pensions Act (1995) available at: http://www.legislation.gov.uk/ukpga/1995/26/schedule/4/enacted.

UNAIDS (2019) *Global HIV and AIDS statistics — 2019 fact sheet*, available at: http://www.unaids.org/sites/default/files/media_asset/UNAIDS_FactSheet_en.pdf.

United Nations (2002) *Madrid international plan of action*, available at: https://www.un.org/development/desa/ageing/madrid-plan-of-action-and-its-implementation.html.

United Nations (2013) *Definition of the indicators of population ageing: Dependency ratio*, available at: https://esa.un.org/unpd/popdev/AgingProfiles2013/Docs/Definitions_2013.pdf.

United Nations Department of Economic and Social Affairs, Population Division (2015) *World Population Prospects: The 2015 Revision*, available at: https://www.populationpyramid.net/hnp/life-expectancy-at-birth-female-years/2015/

United Nations Economic Commission for Europe (2018) *Active ageing index*, available at: https://www.unece.org/population/aai.html.

Van den Hoonaard, D. (2009) 'Widowers' strategies of self-representation of during research interviews', *Ageing & Society*, 29: 257–76.

Van den Hoonaard, D.K. (1997) 'Identity foreclosure during women's experiences of widowhood as expressed in autobiographical accounts', *Ageing & Society*, 17(5): 533–51.

Von Herbay, A. (2014) 'Otto Von Bismarck is not the origin of old age at 65', *The Gerontologist*, 54 (1): 5, available at: https://doi.org/10.1093/geront/gnt111.

Wagner, L.W., McDonald, S.M., and Castle, N.G. (2012) 'Impact of voluntary accreditation on deficiency citations in US nursing homes', *The Gerontologist*, 52(4): 561–70, available at: https://doi.org/10.1093/geront/gnr136.

Wagner, M., Johann, D., and Kritzinger, S. (2012) 'Voting at 16: Turnout and the quality of vote choice', *Electoral Studies*, 31: 372–83.

Walker, A. (2012) 'The new ageism', *The Political Quarterly*, 83(4): 812–19.

Walker, A. (1981) 'Towards a political economy of old age', *Ageing & Society*, 1(1): 73–94.

Ward, R. (2015) 'Hair and age', in Twigg, J., and Martin, W. (eds.) (2015) *Routledge handbook of cultural gerontology*, London: Routledge.

Ward, R., and Campbell, S. (2013) 'Mixing methods to explore appearance in dementia care', *Dementia*, 12(2): 337–47.

Ward, R., and Holland, C. (2011) 'If I look old, I will be treated old: Hair and later life image dilemmas', *Ageing & Society*, 31: 288–307.

Weiner, M., and Teitelbaum, M. (2001) *Political demography, demographic engineering*, New York: Berghahn Books.

Weller, C., Wenger, J., Lichtenstein, B., and Arcand, C. (2018) 'Push or Pull: Changes in the relative risk and growth of entrepreneurship among older households', *The Gerontologist*, 58(2): 308–19.

West, L., Cole, S., Goodkind, D., and He, W. (2014) *65+ in the United States: 2010 US Census Bureau Report*, Government Printing Office: Washington DC.

Westbrook, L., and Schilt, K. (2014) 'Doing gender, determining gender: Transgender people, gender panics and the maintenance of the sex/gender/ sexuality system', *Gender & Society*, 28(1): 32–57.

White Riley, M. (1971) 'Social gerontology and the age stratification of society', *The Gerontologist*, 11(1): 79–87.

WHO (World Health Organization) (2012) *Active ageing: A policy framework*, available at: https://extranet.who.int/agefriendlyworld/wp-content/ uploads/2014/06/WHO-Active-Ageing-Framework.pdf.

WHO (World Health Organization) (2019) *Dementia*, available at: https://www. who.int/news-room/fact-sheets/detail/dementia.

WHO (World Health Organization) (nd) *About the global network for age-friendly cities and communities*, available at: extranet.who.int/agefriendlyworld/who- network/.

Willetts, D. (2010) *The pinch: How the baby-boomers took their children's future and how they can give it back*, London: Atlantic Books.

Wilson, D.H., Walsh, P.G., Sanchez, L., Davis, A.C., Taylor, A.W., Tucker, G., and Meagher, I. (1999) 'The epidemiology of hearing impairment in an Australian adult population', *Int. J. Epidemiol*, 28: 247–52, doi: 10.1093/ije/28.2.247.

Wolfenson, D. (2017) 'The risks to LGBT elders in nursing homes and assisted living facilities and possible solutions', *Tulane Journal of Law and Sexuality: Review of Sexual Orientation and Gender Identity in the Law*, 26: 123–32.

Wolpert, L. (2011) *You're looking very well: The surprising nature of getting old*, London: Faber and Faber.

World Bank (1994) *Averting the old age crisis: Policies to protect the old and promote growth*, New York: Oxford University Press.

World Bank (2018) *Life expectancy at birth*, available at: https://data.worldbank.org/indicator/sp.dyn.le00.in.

Worldbank.org (2012) *Poland: Aging and the economy*, http://www.worldbank.org/en/news/opinion/2012/06/14/poland-aging-and-the-economy.

Yang, J., Ogasa, T., Ohta, Y., Abe, K., and Wu, J. (2010) 'Decline of human tactile angle discrimination in patients with mild cognitive impairment and Alzheimer's disease', *J Alzheimer's Dis*, 22(1): 225–34.

Zhou, F., Ting, Y., Ronghui, D., Guohui, F., Ying, L. and Zhibo, L. (2020) 'Clinical course and risk factors for mortality of adult inpatients with COVID-19 in Wuhan, China: A retrospective study' *The Lancet*, 395 (10229): 1054–62.

Index